W9-BCE-174

Playground Safety Is No Accident: Developing a Public Playground Safety and Maintenance Program

by Kenneth S. Kutska, CLP, CPSI

Kevin J. Hoffman, ARM, CPSI

Antonio C. Malkusak, CPSI

2nd Edition

LIBRARY
UNIVERSITY OF ST. FRANCIS
JOLIET, ILLINOIS

This manual provides practical information concerning the subject matters covered. It is sold with the understanding that neither the publisher nor the writers are rendering legal advice or other professional service. Both the law and professional standards and guidelines change regularly, and may vary from state to state and from one locality to another. You should consult a competent attorney in your state if you are in need of specific legal advice concerning any of the subjects addressed in this manual.

Copyright© 1998 NRPA/NPSI/PDRMA

All rights reserved.

ISBN 0-929581-32-6

© NRPA/NPSI/PDRMA

796.0694
P723
2ed.

Table of Contents

© NRPA/NPSI/PDRMA

Appendix A - Blank Playground Inspection Forms _____ A-1

Appendix B - Case Study of Northside Park _____ B-1

Bibliography/Acknowledgments

© NRPA/NPSI/PDRMA

About the Authors

Kenneth S. Kutska, CLP, CPSI

Ken Kutska has more than 28 years of full time experience in all aspects of Park Operations Management of which he has spent the past 25 years as the Superintendent of Parks and Planning for the Wheaton Park District.

Ken has been an active member of the Illinois Park and Recreation Association and the National Recreation and Park Association for which he served as President in 1995. He was the first National Playground Safety Institute Chair, a position he held for three years. Ken remains on the board of the NRPA NPSI Program, is an NPSI instructor and contributing author to the NPSI program text books.

Ken's interest and involvement in public playground safety peaked in 1985 with his involvement in the Park and Natural Resource Management Section of IPRA's efforts to develop a Public Playground Safety Inspection Checklist.

Ken is a member of the ASTM F15.29 Subcommittee on public playground equipment which has the responsibility to develop voluntary playground safety standards since 1989. He and was named vice-chair in June, 1992.

Kevin J. Hoffman, ARM, CPSI

Kevin Hoffman is currently the Loss Control Manager at the Park District Risk Management Agency (PDRMA) which is an intergovernmental risk management pool created under the Illinois statute to provide property, liability, and worker's compensation coverages to its 124 members.

After graduating from Northern Illinois University with a major in Industrial Safety Management, Kevin went on to work for the Federal Aviation Administration (FAA), a worker's compensation insurance carrier in Loss Control Management, and as the Risk Manager at four Illinois park districts. In 1991, Kevin achieved the Associate in Risk Management (ARM) designation from the Insurance Institute of America.

Kevin is responsible for the development of park playground safety programs at PDRMAs 1000 playground sites. Kevin has attended ASTM F15.29 meetings for the development of voluntary playground safety standards and has spoke at Early National Playground Safety Institutes and other playground safety seminars. Kevin has authored chapters in the NPSI text Play It Safe Anthology on Inspecting Playgrounds.

Antonio C. Malkusak, ASLA, CPSI

Tony Malkusak is currently a Landscape Architect and Playground Consultant with MMS Consultants, Inc., in Iowa City, Iowa. He has over 14 years of experience in the field of parks and recreation, his expertise being in design, inspection audits and staff training for public agencies.

Tony is a graduate from the University of Illinois, where he earned his degree in Landscape Architecture in 1985. From there, he worked for the Wheaton, Illinois Park District and the Waukegan, Illinois Park District as a Landscape Architect and Parks Supervisor, respectively. In 1992, he relocated to Baltimore, Maryland where he was President and Safety Consultant for Playground Design and Safety, Inc. While there, Tony worked with several agencies developing and implementing their safety management programs, one of which was the New Jersey Park and Recreation Association's statewide Safety Audit and Access Program. There 250 playgrounds were inspected throughout the state of New Jersey to determine compliance with ASTM and CPSC guidelines.

Tony is a Certified Playground Safety Inspector and is an executive board committee member for the NPSI Program. He is also a member of the ASTM F15.29 Subcommittee on public playground equipment and is a member of the American Society of Landscape Architect's Professional Interest Group for Parks and Recreation.

Acknowledgments:

On behalf of the National Recreation and Park Association (NRPA), we would like to thank the following companies and individuals for their generous contributions. Their support is not intended to reflect or misrepresent their positions or company policy on public playground safety. This support has enabled NRPA to develop the National Playground Safety Institute's Certified Playground Safety Inspector courses and exam.

Honorary Members:
BCI Burke, Inc.
Iron Mountain Forge/Little Tikes
Landscape Structures

Benefactor:
Fibar Group

Patrons:
Park District Risk Management Agency
Playworld Systems

Contributors:
Columbia Cascade
Gametime
Kompan, Inc/Big Toys, Inc.
PCA Industries, Incorporated
Playground Environments, Inc.
Quality Industries, Inc.

Donor:
Carlisle Tire and Rubber Co.

Friends:
American Playtime Systems
Playsystems, Inc.
Steel Systems, Inc.
Zeager Bros., Inc.

Special thanks are expressed to the Park District Risk Management Agency (PDRMA) for their extensive financial and clerical support in publishing the second edition of this handbook.

With special thanks to Anne Hoffman of Hoffman Writing and Editing, Glenview, Illinois, for desktop publishing and editing advice in the first edition of this handbook.

Playground Safety Is No Accident: Developing a Public Playground Safety and Maintenance Program

by Kenneth S. Kutska, CLP, CPSI

Kevin J. Hoffman, ARM, CPSI

Antonio C. Malkusak, CPSI

Preface

While play and children are a familiar part of life in most communities, play remains largely misunderstood. Perhaps it is our familiarity with children at play that allows us to grow indifferent to its significance. We sometimes think of play as the opposite of work, implying that play is not to be taken seriously. Some have established greater credibility for the activity of play by referring to it as children's work.

Today we know that a child's playground is the environment for learning and development. All children experience growth through a series of social, emotional, intellectual, and physical stages. Each child develops at his or her own pace, and because of this diversity it is important that we provide diversity in the play environment that can meet the developmental needs of all children.

Diversity in a child's play environment will create challenges for some, but may create hazards for others. Hazards may arise through inappropriate design, by adults who are not properly supervising children's play, vandalism, or by improper maintenance practices. Regardless of the causes of these hazards, hundred of thousands of children will be injured on public playgrounds annually.

Ignorance of current playground standards and practices will not absolve your agency from the potential liabilities that exist when operating a playground. In addition, many states will not recognize the "grandfathering" of older playground equipment as a defense measure following a loss. The best and most effective way to reduce the number of playground injuries is to develop a comprehensive playground safety program with the elements contained in this publication.

During the past twenty years, much information has been developed on the subject of public playground safety. However, very few resources provide the practical tools to improve maintenance procedures and help to identify and eliminate safety problems on the public playground.

Since its first printing in 1992, this publication has been used by many public and private organizations such as school districts, public health departments, cities, park districts and consultants as the foundation in developing their comprehensive playground safety programs. They have also been able to use many concepts in this publication to build and strengthen existing playground safety programs. Many of these concepts have been adopted by the National Recreation and Park Association's National Playground Safety Institutes Certification Programs. There are more than 4,500 Certified Playground Safety Inspectors at the time of this printing.

The updating of the ASTM 1487 Standard Consumer Safety Performance Specification for Playground Equipment for Public Use, the 1997 Consumer Products Safety Commissions Handbook for Public Playground Safety, and requests from publication users for an updated edition has led us to the second printing.

This publication was developed to provide a model for public agencies to eliminate hazards on the playground. By bringing together most of the common playground safety concerns into one comprehensive program.

We hope that you will use this information to improve or develop a comprehensive public playground safety and maintenance program for your agency.

© NRPA/NPSI/PDRMA

x

© NRPA/NPSI/PDRMA

Developing a Comprehensive
Public Playground Safety Program

Overview

As public entities across the nation begin to implement public playground safety measures as outlined in the 1997 U.S. Consumer Products Safety Commission Handbook for Public Playground Safety and the American Society for Testing and Materials (ASTM) F1487-95, the bottom line is that no agency wants any playground user to experience an accident, especially one which results in a fatality or a permanently debilitating injury.

It is the continued commitment and efforts of those responsible for the design, care, and operation of public playgrounds and the playground manufacturing industry to eliminate playground area hazards while not totally eliminating the element of risk, which is an integral part of a child's play environment, motor skill development, and learning experience.

There is a major difference between a playground hazard and a risk. A hazard is a danger which may not be foreseen. Risk involves choice, including a level of risk in relation to the age of the user. For example, school age children ages 5 to 12 are at risk and may fall while running to a playground on a hard paved surface and experience a skinned knee or a bump to the head. Most children are willing to accept this risk of injury and would continue to run on hard surfaces as part of their normal play activities. The same is true for adults who drive cars every day, knowing that more people are killed as a result of automobile accidents than of any other type of accident.

We all assume a certain level of risk in everything we do. It is an ongoing challenge to continually evaluate our risk-filled environment and to take reasonable precautions to protect us from our own actions.

Because changes are needed to maintain a reasonable level of safety on playgrounds while not eliminating the element of risk, it is easy to see how the United States Consumer Product Safety Commission's guidelines for public playground safety have evolved through the 1980's and 1990's. In addition, ASTM has developed voluntary industry standards for public playground safety. These current voluntary standards will evolve into the standard of care for designing and managing public playgrounds. In fact, a number of states have adopted the CPSC Guidelines as law. During this evolution process, and given today's societal attitude towards public responsibilities, it is reasonable to expect that there would always be the threat of a legal challenge to determine a public agency's responsibility to comply with playground industry safety guidelines or standards and to provide due care. For these reasons, it is important that each agency develop a plan to comply with all current playground safety guidelines and standards.

In order to create a safe play environment for children, and to provide as much protection as possible for the agency's defense in the event of a legal challenge, it has become necessary to develop and adopt some form of a comprehensive public playground safety program.

The written materials contained in this playground safety handbook include information on how to establish or improve a public playground safety program. All information contained in this document should be customized to reflect an agency's own policies, procedures, management levels, locations, etc. to improve its effectiveness.

NOTE: These materials do not address how to test for compliance with:
- Design compliance with the soon to be released access board's recommendations
- Toxic materials in children's play environment such as:
  - No more than 0.05% lead by weight in friable paint; OR
  - Presence of toxic wood preservatives such as creosote, petachlorophenol, tributyltinoxide.

© NRPA/NPSI/PDRMA

Where Do You Begin?

Most public agencies are now facing a real dilemma in their attempt to meet current playground safety guidelines, avoid potential legal liabilities arising from non-compliance with these guidelines, balance budgets, and still provide a reasonably safe, enjoyable playground environment for children in their communities. Some jurisdictions are now legislated to comply with a specified standard of care.

The first thing **not** to do is simply remove all existing playground equipment that does not meet the newly released 1997 Consumer Products Safety Commission Playground Safety Guidelines or the ASTM F1487-95 Standard. Before you remove playground equipment, discuss your rational with your risk manager, attorney, board, elected officials and community. The negative impact a mass removal of playground equipment would have on our communities would likely outweigh much of the injury potential that exists on most playground equipment. However, it is critical that public agencies take action to minimize hazards on existing equipment that are known to cause serious injuries or death.

The **first step** is to identify any equipment within your agency's jurisdiction that is known to have caused a reported injury because of poor maintenance, lack of repairs, or poor design that is not in compliance with the CPSC Guidelines and ASTM Standard. If the causes of these injuries have not been corrected, they should be corrected or the specific piece of equipment should be removed.

The **second step** is to remove any existing playground equipment that is not recommended for use on public playgrounds in the CPSC guidelines and ASTM Standard. These include:

- ❑ Heavy animal figure swings
- ❑ Multiple occupancy swings (excluding tire swings)
- ❑ Rope swings
- ❑ Swinging exercise rings and trapeze bar swings

You should also:

- ❑ Cover or replace exposed concrete footings
- ❑ Remove cement landing pads in use zones
- ❑ Evaluate older playground equipment for lead content in paint.

The **third step** is to ensure that adequate depths of surfacing material exist below each piece of playground equipment (see chart on following page). It has been widely documented that almost 70% of all playground injuries can be avoided or minimized by providing soft landing materials of sufficient depth below playground equipment.

The **fourth step** is to identify any tall equipment that would require a landing surface that exceeds the maximum fall height of your underlying protective surfacing material. Agencies should consider removing this equipment unless a tested surfacing material that meets the (ASTM F1292) 200G and 1000 HIC impact standard is available and placed below this equipment with an acceptable use zone. The chart on the following page reflects the impact attenuation properties and maximum fall heights for the loose materials most commonly used beneath playground equipment.

2

© NRPA/NPSI/PDRMA

Critical Heights (in feet) of Tested Materials

Material	Uncompressed Depth			Compressed Depth
	6 inch	9 inch	12 inch	9 inch
Wood Mulch	7	10	11	10
Double Shredded Bark Mulch	6	10	11	10
Uniform Wood Chips	6	7	>12	6
Fine Sand	5	5	9	5
Course Sand	5	5	6	4
Fine Gravel	6	7	10	6
Medium Gravel	5	5	6	5

(From **Handbook for Public Playground Safety,** U.S. Consumer Product Safety Commission)

The **fifth step** is to adjust playground borders and/or when possible relocate equipment to accommodate CPSC and ASTM Layout and Spacing Guidelines (use zone requirements).

The **sixth step** is to identify and repair existing hazards on playground equipment by beginning or improving your regular playground inspection and maintenance program. A major playground equipment manufacturer study alleged that 28% of playground accidents were caused by inadequate maintenance practices by playground operators. Inadequate maintenance inspections and follow-up corrective procedures are a common cause of playground accidents. The resulting lack of inspections or poor documentation may be a basis for legal actions against a public agency.

The **seventh step** is to conduct a comprehensive playground safety audit of each playground site to determine its compliance with the 1997 CPSC handbook and the current ASTM standards. This audit will assist agencies developing playground replacement schedules by identifying and prioritizing serious hazards in existing playground equipment and park/playground sites as a whole. The results of the audit will also identify some conditions that are correctable by agency staff as well as those that may be abated by contacting manufacturers for retrofit upgrades. Because standards have changed throughout the last twenty years and may be law in some states, it is suggested that you review with your legal counsel which standards apply to your playgrounds.

The **eighth step** is to formalize your playground maintenance program policies and procedures. The information contained in this publication should help you in this regard by providing usable forms and suggested procedures that can be customized into your current playground maintenance program.

The **ninth step** is to establish a long term action plan to upgrade playground sites that is reflected in your agency's capital equipment replacement program, existing staff resources, and maintenance/repair budget.

The **tenth step** and the most important part of this project is the ongoing commitment of each and every person who is actively involved in providing safe and challenging playgrounds in your community.

These steps represent a multi-year process which should address all your playground safety needs now and in the future. Your written plan will not exempt your agency from liability, but it should minimize the exposure to the court's larger cash awards or settlements which threaten the financial stability of every entity. But most importantly, this process will avoid the likelihood of an unfortunate accident to some unsuspecting child.

Without the long term commitment of all of your agency's resources and the support of the policy makers and the administrative staff, a public playground safety and loss containment program cannot reach its potential.

Once your plan is complete, your work has just begun. This plan must be reviewed regularly as standards, resources, personnel and the concept of play itself often change without notice. Developing a comprehensive public playground safety and maintenance program is a dynamic process that will continue as long as your agency provides play spaces for children.

© NRPA/NPSI/PDRMA

Outlining a Written Public Playground Safety Program

The following outline is provided to illustrate some of the major components that should be included and documented in a comprehensive public playground safety program. Additional information on these topics will be covered later in this publication.

A.   Major Policies and Procedures

  1. Public Playground Safety Policy Statement

  2. Site inspection frequency rationale

  3. Public playground safety inspection forms with instructions

  4. Procedures for correcting known playground safety hazards

  5. Employee requirements related to public playground safety program

  6. Staff training guidelines

  7. Guidelines for storage of playground documents

  8. Playground signage

  9. Playground accident investigations

B.   Playground documentation and records that should be maintained:

  1. A current copy of the agency's playground safety program

  2. Copies of all current industry public playground safety guidelines or standards

  3. Copies of all staff training records

  4. All individual playground site history files by location

© NRPA/NPSI/PDRMA

Developing a Playground Safety Policy

As in any organization, safety and risk management programs can only be effective if supported by the governing board, by top management, and by those persons down the organizational chart who are responsible for implementing the day to day aspects of the safety program.

To begin the process, an agency should develop a written public playground safety policy statement. A written playground safety policy statement is an effective tool for communicating to the public and agency staff the purposes of the playground safety program. It also should generally outline what actions persons throughout the organization must take to make the program successful.

A well designed playground safety policy statement should include the following elements:

- ❑ The policy statement should be simply written and clearly include the philosophies and objectives of the agency's playground safety program.

- ❑ It should be signed and supported by top management by providing the resources necessary to accomplish the goals of the playground safety program.

- ❑ It should provide for program continuity of playground related loss exposures between all sites and departments involved within the organization.

- ❑ It should facilitate the lines of communication between departments included in playground risk management.

The playground safety policy statement should be approved by an agency's governing board, chief executive, or other top management positions. This top management commitment is vitally important to the long term success of a playground safety program since top management will be ultimately responsible for providing the resources necessary to implement and sustain a comprehensive playground safety program.

The completed playground safety policy statement should be made available to all agency staff and be included in playground safety training materials.

The following is a sample public agency playground safety statement.

© NRPA/NPSI/PDRMA

Sample Public Playground Safety Policy Statement

Any Town's Public Playground Safety Policy

In the continuing effort by **Any Town** to provide quality, well maintained, clean, and safer parks and facilities for the public, **Any Town** has developed the following standard operating procedures to protect and preserve its unsupervised public playground facilities and its users. This program may only be accomplished through a commitment to a public playground safety program which assures that every attempt will be made to eliminate playground hazards while not totally eliminating the element of risk which is an essential part of any successful children's play and learning environment.

To guarantee the continued success of this program, the following guidelines will be adhered to by all **Any Town** departments and staff:

- All playground sites will be subject to the playground safety program.

- All equipment shall be installed according to manufacturer specifications.

- **Any Town** shall provide reasonable resources to ensure prudent and timely inspections and repairs as determined necessary by the playground safety program.

- All play equipment shall be inspected, repaired, and maintained by agency employees on a regular basis with the necessary documentation.

- All playground equipment purchasers, installers, inspectors, and maintenance employees performing repairs shall be trained in accordance with the agency's public playground safety training program, in order to maintain the playground equipment in substantial compliance with the current standard of care.

- All equipment shall be purchased from an International Playground Equipment Association (IPEMA)* certified playground equipment manufacturer with adequate product liability insurance.

This Playground Safety Policy is subject to review and revision as required. (Revision date March, 1998.)

---

*IPEMA Certification – Third party voluntary certification program of a manufacturer's compliance with the current ASTM Standard.

© NRPA/NPSI/PDRMA

The Playground Safety Audit Process

What is a Playground Safety Audit?

The playground safety audit form is a comprehensive document that will assist public agencies in identifying a wide range of known playground hazards based on the 1997 CPSC Handbook for Public Playground Safety and the ASTM F1487-95 voluntary industry performance standard for public playgrounds. It will also help an agency determine where the most serious and potentially life threatening hazards exist on specific types of playground equipment, as well as the park and playground environment as a whole. This is accomplished by assigning index points to specific types of playground safety concerns based on their potential to cause serious injury or loss of life.

The following index points and corresponding levels used in the playground audit form are listed in the table below.

Key to Assigned Index Points on Audit Form		
Priorities	**Points**	**Condition likely to cause:**
Priority 1	10 or more	Permanent disability, loss of life or body part
Priority 2	5	Serious injury or illness resulting in temporary disability
Priority 3	1	Minor (non-disabling) injury

Using the Results of the Playground Safety Audit

Once completed, the playground safety audit can be used in many ways to reduce safety concerns that exist in playground areas and develop long term planning strategies.

The following are some specific examples:

1. It can help to identify and prioritize any life threatening or serious hazards that can be corrected by your own agency personnel. For example, adding surfacing materials where inadequate, repairing broken equipment, removing playground equipment not recommended for use on public playgrounds, etc. (Priority 1 Concerns)

2. It can help to identify playground equipment design flaws that may be correctable by contacting the playground manufacturer to see if retrofit parts are available to eliminate an existing safety concern. For example, adding infills between step platforms to eliminate entrapment hazards, replacing barrier walls that create entrapment hazards, etc. (Priority 1 Concerns)

3. It can assist agencies in developing and prioritizing their comprehensive playground replacement schedules. By identifying safety concerns on specific types of playground equipment and entire park/playground sites based on their index scores, the agency can make better decisions on where to best spend available funds to eliminate the most serious playground safety concerns *first*.

4. It can demonstrate the agency's plan of action to meet current playground safety standards in good faith. Your efforts in auditing to identify playground safety concerns and acting to remove or minimize these hazards will significantly assist you in defending your agency in the event of an accident that leads to litigation. It will likely take many years for most public agencies to fully comply with the new CPSC and ASTM voluntary standards because the funds will likely not be available to update existing playground equipment immediately. But, simply taking a position that funds are not available will probably not absolve an agency of potential liability if no plan to identify and correct existing playground safety concerns is developed.

5. It can help to prevent serious playground injuries. Agencies can identify and direct their immediate attention to the most serious existing playground safety concerns and spend available funds to eliminate these known hazards.

The benefits of this playground safety audit are many. All agencies with playground equipment should conduct a playground safety audit as soon as possible to evaluate the safety of existing playground equipment and the immediate playground environment.

Examples of Priority Ratings Based on Potential to Cause Serious Injury:

Priority 1

- Swinging wheelchair platforms in an unsecured and unsupervised setting
- Merry-go-rounds (whirls) with open platform seating
- Exposed concrete footers
- Asphalt surfacing within fall zone of play equipment
- Ten foot high free standing slide without a transition platform
- Metal animal swings
- Severely worn S-hooks
- Handholds used for supporting users weight turn and move when in use
- Swings are attached to composite play structure
- Entanglement hazards at the top of slides
- Entrapment openings between metal rungs or wood members on the roof of a log cabin climbing structure

Priority 2

- Broken bench on picnic table board
- Broken swing chain
- Worn and cracked rubber belt swing seat
- Surfacing containment barrier creates a trip hazard
- There are one belt and one bucket swing in the same swing bay
- Loose hardware

Priority 3

- Litter and debris scattered throughout the playground
- Surfacing material can be found scattered on the playground perimeter walkways
- Lack of trash receptacles
- A shady area is not provided
- Users cannot get to the playground via an accessible route
- There is no regulatory or information signage for the play area
- The pre-school tube slide diameter is 20" instead of the 23" minimum.
- Metal equipment is showing rust and paint is chipping and worn off in several areas
- Several bolts protrude below decks and platforms between 3 and 4 threads, but pass the protrusion test gauge
- Wood components with excessive dislodgable wood treatment

© NRPA/NPSI/PDRMA

How to Conduct a Playground Safety Audit

This section explains how to conduct a playground safety audit, including recommendations on staff training, documenting serious concerns, the tools needed, and how to use the audit form itself.

Audit Consistency and Staff Training

If possible, all agency playground safety audits should be performed by a group of two persons to help maintain a high level of consistency during the process. If more than one audit team or person will be performing the audits, at least two playground sites should be audited jointly so that the playground auditors will be in agreement on the interpretation of the audit questions.

The playground safety auditor must be committed to this important project. If the employee is not, the audit data will be unreliable and inappropriate decisions may be made in allocating the substantial financial resources often needed to eliminate existing playground safety concerns.

Agency staff who will be responsible for conducting the playground safety audits should be trained in basic playground safety principles. (**See Staff Training in Maintaining Parks and Playgrounds**, page 90). It is preferred that a certified playground safety inspector (CPSI) as certified by the National Recreation and Park Association's National Playground Safety Institute (NPSI) conduct the audit. At minimum, the auditors should have the following basic knowledge and abilities:

- The ability to read and write clearly.
- The ability to physically climb onto play equipment structures.
- The ability to work with minimal supervision.
- The ability to use and interpret measuring devices, gauges, and site plans.
- Be trained in current playground safety guidelines and have a working understanding of them.

Documenting Serious Playground Concerns Identified During the Audit

The inspector conducting a playground safety audit should be prepared to make a list of any serious playground safety concerns noted during the audit process that can be corrected by agency staff. A comments page is provided at the end of the audit form to make notes during the audit. A list of immediate safety concerns should be promptly turned over to a supervisor responsible for directing agency maintenance staff in addressing playground safety concerns. All playground repairs should be documented and maintained in the playground site history file.

Some common agency correctable playground safety concerns that should receive immediate attention include:

- Inadequate surfacing material depths
- Broken or damaged equipment
- Vandalism
- The removal of existing playground equipment not intended for public playground use by CPSC

Audit Tools and Equipment

When preparing to conduct a playground safety audit, it is important that the following tools and other equipment be available so that all questions included in the audit form can be fully evaluated. It is suggested that the auditor wear a carpenter's tool belt or have a canvas bag available to hold the many tools needed during the audit.

- Blank audit forms and copy of instructions

- Copy of 1997 CPSC Handbook for *Public Playground Safety*

- Copy of ASTM F1487-95 Standard

- Pens or pencils and clipboard

- Site plans, drawings, photographs of site, etc.

- Small hand shovel or soil probe core sampler

- Camera

- 100 foot measuring tape or measuring wheel

- 12 foot measuring tape or landscaper's yardstick

- Protrusion gauges

- Partially bounded opening head and neck entrapment probe (fish probe)

- Small torso template or probe

- Large head template or probe

- 5/16" rod or articulated finger probe

- 3/16" neoprene rod

- 5/8" rod

- Carpenter's level (smart level) or mechanical level to measure angles and slope

- Pointed screw driver, awl, or forester's increment bore

- Claw hammer (to pound in nail protrusions or assist in digging through compacted surfacing)

- Caliper to measure outside diameter of pipe

- Automotive feeler gauges

© NRPA/NPSI/PDRMA

Directions for Using the Playground Safety Audit Form

Before the playground auditor begins auditing a playground site, they should review the following directions on using the playground audit form to help ensure that each part will be completed correctly. Remember, this form is to be used to audit only those items within the playground use zone and those items immediately adjacent and continuous to the playground. Example: Fitness equipment is not considered playground equipment, but if it were located adjacent to a playground separated by only a sidewalk, it is likely that children would use this apparatus as play equipment. In this case, this equipment should be audited to determine its compliance with CPSC and ASTM Standards.

1. **Getting Started with the Form**

   Fill in the background information for each playground site as indicated, including the park name, date, inspector name, start/finish times, etc.

2. **Special Notes on Completing the Form**

   a. When reading the audit questions, a negative response will result in "full" index points being given. Positive responses will result in a zero being given for that question.

   b. If the auditor finds that a type of playground equipment exists at a park site and is not included in the "specific conditions section, B" of the audit form, the Specific Equipment Index Point (SEIP) Form should be used. An individual SEIP Form should be used for each piece of equipment that does not fit into the specific conditions section. The auditor should use the SEIP Form to evaluate various potential safety concerns on the playground equipment using the index points. The index points should be added and placed in the section subtotal box. Examples include talk tubes, clatter bridge, free standing play panels, etc. The following instructions will give further examples of specific play equipment that pertains to each category listed in Section "B, Specific Conditions".

   c. When completing the "specific conditions section, B" of the audit form (starts with slides), the playground auditor may, for example, find four slides at a particular playground site. The auditor should evaluate all slides collectively in the slide section of the form and provide full index points whenever a deficiency is noted on any one of the four existing slides. Only provide the index points listed. Do not multiply the possible index points by four. To differentiate where and on which slide the deficiency exists, the auditor must carefully note the location and type of deficiency for each slide in the Comments Column and again on the Comments Summary at the end of the audit form. It is important to note the type and location of specific safety concerns on each slide, especially when evaluating multiple pieces of the same equipment. This will greatly assist maintenance staff in identifying and correcting slide safety concerns following your audit during the repair phase.

Experience has shown that this method will still provide a quality analysis of the relative safety concerns whether it is for a particular playground site or for all sites when developing a playground replacement schedule. Again, it is imperative that all safety concerns be noted in the comments summary for follow-up and correction (especially when multiple pieces of the same equipment exist at one playground).

Finally, the most important consideration is consistency and accuracy in answering all questions on each playground audit form and all site audits performed. Without audit consistency, the resulting data will be flawed, making it difficult to make accurate inferences about playground sites.

3. **The following is an overview for each major category that will be evaluated on the audit form.**

Question 1

Indicate the type of playground environment that is being inspected. Circle the appropriate playground category that best fits the description below.

Definitions:

    a. <u>Public school playground</u> - any playground located on the grounds of a public school.

    b. <u>Private school playground</u> - any playground located on the grounds of a private school.

    c. <u>Day care playground</u> - a playground located on the grounds of a day care center.

    d. <u>Community park</u> - typically a large park area that offers a variety of recreational opportunities in addition to playground sites. Is often designed to serve the recreational needs of a larger geographical area and community population than a neighborhood or recreation facility park.

    e. <u>Neighborhood park/tot lot</u> - a public playground located in a neighborhood environment to serve a limited geographical area of residents.

    f. <u>Other</u> - if the playground audit form will be used on a playground site that does not meet the above definitions, please specify. For example, neighborhood playgrounds located at a community recreation center or a fast food restaurant.

Question 2

Indicate the type and number of specific play equipment that exist at the playground site being audited. Simply indicate in the provided spaces the appropriate numbers. This question will provide documentation on the actual playground equipment located at the park site on the day the audit is conducted.

Question 3

Evaluate how close common potential playground border factors are from the playground site. Index points are assigned based on the actual distance the border concerns are from the border of the playground. This information can be helpful in identifying existing playground design problems that may need immediate or future consideration.

The points in the third column are added, resulting in the total score for question three. Use the comments section to make important notes that will help the auditor to summarize the results and develop a plan of appropriate action to address all deficiencies in a timely fashion.

Questions 4-14

Evaluate the playground's general environment safety concerns, and assign index points when appropriate.

Special Note: This audit does not address how to test for lead paint which has been banned for some time. Friable paint containing more than 0.06% lead by weight should be targeted for lead hazard control. Only qualified testing laboratories should be used.

© NRPA/NPSI/PDRMA

Also, test methods for evaluating wood treatment is not addressed. Wood preservatives such as creosote, petachlorophenol and tributyl tin oxide are considered toxic and should not be used.

Owner/operators should be aware of these and other toxic substances not recommended for use on children's products. You should contact product manufacturers if you have questions. Contact CPSC for further testing information on lead paint and related substances.

Add points given and fill in section subtotal box.

Questions 15-17   Evaluate the age/size appropriate design by assigning index points when appropriate. Question 16 has a possible 110 points.

Add points given and fill in section subtotal box.

Questions 18-22   Evaluate the playground protective surfacing site by assigning index points when appropriate.

Add points given and fill in section subtotal box.

Questions 23-28   Evaluate the use zone safety concerns by assigning index points when appropriate.

Add points given and fill in section subtotal box.

Questions 29-43   Evaluate accessibility design concerns by assigning index points when appropriate.

Add points given and fill in section subtotal box.

The auditor shall indicate in the Comments Section and Audit Summary Report in your opinion whether the playground site is accessible. We suggest this simple 3-point test:

- Does the user have access to,

- Through, and

- Onto accessible and usable playground equipment. Refer to the Access Board's Accessibility Guidelines for play areas.

Questions 44-62   Evaluate slide safety concerns by assigning index points when appropriate.

Add the slide section points given and fill in the section subtotal box.

Questions 63-77   Evaluate climbing equipment safety concerns by assigning index points when appropriate. (Includes crawl through tunnels, turning bars, corkscrew type climbers, looped and/or rung incline cable climbers, arch climbers, parallel bars, suspension bridges, balance beams, stepping columns, chain walk, cargo net, any flexible climbing equipment, etc.)

Add the climbing equipment section points and place that point total in the section subtotal box.

Questions 78-96   Evaluate the upper body climbing equipment safety concerns by assigning index points when appropriate. Includes fireman's sliding pole, ring treks, track rides, horizontal ladders, climbing ropes, and other equipment that requires the user to support their body weight primarily by hands and arms.

Add the upper body climbing equipment section points and place that point total in the section subtotal box.

Questions 97-108   Evaluate stairway and ladder safety concerns by assigning index points when appropriate. Includes transfer stations, transfer steps, vertical rung ladders, and other equipment where feet and legs primarily support the user.

Add the stairway and ladder equipment section points and place that point total in the section subtotal box.

Questions 109-120   Evaluate deck and platform safety concerns by assigning index points when appropriate. Includes guard rails, barrier walls, and play panels, both passive and active when elevated on a deck, also includes ramps or inclined ramps attached to decks.

Add the deck and platform equipment section points and place that point total in the section subtotal box.

Questions 121-139   Evaluate swing equipment safety concerns by assigning index points when appropriate. Includes all to-fro swings, i.e., infant swing seats, belt type, and rotating swings, i.e., tire swings.

Add the swing equipment section points and place that point total in the section subtotal box.

Questions 140-159   Evaluate rocking and rotating equipment safety concerns by assigning index points when appropriate. (Includes see-saws, spring riders, any spring centering device platform or riders, whirls (merry-go-rounds), log rolls, piroet spinners, backhoe diggers, etc.)

Add the rocking and rotating equipment questions and place that point total in the section subtotal box.

Questions 160-169   Evaluate sand play safety concerns by assigning index points when appropriate. Includes elevated sand tables, water tables, etc.

Add the sand play section points and place that point total in the section subtotal box.

☞   **NOTE:** If you have completed all questions on the Audit Form and have not included all play components (such as talktubes, ground level play panels or clatter bridges, etc.), use the SEIP form to evaluate the equipment. Place the SEIP form score in Section C on the Audit Summary Form.

4.   Completing the Audit Summary

Please have a copy of the Audit Summary Form with you as you read these instructions.

To assist you in completing the Audit Summary Form, the following definitions relate to the column headings and sections on the Audit Summary Form.

- **"Possible Index Points"** column heading at the top of the form: Refers to the "Total Maximum Points Possible" for each section (A, B, C) relating to questions on the audit form.

- **"Actual Index Points"** column heading at the top of the form: Refers to the Actual Index Points that are applicable at the playground site that has been audited. For Section A,

© NRPA/NPSI/PDRMA

"General Conditions" these questions will always apply at all playground sites and have been permanently placed in the Actual Index Points column. However, in Section B, if you do not have any sand play areas at the site being audited, you would not move the 271 points into the "Actual Index Points" column. This, in effect, would reduce the "Actual Index Points" sub-total in Section B by 271 points.

- **"Index Points Given" column heading at the top of the form:** Refers to the Index Points given or scored for each section (A, B, C sub-categories) for the playground site being audited. For example, you may only have scored 90 of the 110 possible points for the Use Zone. The 90 points should be placed in the Index Points Given column for Use Zone in Section A.

- **"Section Subtotals (A, B, C):** Each section subtotal has a space to place the sum of the "Actual Index Points" and the "Index Points Given" for each individual section (A - General Conditions, B - Specific Conditions, and C - SEIP Forms) on the summary form.

- **"Site Total":** This section lists the final composite figures for the "Actual Index Points" and "Index Points Given" columns. The section subtotals (A, B, C) are added together to determine the site totals.

- **"Audit % Rating" Column:** Refers to the final percentage rating for the site in the lower right corner of the form in the Site Total Section. This number is calculated by dividing the sum total of the "Index Points Given" by the sum total of the "Actual Index Points" Column.

    a. When the entire audit form has been completed, turn to the audit summary page. Next, write in the "Actual Index Points" for Sections B and C for equipment that exists at the playground site you have audited. If the equipment or play components do not exist at the playground audited, place a "0" in the Actual Index Points Column for that corresponding section.

    b. Add the Actual Index Points for Section B "Specific Conditions" and place this number in the Section B sub-total box. Next, add the Actual Index Points for Section C (if applicable) and place this figure in the Section C sub-total box.

    When completed, add together Sections A, B, C, subtotals and place the site total for the "Actual Index Points" column at the bottom of the page.

    c. Place the total of Index Points Given for each sub-section category listed under Sections A, B, C, from the audit form into the "Index Points Given" column.

    Next, add the "Index Points Given" for each section (A, B, C) and place the composite figure in the section sub-totals for each.

    Next, add the Section A, B, C, sub-totals together and this will give you the site total for all Index Points Given for each section.

    d. To determine the "Audit Percentage Rating" for the entire playground site, **divide the Index Points Given site total by the Actual Index Points total to determine the Final Audit Percentage Rating.**

    When all sites are completed, transfer the results including the Audit Percentage Rating figure to the "Playground Audit Score Summary Form for All Agency Sites."

5. **Comments Section**

5. Comments Section

The playground auditor should list in the comments section any information that may be necessary to further qualify, interpret, or document any portions of the audit process. It is very important that the auditor list very specific descriptions in this section to document a playground safety concern identified during the audit process.

For example, "The audit was conducted on a dry day and it was difficult to identify any drainage concerns, or a serious safety concern was noted during the audit process that should be corrected immediately by agency staff". Another example might be that a swing labeled "1" is the swing with a cut belt swing seat that needs to be replaced.

Upon completion of the Audit and the Audit Summary Form, the Auditor should transfer the audit notes and comments from the comments column to the "Comments Summary Form". This process will create a comprehensive list of concerns that will provide the playground safety team with a concise overview of the audit findings.

6. Documentation of Report

The auditor should print his/her name and also sign the bottom of the audit form.

The playground supervisor should print his/her name and sign and date the bottom of the audit form when received and reviewed.

A copy of the audit form should be placed in the site history file for each playground.

7. Information Release Waiver

This information release waiver should be clearly printed on the playground audit form to help protect against its accidental release during litigation.

© NRPA/NPSI/PDRMA

Playground Safety Audit Form

(revised March, 1998)

Playground Name/ID Number_____

Injuries to children may occur from many types of playground equipment and environmental conditions. The checklist on the following pages will help you to assess and correct safety concerns that may be present on or near your playground. While it does not cover every potential safety concern in a children's environment, it is an overview of most known playground safety concerns. The checklist does not apply to home playground equipment, amusement park equipment, or to equipment normally intended for sports use. The checklist also does not address the many important issues of child development that pertain to play.

The playground audit form is not a regulatory standard, but a compilation of suggested guidelines based upon the *Handbook for Public Playground Safety* written by the Consumer Product Safety Commission (CPSC) (Revised 1997), *American Society for Testing and Materials* (ASTM) F1487-95 Standard, and expert opinions from consultants in the field of playground safety.

Acknowledgments

From the "Statewide Comprehensive Injury Prevention Program" (SCIPP), Department of Public Health, 150 Trecost Street, Boston, MA   02111

Adapted as Wheaton Park District's "Initial Playground Safety Audit" September, 1989, Revised December 20, 1990 and November, 1991, Ken Kutska.

Edited and updated June, 1992, by Ken Kutska, CLP, and Kevin Hoffman, ARM, Park District Risk Management Agency.

Edited and updated March, 1998, by Ken Kutska, CLP, CPSI; Kevin Hoffman, ARM, CPSI, and Tony Malkusak, CLP, CPSI.

ASTM
American Society for Testing and Materials
100 Barr Harbor Drive
West Conshohocken, Pennsylvania 19428
(610)832-9585

U.S. CPSC
Consumer Product Safety Commission
Washington, DC 20207
(1-800-638-CPSC)

National Playground Safety Institute, NPSI
22377 Belmont Ridge Road
Ashburn, VA 20148
(703) 858-0784
www.nrpa.org

© NRPA/NPSI/PDRMA

Background Information:

Playground/Park: _____ Date of Audit: _____

Site Location: _____ Agency: _____

Equipment Type: _____ Surfacing: _____

Inspected By: _____ Ages of Intended Users: _____

General Environment:

1. **Category of playground (circle all that apply):**

- Public School
- Private School
- Day Care

- Community Park
- Neighborhood Park/Tot Lot
- Other (please specify)_____

2. **Equipment Inventory. Indicate the number of equipment pieces that exist.**

A. Composite play structure	B. Free standing equipment	C. Site amenities
• Stairways and Step Ladders _____	• Swings (to-fro) _____	• Benches _____
• Vertical Rung Ladders _____	• Tire Swings _____	• Tables _____
• Rigid Climber _____	• Seesaws _____	• Fountains _____
• Flexible Climber _____	• Slides _____	• Bike Rack _____
• Decks and Platforms _____	• Rigid Climbers _____	• Wheelchair Parking _____
• Play Panel _____	• Flexible Climbers _____	
• Slides _____	• Upper Body Equipment _____	• Signs _____
• Sliding Pole _____	• Rocking Equipment _____	• Trash Receptacles _____
• Horizontal Ladder _____	• Whirl _____	• Fencing _____
• Horizontal Rings _____	• Sand Play Area _____	• Other _____
• Track Ride _____	• Blackhoe Digger _____	• Other _____
• Crawl Tunnel _____	• Play Panels _____	
• Clatter Bridge/Bridges _____	• Other _____	
• Ramps _____	• Other _____	
• Transfer Stations _____	• Other _____	
• Roofs _____		
• Other _____		

© NRPA/NPSI/PDRMA

3.   Playground Border Factors:

Directions: Determine which playground border concerns exist and circle them. In the second column, indicate the actual distance the item is from the playground border. In the third column, assign index points based on the distance each potential border concern is from the nearest playground border (see Key to Border Concern Points).

Key to Border Concern Points:
Within 100 feet   (5 points)
101-199 feet   (2 points)
200 feet or more (0 points)

Playground Border Concerns Measurements or Distances	Distance from Play Edge	Index Points Given	Comments
1st public street			
2nd public street			
3rd public street			
4th public street			
Streets with heavy traffic			
Water (ponds/stream/drainage ditch)			
Soccer/football field			
Baseball/softball field from home plate			
Basketball court			
Parking lots			
Railroad tracks			
Trees (not pruned up at least 7')			
Golf course			
Other (specify) _____			
Point Total for Question 3:			

© NRPA/NPSI/PDRMA

General Conditions	Possible Index Points	Index Points Given	Comments

General Environment Concerns

	General Conditions	Possible Index Points	Index Points Given	Comments
4.	The playground can be accessed safely by a sidewalk that is free of standing water, sand, pea gravel & low hanging branches.	5		
5.	If needed, a suitable barrier (fence) is provided for border concerns within 100' of playground edge. See question 3 for list of possible border concerns (CPSC 6.1).	20		
6.	Seating (benches, outdoor tables) is in good condition (free of splinters, missing hardware or slats, protruding bolts, etc.).	1		
7.	Signs give information about: • regulations on the use of the playground (hours, pets, specific rules, etc.). • name and phone number of playground owner (to report problems). • age appropriateness of equipment. (CPSC 6.3)	15		
8.	Signs on all bordering roads advise motorists that a playground is nearby.	5		
9.	Trash receptacles are provided and located outside of the play area.	1		
10.	Poisonous plants are removed from play area.	10		
11.	Shaded area is provided.	1		
12.	The play area is visible to deter inappropriate behavior (CPSC 6.2).	5		
13.	The play area is free from lead in paint(maximum 0.06% lead by dry weight) (CPSC 8.1).	20		
14.	The play area is free from toxic materials and preservatives (CPSC 8.1).	20		
	Section Subtotal	103		

© NRPA/NPSI/PDRMA

General Conditions	Possible Index Points	Index Points Given	Comments

Age/Size Appropriateness Design

		Possible Index Points	Index Points Given	Comments
15.	Net, chain, arch or tire climbers are not the sole means to access play equipment for 2-5 yr. old users (ASTM 7.2.2.1).	10		
16.	Play equipment not recommended for 2-5 yr. old users: chain or cable walks, free standing arch climbers, free standing climbing events with flexible components, fulcrum seesaws, log rolls, long spiral slides, overhead rings, parallel bars, swinging gates, track rides and vertical sliding poles (CPSC 6.3).	10 pts. for each item found (Possible 110 pts.)		
17.	The play area has signs that inform users of intended user age group (CPSC 6.3).	20		
	Section Subtotal	**140**		

Playground Protective Surface

		Possible Index Points	Index Points Given	Comments
18.	All elevated play equipment (slides, swings, bridges, seesaws, climbing apparatus, etc.) has proper depth of impact-absorbing material underneath the structure. Refer to CPSC and ASTM F1487-95 and ASTM 1292 for specifications on conforming protective surface type, critical fall heights and how far surfacing should extend from structure (CPSC Section 4).	20		
19.	Surfaces are inspected at least weekly and raked to prevent them from becoming packed down and to remove hidden hazards (e.g. litter, sharp objects, animal feces). (Daily=0 points, weekly=5 pts, monthly=10 pts, seasonally=20 pts, annually=40 pts) (CPSC 7.2).	40 20 10 5 0		
20.	Loose materials are replenished as recommended to maintain adequate depth and coverage (annually=10, seasonally=5, monthly or less=0) (CPSC 7.2).	10 5 0		
21.	Standing water is not found within any of the use zones (CPSC 6.1).	20		

General Conditions	Possible Index Points	Index Points Given	Comments

Playground Protective Surface, cont.

	General Conditions	Possible Index Points	Index Points Given	Comments
22.	For equipment installed after 1995, manufacturer's sign attached to equipment stating equipment must be installed over impact absorbing surface (ASTM 14.3).	10		
	Section Subtotal	**150**		

<u>Note</u>: **If playground protective surface inspections are not documented in writing; <u>add 50 points</u> to section subtotal.**

Use Zone

	General Conditions	Possible Index Points	Index Points Given	Comments
23.	There is a minimum use zone of 6' in all directions for all equipment. Use zones for adjacent pieces of play equipment may overlap if the adjacent designated play surfaces are less than 30" above the protective surface. If either adjacent structure exceed 30", the minimum distance between the structures should be 9'. Rocking/springing equipment intended for users to stand upon is no less than 7'. Swings, slide exits, and moving equipment other than less than 30" high rocking equipment shall not overlap use zones. (CPSC 5.1.1, ASTM 9.2.1, 9.5.2.1).	20		
24.	Swings with enclosed swing seat or bucket, use zone to the front and to the rear shall be a minimum distance of 2W, where W equals the distance from the top of the occupant's sitting surface to the pivot-point on the swing (CPSC 5.1.3, ASTM 9.4.1.2).	20		
25.	Belt swings' use zone to the front and to the rear shall be a minimum distance of 2X, where X equals the distance from the top of the protective surface to the pivot-point on the swing (CPSC 5.1.3, ASTM 9.4.1.1).	20		
26.	Slides have adequate space from other equipment at the bottom (height of slide plus 4' from the reduced gradient, or 6' from edge of slide; whichever is greater, but not more than 14'). (CPSC 5.1.2, ASTM 9.6.2, 9.6.2.1, Fig. A1.32).	20		

© NRPA/NPSI/PDRMA

General Conditions	Possible Index Points	Index Points Given	Comments

Use Zone, cont.

		Possible Index Points	Index Points Given	Comments
27.	The use zone for a rotating swing (tire swing) shall be a minimum of 6' in all directions of the support structure plus a minimum horizontal distance in all directions equal to the distance between the pivot point to the top of seat plus 6' (CPSC 5.1.3, 5.1.4, ASTM 9.4.2).	20		
28.	Barriers between equipment are installed so as not to create a trip hazard and are free of protrusions, splinters, sharp edges, etc. and are outside equipment use zone (CPSC 9.7).	10		
	Section Subtotal	**110**		

Accessibility

NOTE: The purpose of this audit form, with regard to accessibility, is to allow the audit inspector to determine compliance of the play area with ASTM F 1487-95. The goal of the inspector is to determine if a person with a disability has access to, on and through the equipment and play area. This audit form is not intended to assess design compliance with the soon to be released access board report.

The auditor shall indicate in the comments column and audit summary report, in your opinion, whether or not the playground is accessible per this simple three part question. Does the user have access to, through, and onto the playground equipment?

29.	The playground has an accessible route with a maximum horizontal slope of 1:20 (greater than 1:20 would be considered a ramp) and a maximum cross-slope of 1:50 (access to and around the playground area is at least 60" wide) (ASTM 10.1.3).	10		
30.	Ramps are 36" wide minimum; with a slope between 1:20 and 1:12 and maximum horizontal run of 12 feet (ASTM 10.2.2.1, 10.2.2.2).	10		
31.	Landings are 60" minimum diameter at bottom and top of each run; landings with play components shall have area 30" x 48" to park wheelchair while not reducing adjacent circulation path to less than 36" (ASTM 10.2.2.4).	10		
32.	For ramps, either the barrier extends to within 1 inch of the ramp surface or a curb stop exists that projects a minimum of 2" above the ramp. (ASTM 10.2.2.8).	20		
33.	For ramps higher than 30" (designed for 2-5 yr. olds) or higher than 48" (designed for 5-12 yr. olds) barriers are provided (ASTM 7.4.4, 10.2.2.5).	20		

LIBRARY
UNIVERSITY OF ST. FRANCIS
JOLIET, ILLINOIS

General Conditions	Possible Index Points	Index Points Given	Comments
Accessibility, cont.			
34. For ramps > 30" H (designed for 2-5 yr. olds) or > 48" H (designed for 5-12 yr. olds) handrails are provided on each side of a ramp at a height between 26-28". For ramps less than or equal to 30" H and 48" H (for 2-5 and 5-12 yr. olds, respectively) two handrails are provided on each side that are between 12-16" H and 26-28" H (ASTM 7.4.3, 10.2.2.6, 10.2.2.7).	20		
35. Transfer point height is between 14-18" with a clear width of minimum 24" and depth of no less than 14". Transfer point steps are a maximum of 8" high with handholds (ASTM 10.2.3.1-10.2.3.3, 10.3.1).	10		
36. Transfer pts. have; wheelchair turning space at base of transfer point; a clear space area of 60" minimum. T-shaped area in accordance with ASTM Fig. A1-39a (ASTM 10.2.4.1).	10		
37. The playground use zone has an accessible safety surface (ASTM 10.1.2).	10		
38. Accessible restroom facilities, accessible seating, accessible drinking fountain and shade are located in or near the play area.	1		
39. Wheelchair accessible platforms: single wheelchair passage 36"; two wheelchair passage 60"; single wheelchair and 1 able-bodied user 44"; openings between deck not greater than 0.50" (ASTM 10.2.5.1-10.2.5.4).	10		
40. Accessible play opportunities designed with different access and egress points, such as slides, allow the user to return unassisted to access the original transfer point (ASTM 10.3.2.1).	10		
41. Vertical leg clearance is not less than 24" for equipment that requires a wheelchair user to pull partially under, such as sand tables, with a top playing surface of no greater than 30" (ASTM 10.3.2.2).	10		

© NRPA/NPSI/PDRMA

General Conditions	Possible Index Points	Index Points Given	Comments
Accessibility, cont.			
42. Wheelchair accessible upper body equipment, such as horizontal ladders and rings, are less than or equal to 54" high (ASTM 10.3.2.3).	10		
43. Wheelchair accessible manipulative equipment, such as interactive panels, are between 9"-48" H for side reach and 20"-36" H for front reach from the accessible surface (ASTM 10.3.2.4, 10.3.2.5).	10		
Section Subtotal	**171**		

© NRPA/NPSI/PDRMA

Specific Conditions	Possible Index Points	Index Points Given	Comments

- **Important:** For the following audit sections, if multiple types of the same equipment exists (such as two swing sets), you can apply the questions to all multiple pieces of equipment as a whole. However, no more than full index points should be applied if a negative response exists on more than one piece of the same equipment. Also, deficiencies on a specific piece of equipment should be noted in the comments section for repair or future consideration.

Slides

	Specific Conditions	Possible Index Points	Index Points Given	Comments
44.	Slides are accessed by stairs, step ladders, or platforms which are evenly spaced, less than 12" apart, and pass the entrapment test. Refer to ASTM F 1487 Table 2 (CPSC 12.4.2).	10		
45.	There is a flat surface the width of the slide bed at the top of the slide to help position the child for sliding (min. 22" deep going back from the slide bedway and min. 12" wide for 2-5 yr. old users and a min. 16" for 5-12 yr. old users) (CPSC 12.4.3, ASTM 8.5.2.2, 8.5.2.3, 8.5.4.3).	10		
46.	There are sufficient safety barriers at the top of the slide to prevent falls, with hand holds to assist standing to sitting transition and a means to channel the user to the sitting position before slide entry (CPSC 12.4.3, ASTM 7.4, 8.5.3).	15		
47.	Sides of bedways are at least 4" high (CPSC 12.4.4, ASTM 8.5.4.4).	15		
48.	No portion of the angle of the sliding surface exceeds 50 degrees with the average angle of 30 degrees or less (CPSC 12.4.4, ASTM 8.5.4.2).	10		
49.	A flat sliding surface (run out zone) at the bottom of the slide is a min. of 11" long at transition point and angle is less than 5 degrees from the horizontal plane (CPSC 12.4.5, ASTM 8.5.5.1, 8.5.5.2).	10		
50.	For slides greater than 4' high, designed for 5-12 yr. olds, the slide exit height is between 7" and 15" above the protective surfacing material (CPSC 12.4.5, ASTM 8.5.5.3).	10		

© NRPA/NPSI/PDRMA

	Specific Conditions	Possible Index Points	Index Points Given	Comments

Slides cont.

	Specific Conditions	Possible Index Points	Index Points Given	Comments
51.	For slides 4' high or less and designed for 2-5 yr. olds, the slide exit height does not exceed 11" above the protective surfacing material (CPSC 12.4.5, ASTM 8.5.5.3).	10		
52.	Tube slides have a minimum diameter equal to or greater than 23" (CPSC 12.4.8, (ASTM 8.5.4.7).	5		
53.	Only short spiral slides, with one turn or less, are recommended for 2-5 yr. old users (CPSC 12.4.7).	5		
54.	A clear area, height of 60" along slide chute and width of 21" from inside edge of siderail including the transition platform. No obstacles or protrusions project more than 1/8" perpendicular to the plane of the initial surface. Underside of slide bedway is exempt (ASTM 8.5.6.1, figures A1.16 and A1.22).	20		
55.	On roller slides, no opening allows a 3/16" rod to enter (ASTM 8.9.2.1).	10		
56.	If the slide is made in several pieces, the sliding surface has no gaps or rough edges at the top of the slide or at section seams which could entangle clothing or trap foreign material (CPSC 12.4.3, 12.4.4).	20		
57.	The sliding surface faces away from sun or is located in the shade and isn't made of wood or fiberglass (CPSC 12.4.4).	10		
58.	Pinch, Crush and Shear Points (CPSC 9.5, ASTM 6.4): • Equipment is free of sharp edges. • There are no open holes in the equipment forming traps (e.g. at the ends of the tubes). • There are no pinch, crush or shear points.	10 10 10		
59.	Protrusions (CPSC 9.2, ASTM 6.2): • No components fail protrusion test. • Nuts, bolts and screws are recessed, covered or sanded smooth and level.	10 10		

© NRPA/NPSI/PDRMA

Specific Conditions	Possible Index Points	Index Points Given	Comments
Slides cont.			
60. Entanglements/Entrapment Angles (CPSC 9.4, 9.6, ASTM 6.3):			
• No more than two threads of the fastener protrude through any nut.	10		
• No obstacles or protrusions project upwards from a horizontal plane extending more than 1/8" perpendicular to the plane of the initial surface.	10		
• There are no open "V" entrapment angles on any part of the equipment. See Figs. A1.3-4 in ASTM F 1487.	10		
61. Head Entrapments (CPSC 9.6, ASTM 6.1):			
• No components fail the entrapment test.	10		
• There are no partially bounded openings. See Figs. A1.6a-A1.10 in ASTM F 1487.	10		
62. Hardware:			
• Nuts and bolts are tight and not able to be loosened without tools. Upon close inspection, they show no loose play or excessive wear (CPSC 8.2).	10		
• Equipment is free of rust and chipping paint (CPSC 8.1).	5		
• Equipment is free of sharp edges, splinters or rough surfaces and shows no excessive wear (CPSC 9.1).	10		
• Ropes, chains and cables have not frayed or worn out (CPSC 7.2).	10		
• Equipment has not shifted or become bent (CPSC 8.1).	10		
• There is no corrosion or visible rotting at points where equipment comes into contact with ground surface (CPSC 7.2, 8.1).	10		
• No components are missing. All parts of the equipment are present and in good working order with no loose play or excessive wear in moving parts (CPSC 7.2, 8.1).	20		
• Handgrips are between 0.95" and 1.55" in diameter (CPSC 10.2.1).	10		
• Footings for equipment are stable and buried below ground level or covered by surfacing materials (CPSC 9.7).	20		
• Equipment is free of any litter, debris and surfacing material (ASTM 7.1.2).	20		
• Equipment use zone is free of litter and debris (CPSC 7.2).	10		
Section Subtotal			

© NRPA/NPSI/PDRMA

Specific Conditions	Possible Index Points	Index Points Given	Comments

Climbing Equipment

	Specific Conditions	Possible Index Points	Index Points Given	Comments
63.	Handholds stay in place when grasped (CPSC 10.4).	20		
64.	Climbing bars and handrails are between 0.95"-1.55" in diameter (CPSC 10.2.1, ASTM 8.2.1).	10		
65.	Flexible access equipment anchoring devices are below level of playing surface (CPSC 12.1.3, ASTM 7.2.2.2).	10		
66.	Flexible climbing devices used as access for use by 2-5 yr. olds, readily allows users to bring feet to the same level before ascending to the next level (ASTM 7.2.2.4).	5		
67.	Climbers don't have climbing bars or other structural components in the interior of the structure onto which a child may fall from a height of greater than 18" (CPSC 12.1.2).	20		
68.	Accesses which don't have side handrails, such as rung ladders, arch or flexible climbers, are to have alternate hand-gripping support at transition (CPSC 10.4, ASTM 7.3.2).	10		
69.	Rung ladders, arch and flexible climbers used as access, are not above the designated play surface it serves (no trip hazard) (ASTM 7.3.3).	10		
70.	Balance beam maximum height from the playing surface is 12" for 2-5 yr. old users and 16" for 5-12 yr. old users (CPSC 12.1.8, ASTM 8.1.1).	5		
71.	No obstacles or protrusions project upwards from a horizontal plane extending more than a 1/8" perpendicular to the plane of the initial surface. See ASTM F1487 fig. A1.13 (CPSC 9.3, ASTM 6.3.2.1).	20		

© NRPA/NPSI/PDRMA

Specific Conditions	Possible Index Points	Index Points Given	Comments

Climbing Equipment, cont.

Specific Conditions	Possible Index Points	Index Points Given	Comments
72. All components of crawl through tunnels are secure and firmly fixed. The tunnel has two safe, clear exits and is designed to drain freely.	20		
73. Pinch, Crush and Shear Points (CPSC 9.5, ASTM 6.4): • Equipment is free of sharp edges. • There are no open holes in the equipment forming traps (e.g. at the ends of the tubes). • There are no pinch, crush or shear points.	10 10 10		
74. Protrusions (CPSC 9.2, ASTM 6.2): • No components fail protrusion test. • Nuts, bolts and screws are recessed, covered or sanded smooth and level.	10 10		
75. Entanglements/Entrapment Angles (CPSC 9.4, 9.6, ASTM 6.3): • No more than two threads of the fastener protrude through any nut. • No obstacles or protrusions project upwards from a horizontal plane extending more than 1/8" perpendicular to the plane of the initial surface. • There are no open "V" entrapment angles on any part of the equipment. See Figs. A1.3-4 in ASTM F 1487.	10 10 10		
76. Head Entrapments (CPSC 9.6, ASTM 6.1): • No components fail the entrapment test. • There are no partially bounded openings. See Figs. A1.6a-A1.10 ASTM F 1487.	10 10		
77. Hardware: • Nuts and bolts are tight and not able to be loosened without tools. Upon close inspection, they show no loose play or excessive wear (CPSC 8.2). • Equipment is free of rust and chipping paint (CPSC 8.1). • Equipment is free of sharp edges, splinters or rough surfaces and shows no excessive wear (CPSC 9.1). • Ropes, chains and cables have not frayed or worn out (CPSC 7.2). • Equipment has not shifted or become bent (CPSC 8.1).	10 5 10 10 10		

© NRPA/NPSI/PDRMA

Specific Conditions	Possible Index Points	Index Points Given	Comments

Climbing Equipment, cont.

Specific Conditions	Possible Index Points	Index Points Given	Comments
77. Hardware, cont.			
• There is no corrosion or visible rotting at points where equipment comes into contact with ground surface (CPSC 7.2, 8.1).	10		
• No components are missing. All parts of the equipment are present and in good working order with no loose play or excessive wear in moving parts (CPSC 7.2, 8.1).	20		
• Handgrips are between 0.95" and 1.55" in diameter (CPSC 10.2.1).	10		
• Footings for equipment are stable and buried below ground level or covered by surfacing materials (CPSC 9.7).	20		
• Equipment is free of any litter, debris and surfacing material (ASTM 7.1.2).	20		
• Equipment use zone is free of litter and debris (CPSC 7.2).	10		
Section Subtotal	**365**		

Upper Body Climbing Equipment

Specific Conditions	Possible Index Points	Index Points Given	Comments
78. Upper body climbing equipment, other than turning bars, not recommended for 2-5 yr. old users (CPSC 6.3, ASTM 8.3.1).	10		
79. Upper body climbing equipment maximum height is 84" for 5-12 yr. old users (CPSC 12.1.5, ASTM 8.3.4).	10		
80. Maximum distance between rungs for upper body equipment is 15" and openings pass the entrapment test (CPSC 9.6, 12.1.5, ASTM 8.3.2).	10		
81. Overhead swinging rings pass the entrament test and chain is maximum length of 12" (CPSC 9.6, 12.1.5).	10		
82. Climbing ropes are secured at both ends and are not capable of being looped back on itself creating a loop with an inside perimeter of greater than 5" (CPSC 12.1.7, ASTM 6.5.1).	20		

Specific Conditions	Possible Index Points	Index Points Given	Comments

Upper Body Climbing Equipment, cont.

	Specific Conditions	Possible Index Points	Index Points Given	Comments
83.	Horizontal take-off distance from landing structure to first handhold of upper body equipment is no greater than 10"; if access and egress is by rungs, horizontal distance to first rung is at least 8", but no greater than 10" (ASTM 8.3.3).	10		
84.	Maximum ht. of take off/landing for upper body equipment is 36" for 5-12 yr. old users (ASTM 8.3.5).	10		
85.	There are no single non-rigid components (cable, rope, wire, or similar component) suspended between play units or from the ground to the play unit within 45 degrees of horizontal, unless it is above 7 ft. from the playground surface and is a minimum of 1" at its widest cross-section dimension. It is recommended that the suspended components be brightly colored or contrast with surrounding equipment (CPSC 9.8, ASTM 6.5).	10		
86.	Sliding pole clearance from structures is between 18" and 20" (CPSC 12.1.6, ASTM 8.4.1).	10		
87.	Sliding pole is a minimum of 38" above the access structure, 60" min., recommended (CPSC 12.1.6, ASTM 8.4.3).	10		
88.	Sliding pole is a maximum 1.9" in diameter and continuous with no protruding welds or joints within sliding area (CPSC 12.1.6, ASTM 8.4.4, 8.4.5).	10		
89.	Track rides not recommended for 2-5 yr. old users (CPSC 6.3, ASTM 8.13.5).	20		
90.	Track rides; the lowest portion of the hand gripping component is a minimum 64" above protective surface with maximum height of 78" (ASTM 8.13.1).	10		
91.	Underside of track beam is a minimum of 78" above the protective surfacing (ASTM 8.13.2).	5		

© NRPA/NPSI/PDRMA

Specific Conditions	Possible Index Points	Index Points Given	Comments

Upper Body Climbing Equipment, cont.

Specific Conditions	Possible Index Points	Index Points Given	Comments
92. Pinch, Crush and Shear Points (CPSC 9.5, ASTM 6.4): • Equipment is free of sharp edges. • There are no open holes in the equipment forming traps (e.g. at the ends of the tubes). • There are no pinch, crush or shear points.	10 10 10		
93. Protrusions (CPSC 9.2, ASTM 6.2): • No components fail protrusion test. • Nuts, bolts and screws are recessed, covered or sanded smooth and level.	10 10		
94. Entanglements/Entrapment Angles (CPSC 9.4, 9.6, ASTM 6.3): • No more than two threads of the fastener protrude through any nut. • No obstacles or protrusions project upwards from a horizontal plane extending more than 1/8" perpendicular to the plane of the initial surface. • There are no open "V" entrapment angles on any part of the equipment. See Figs. A1.3-4 in ASTM F 1487.	10 10 10		
95. Head Entrapments (CPSC 9.6, ASTM 6.1): • No components fail the entrapment test. • There are no partially bounded openings. See Figs. A1.6a-A1.10 in ASTM F 1487.	10 10		
96. Hardware: • Nuts and bolts are tight and not able to be loosened without tools. Upon close inspection, they show no loose play or excessive wear (CPSC 8.2). • Equipment is free of rust and chipping paint (CPSC 8.1). • Equipment is free of sharp edges, splinters or rough surfaces and shows no excessive wear (CPSC 9.1). • Ropes, chains and cables have not frayed or worn out (CPSC 7.2). • Equipment has not shifted or become bent (CPSC 8.1). • There is no corrosion or visible rotting at points where equipment comes into contact with ground surface (CPSC 7.2, 8.1).	10 5 10 10 10 10		

© NRPA/NPSI/PDRMA

Specific Conditions	Possible Index Points	Index Points Given	Comments

Upper Body Climbing Equipment, cont.

Specific Conditions	Possible Index Points	Index Points Given	Comments
96. Hardware, cont. • No components are missing. All parts of the equipment are present and in good working order with no loose play or excessive wear in moving parts (CPSC 7.2, 8.1).	20		
• Handgrips are between 0.95" and 1.55" in diameter (CPSC 10.2.1).	10		
• Footings for equipment are stable and buried below ground level or covered by surfacing materials (CPSC 9.7).	20		
• Equipment is free of any litter, debris and surfacing material (ASTM 7.1.2).	20		
• Equipment use zone is free of litter and debris (CPSC 7.2).	10		
Section Subtotal	**390**		

Stairways and Ladders

Specific Conditions	Possible Index Points	Index Points Given	Comments
97. Continuous handrails on both sides for stairways >1 tread; on those with only 1 tread, an alternate means of hand support or handrail present. Handrail height is between 22" and 38" (CPSC 10.3.1, ASTM 7.1.4).	10		
98. Children have an easy, safe way to descend equipment when they reach the top. (via platform, stairway, or step ladder) (CPSC 12.1.2).	20		
99. Steps and rungs do not allow for accumulation of water and debris (CPSC 10.2, ASTM 7.1.2).	5		
100. Net, chain, arch or tire climbers not the sole means to access equipment for play areas for 2-5 yr. old users (CPSC 12.1.3, ASTM 7.2.2.1).	10		
101. Steps and rungs are evenly spaced within a tolerance of ±0.25 inches and horizontal within a tolerance of ±2 degrees. This includes the spacing between the top step or rung and the surface of the platform (ASTM 7.1.1).	10		

© NRPA/NPSI/PDRMA

Specific Conditions	Possible Index Points	Index Points Given	Comments
Stairways and Ladders, cont.			
102. Openings between steps or rungs and between the top step or rung and underside of a platform pass the testing requirements for head entrapment (CPSC 9.6.1, 10.2, ASTM 6.1)	20		
103. All stairways, step ladders and rung ladders, as it relates to the intended users, conform with access slope; tread, rung, and ramp width; tread depth; rung diameter; and vertical rise specifications as per ASTM F1487 Table 2 (CPSC 10.2).	10		
104. Pinch, Crush and Shear Points (CPSC 9.5, ASTM 6.4): • Equipment is free of sharp edges. • There are no open holes in the equipment forming traps (e.g. at ends of the tubes). • There are no pinch, crush or shear points.	10 10 10		
105. Protrusions (CPSC 9.2, ASTM 6.2): • No components fail protrusion test. • Nuts, bolts and screws are recessed, covered or sanded smooth and level.	10 10		
106. Entanglements/Entrapment Angles (CPSC 9.4, 9.6, ASTM 6.3): • No more than two threads of the fastener protrude through any nut. • No obstacles or protrusions project upwards from a horizontal plane extending more than 1/8" perpendicular to the plane of the initial surface. • There are no open "V" entrapment angles on any part of the equipment. See Figs. A1.3-4 in ASTM F1487.	10 10 10		
107. Head Entrapments (CPSC 9.6, ASTM 6.1): • No components fail the entrapment test. • There are no partially bounded openings. See Figs. A1.6a-A1.10 in ASTM F 1487.	10 10		
108. Hardware: • Nuts and bolts are tight and not able to be loosened without tools. Upon close inspection, they show no loose play or excessive wear (CPSC 8.2). • Equipment is free of rust and chipping paint (CPSC 8.1).	10 5		

© NRPA/NPSI/PDRMA

Specific Conditions	Possible Index Points	Index Points Given	Comments

Stairways and Ladders, cont.

Specific Conditions	Possible Index Points	Index Points Given	Comments
108. Hardware, cont.:			
• Equipment is free of sharp edges, splinters or rough surfaces and shows no excessive wear (CPSC 9.1).	10		
• Ropes, chains and cables have not frayed or worn out (CPSC 7.2).	10		
• Equipment has not shifted or become bent (CPSC 8.1).	10		
• There is no corrosion or visible rotting at points where equipment comes into contact with ground surface (CPSC 7.2, 8.1).	10		
• No components are missing. All parts of the equipment are present and in good working order with no loose play or excessive wear in moving parts (CPSC 7.2, 8.1).	20		
• Handgrips are between 0.95" and 1.55" in diameter (CPSC 10.2.1).	10		
• Footings for equipment are stable and buried below ground level or covered by surfacing materials (CPSC 9.7).	20		
• Equipment is free of any litter, debris and surfacing material (ASTM 7.1.2).	20		
• Equipment use zone is free of litter and debris (CPSC 7.2).	10		
Section Subtotal	**320**		

Decks and Platforms

Specific Conditions	Possible Index Points	Index Points Given	Comments
109. Unless an alternate means of access is provided, the maximum difference in height between stepped platforms for 2-5 yr. olds is 12" and for 5-12 yr. olds is 18" (CPSC 11.7, ASTM 7.4.5.1).	20		
110. There is a 29" high (min.) protective perimeter barrier around 2-5 yr. old users' equipment that is more than 30" above the underlying surface (CPSC 11.5, ASTM 7.4.4.1, 7.4.4.3).	10		
111. There is a 38" high (min.) protective perimeter barrier on all elevated surfaces 48" above the underlying surface for 5-12 yr. old users' equipment (CPSC 11.5, ASTM 7.4.4.1, 7.4.4.3).	10		

© NRPA/NPSI/PDRMA

Specific Conditions	Possible Index Points	Index Points Given	Comments

Decks and Platforms, cont.

Specific Conditions	Possible Index Points	Index Points Given	Comments
112. The space between slats of protective barriers and guardrails is not between 3-1/2" and 9" and passes the entrapment test (CPSC 9.6, ASTM 6.1).	10		
113. Guardrails or protective barriers are present on all elevated surfaces greaterthan 20" above the underlying surface for 2-5 yr. old users' equipment (29" top edge, 23" lower edge) (CPSC 11.4, ASTM 7.4.3.1-7.4.3.4).	10		
114. Guardrails or protective barriers are present for all elevated surfaces 30" above the underlying surface for 5-12 yr. old users' equipment (38" top edge, 24" high lower edge) (CPSC 11.4, ASTM 7.4.3.1-7.4.3.4).	10		
115. No partially bounded openings are projecting upwards from the horizontal plane that are greater than 1 7/8" or less than 9" and fail the test method for partially bounded openings. See ASTM F1487 Figures A1.6a-A1.10 (CPSC Fig. 8, ASTM 6.1.4).	20		
116. Pinch, Crush and Shear Points (CPSC 9.5, ASTM 6.4): • Equipment is free of sharp edges. • There are no open holes in the equipment forming traps (e.g. at ends of the tubes). • There are no pinch, crush or shear points.	10 10 10		
117. Protrusions (CPSC 9.2, ASTM 6.2): • No components fail protrusion test. • Nuts, bolts and screws are recessed, covered or sanded smooth and level.	10 10		
118. Entanglements/Entrapment Angles (CPSC 9.4, 9.6, ASTM 6.3): • No more than two threads of the fastener protrude through any nut. • No obstacles or protrusions project upwards from a horizontal plane extending more than 1/8" perpendicular to the plane of the initial surface.	10 10		

© NRPA/NPSI/PDRMA

Specific Conditions	Possible Index Points	Index Points Given	Comments
Decks and Platforms, cont.			
118. Entanglements/Entrapment Angles (CPSC 9.4, 9.6, ASTM 6.3): • There are no open "V" entrapment angles on any part of the equipment. See Figs. A1.3-4 in ASTM F 1487.	10		
119. Head Entrapments (CPSC 9.6, ASTM 6.1): • No components fail the entrapment test. • There are no partially bounded openings. See Figs. A1.6a-A1.10 in ASTM F1487.	10 10		
120. Hardware: • Nuts and bolts are tight and not able to be loosened without tools. Upon close inspection, they show no loose play or excessive wear (CPSC 8.2). • Equipment is free of rust and chipping paint (CPSC 8.1). • Equipment is free of sharp edges, splinters or rough surfaces and shows no excessive wear (CPSC 9.1). • Ropes, chains and cables have not frayed or worn out (CPSC 7.2). • Equipment has not shifted or become bent (CPSC 8.1). • There is no corrosion or visible rotting at points where equipment comes into contact with ground surface (CPSC 7.2, 8.1). • No components are missing. All parts of the equipment are present and in good working order with no loose play or excessive wear in moving parts (CPSC 7.2, 8.1). • Handgrips are between 0.95" and 1.55" in diameter (CPSC 10.2.1). • Footings for equipment are stable and buried below ground level or covered by surfacing materials (CPSC 9.7). • Equipment is free of any litter, debris and surfacing material. • Equipment use zone is free of litter and debris.	10 5 10 10 10 10 20 10 20 20 10		
Section Subtotal	**325**		

© NRPA/NPSI/PDRMA

Specific Conditions	Possible Index Points	Index Points Given	Comments
Swings			
121. All swings, to and fro and rotating swings are not attached to main structure (CPSC 12.6.2, ASTM 8.6.1.1).	20		
122. All flying animal figure swings, multiple occupancy swings (except tire swings), rope swings, and trapeze bars are removed from public playgrounds (CPSC 12.6.4, ASTM 8.7.1).	40		
123. Lightweight enclosed swing seats, are used and all openings meet entrapment criteria (CPSC 12.6.3).	10		
124. All swing seats are made of canvas, rubber, or other lightweight material (CPSC 12.6.2, ASTM 8.6.1.3).	20		
125. There are no open "S" hooks (openings greater than or equal to 0.04") (CPSC 12.6.1).	10		
126. When stationary, all seats same type are level.	1		
127. There are no more than two swings, evenly spaced, in any individual swing bay (CPSC 12.6.2, ASTM 8.6.1.3). Swing seat shall be of the same type in each bay. (CPSC 12.6.3)	20		
128. Swings are at least 24" from each other and 30" away from the frame. See ASTM Figs. A1.23, A1.24 (CPSC Fig. 22, ASTM 8.6.1.5).	20		
129. Vertical distance is at least 12" between underside of occupied seat and protective surface (CPSC 12.6.2, ASTM 8.6.1.5).	1		
130. Swing hangers are spaced wider than seats, not less than 20" (CPSC 12.6.2, ASTM 8.6.1.5).	10		
131. For tire swings, there is at least a 30" safety zone from the crossbeam support structure and the farthest extensions of the swing, and each must have a minimum clearance of 12" from the bottom of the tire to the protective surface (CPSC 12.6.4, ASTM 8.6.1.5).	10		
132. Swing tires have adequate drainage (CPSC 12.6.4).	5		

Specific Conditions	Possible Index Points	Index Points Given	Comments
Swings, cont.			
133. Tire swings are not made of steel belted radial tires (CPSC 12.6.2, ASTM 8.6.2.3).	10		
134. To and fro swings and tire swings are located away from circulation paths (a distance at least equal to the equipment use zone and an additional safety factor for circulation, with this area free of any obstructions) and near the periphery of the playground (CPSC 6.2, ASTM 8.6.1.1, 8.6.2.1).	10		
135. Pinch, Crush and Shear Points (CPSC 9.5, ASTM 6.4): • Equipment is free of sharp edges. • There are no open holes in the equipment forming traps (e.g. at the ends of the tubes). • There are no pinch, crush or shear points.	10 10 10		
136. Protrusions (CPSC 9.2, ASTM 6.2): • No components fail protrusion test. • Nuts, bolts and screws are recessed, covered or sanded smooth and level.	10 10		
137. Entanglements/Entrapment Angles (CPSC 9.4, 9.6, ASTM 6.3): • No more than two threads of the fastener protrude through any nut. • No obstacles or protrusions project upwards from a horizontal plane extending more than 1/8" perpendicular to the plane of the initial surface. • There are no open "V" entrapment angles on any part of the equipment. See Figs. A1.3-4 in ASTM F 1487.	10 10 10		
138. Head Entrapments (CPSC 9.6, ASTM 6.1): • No components fail the entrapment test. • There are no partially bounded openings. See Figs. A1.6a-A1.10 in ASTM F 1487.	10 10		
139. Hardware: • Nuts and bolts are tight and not able to be loosened without tools. Upon close inspection, they show no loose play or excessive wear (CPSC 8.2).	10		

© NRPA/NPSI/PDRMA

Specific Conditions	Possible Index Points	Index Points Given	Comments
Swings, cont.			
139. Hardware, cont.:			
• Equipment is free of rust and chipping paint (CPSC 8.1).	5		
• Equipment is free of sharp edges, splinters or rough surfaces and shows no excessive wear (CPSC 9.1).	10		
• Ropes, chains and cables have not frayed or worn out (CPSC 7.2).	10		
• Equipment has not shifted or become bent (CPSC 8.1).	10		
• There is no corrosion or visible rotting at points where equipment comes into contact with ground surface (CPSC 7.2, 8.1).	10		
• No components are missing. All parts of the equipment are present and in good working order with no loose play or excessive wear in moving parts (CPSC 7.2, 8.1).	20		
• Handgrips are between 0.95" and 1.55" in diameter (CPSC 10.2.1).	10		
• Footings for equipment are stable and buried below ground level or covered by surfacing materials (CPSC 9.7).	20		
• Equipment is free of any litter, debris and surfacing material (ASTM 7.1.2).	20		
• Equipment use zone is free of litter and debris (CPSC 7.2).	10		
Section Subtotal	**422**		

Rotating and Rocking Equipment

Specific Conditions	Possible Index Points	Index Points Given	Comments
140. The seesaws seating surface does not reach more than 5' above the underlying surface ASTM 8.10.6).	10		
141. The seesaw fulcrum is fixed, enclosed or designed to prevent pinching (CPSC 12.3, ASTM 8.10.3).	10		
142. Seesaw handgrips intended to be gripped by one hand have a minimum length of 3" and 2-hands a minimum of 6" and pass the protrusion test (CPSC 12.3, ASTM 8.10.4.1).	10		

Specific Conditions	Possible Index Points	Index Points Given	Comments

Rotating and Rocking Equipment, cont.

	Specific Conditions	Possible Index Points	Index Points Given	Comments
143.	A rubber segment is buried in the surfacing under the seesaw seats unless seesaw uses a spring centering device (CPSC 12.3, ASTM 8.10.2).	10		
144.	Log rolls (not recommended for 2-5yr. old users) have maximum ht. of 18" above the protective surface for 5-12 yr. old users (ASTM 8.12.2, 8.12.3).	20		
145.	Spring rocking equipment seat height is between 14" and 28" (ASTM 8.11.5).	5		
146.	There are no equipment parts that could cause a pinching or crushing injury on spring rocking equipment. Exemption is the attachment area of heavy duty coil springs to the body and base of spring rocking equipment (CPSC 12.5, ASTM 6.4.1.3 [2], 8.11.4).	10		
147.	Handholds stay in place when grasped and pass the protrusion test (CPSC 12.5, ASTM 8.11.2).	10		
148.	Footrests stay in place and pass the protrusion test (CPSC 12.5, ASTM 8.11.3).	5		
149.	Merry-go-rounds are approximately circular, and the distance between the minimum and maximum radii of a noncircular platform does not exceed 2". See Fig. A1.25 in ASTM F1487 (CPSC 12.2, ASTM 8.8.1.1, 8.8.1.2).	10		
150.	Components of the merry-go-round do not extend beyond the platform perimeter (CPSC 12.2, ASTM 8.8.1.2).	10		
151.	There are no openings in the surface of the platform that permit the penetration of 5/16" rod through the surface of the merry-go-round (CPSC 12.2, ASTM 8.8.1.4).	10		
152.	There are no accessible shearing or crushing mechanisms in the undercarriage of the equipment, and the platform does not provide an oscillatory (up and down) motion (CPSC 12.2, ASTM 8.8.1.5).	10		

© NRPA/NPSI/PDRMA

Specific Conditions	Possible Index Points	Index Points Given	Comments
Rotating Equipment, cont.			
153. The peripheral speed of the platform does not exceed 13 feet per second (CPSC 12.2, ASTM 8.8.1.6).	10		
154. There is a minimum of 9" between the protective surface and the underside of a merry-go-round platform with a max. ht. of 14" for the platform surface (CPSC 12.2, ASTM 8.8.1.2, 8.8.1.4).	10		
155. Pinch, Crush and Shear Points (CPSC 9.5, ASTM 6.4): • Equipment is free of sharp edges. • There are no open holes in the equipment forming traps (e.g. at the ends of the tubes). • There are no pinch, crush or shear points.	10 10 10		
156. Protrusions (CPSC 9.2, ASTM 6.2): • No components fail protrusion test. • Nuts, bolts and screws are recessed, covered or sanded smooth and level.	10 10		
157. Entanglements/Entrapment Angles (CPSC 9.4, 9.6, ASTM 6.3): • No more than two threads of the fastener protrude through any nut. • No obstacles or protrusions project upwards from a horizontal plane extending more than 1/8" perpendicular to the plane of the initial surface. • There are no open "V" entrapment angles on any part of the equipment. See Figs. A1.3-4 in ASTM F 1487.	10 10 10		
158. Head Entrapments (CPSC 9.6, ASTM 6.1): • No components fail the entrapment test. • There are no partially bounded openings. See Figs. A1.6a-A1.10 in ASTM F 1487.	 10 10		
159. Hardware: • Nuts and bolts are tight and not able to be loosened without tools. Upon close inspection, they show no loose play or excessive wear (CPSC 8.2). • Equipment is free of rust and chipping paint (CPSC 8.1).	10 5		

Specific Conditions	Possible Index Points	Index Points Given	Comments

Rotating Equipment, cont.

Specific Conditions	Possible Index Points	Index Points Given	Comments
159. Hardware, cont.			
• Equipment is free of sharp edges, splinters or rough surfaces and shows no excessive wear (CPSC 9.1).	10		
• Ropes, chains and cables have not frayed or worn out (CPSC 7.2).	10		
• Equipment has not shifted or become bent (CPSC 8.1).	10		
• There is no corrosion or visible rotting at points where equipment comes into contact with ground surface (CPSC 7.2, 8.1).	10		
• No components are missing. All parts of the equipment are present and in good working order with no loose play or excessive wear in moving parts (CPSC 7.2, 8.1).	20		
• Handgrips are between 0.95" and 1.55" in diameter (CPSC 10.2.1).	10		
• Footings for equipment are stable and buried below ground level or covered by surfacing materials (CPSC 9.7).	20		
• Equipment is free of any litter, debris and surfacing material (ASTM 7.1.2).	20		
• Equipment use zone is free of litter and debris (CPSC 7.2).	10		
Section Subtotal	**385**		

Sand Play Area

<u>Note:</u>   This section is only applicable to sand box areas designated for play. Ground level sand boxes and activity walls require a child to be at ground level. Such ground level activities are excluded from the recommendations for protective surfacing under and around playground equipment. Refer to CPSC 4.4 revised handbook May, 1997.

Specific Conditions	Possible Index Points	Index Points Given	Comments
160. Sand play is located in a shaded area.	1		
161. The sand play area is inspected and raked at least every week for debris and to provide exposure to air and sun.	5		
162. If the sand play area is in a box, it is covered at night to prevent animal excrement contamination.	5		
163. The sand play area does not have standing water 24 hours after a rainfall.	5		

© NRPA/NPSI/PDRMA

Specific Conditions	Possible Index Points	Index Points Given	Comments

Sand Play Area cont.

Specific Conditions	Possible Index Points	Index Points Given	Comments
164. Elevated sand boxes have appropriate use zone with proper impact absorbing material (CPSC 4.4).	20		
165. Pinch, Crush and Shear Points (CPSC 9.5, ASTM 6.4): • Equipment is free of sharp edges. • There are no open holes in the equipment forming traps (e.g. at ends of the tubes). • There are no pinch, crush or shear points.	10 10 10		
166. Protrusions (CPSC 9.2, ASTM 6.2): • No components fail protrusion test. • Nuts, bolts and screws are recessed, covered or sanded smooth and level.	10 10		
167. Entanglements/Entrapment Angles (CPSC 9.4, 9.6, ASTM 6.3): • No more than two threads of the fastener protrude through any nut. • No obstacles or protrusions project upwards from a horizontal plane extending more than 1/8" perpendicular to the plane of the initial surface. • There are no open "V" entrapment angles on any part of the equipment. See Figs. A1.3-4 in ASTM F 1487.	10 10 10		
168. Head Entrapments (CPSC 9.6, ASTM 6.1): • No components fail the entrapment test. • There are no partially bounded openings. See Figs. A1.6a-A1.10 in ASTM F 1487.	10 10		
169. Hardware: • Nuts and bolts are tight and not able to be loosened without tools. Upon close inspection, they show no loose play or excessive wear (CPSC 8.2). • Equipment is free of rust and chipping paint (CPSC 8.1). • Equipment is free of sharp edges, splinters or rough surfaces and shows no excessive wear (CPSC 9.1). • Ropes, chains and cables have not frayed or worn out (CPSC 7.2). • Equipment has not shifted or become bent (CPSC 8.1). • There is no corrosion or visible rotting at points where equipment comes into contact with ground surface (CPSC 7.2, 8.1).	10 5 10 10 10 10		

Specific Conditions	Possible Index Points	Index Points Given	Comments
169. Hardware, cont.			
• No components are missing. All parts of the equipment are present and in good working order with no loose play or excessive wear in moving parts (CPSC 7.2, 8.1).	20		
• Handgrips are between 0.95" and 1.55" in diameter (CPSC 10.2.1).	10		
• Footings for equipment are stable and buried below ground level or covered by surfacing materials (CPSC 9.7).	20		
• Equipment is free of any litter, debris and surfacing material (ASTM 7.1.2).	20		
• Equipment use zone is free of litter and debris (CPSC 7.2).	10		
Section Subtotal	**271**		

Sand Play Area, cont.

© NRPA/NPSI/PDRMA

Specific Conditions	Possible Index Points	Index Points Given	Comments

Specific Equipment Index Points Form (SEIP Form)
Equipment/Component Name: _____

Specific Conditions	Possible Index Points	Index Points Given	Comments
Pinch, Crush and Shear Points (CPSC 9.5, ASTM 6.4): • Equipment is free of sharp edges. • There are no open holes in the equipment forming traps (e.g. at the ends of the tubes). • There are no pinch, crush or shear points.	10 10 10		
Protrusions (CPSC 9.2, ASTM 6.2): • No components fail protrusion test. • Nuts, bolts and screws are recessed, covered or sanded smooth and level.	10 10		
Entanglements/Entrapment Angles (CPSC 9.4, 9.6, ASTM 6.3: • No more than two threads of the fastener protrude through any nut. • No obstacles or protrusions project upwards from a horizontal plane extending more than 1/8" perpendicular to the plane of the initial surface. • There are no open "V" entrapment angles on any part of the equipment. See Figs. A1.3-4 in ASTM F 1487.	10 10 10		
Head Entrapments (CPSC 9.6, ASTM 6.1): • No components fail the entrapment test. • There are no partially bounded openings. See Figs. A1.6a-A1.10 in ASTM F 1487.	10 10		
Hardware: • Nuts and bolts are tight and not able to be loosened without tools. Upon close inspection, they show no loose play or excessive wear (CPSC 8.2). • Equipment is free of rust and chipping paint (CPSC 8.1). • Equipment is free of sharp edges, splinters or rough surfaces and shows no excessive wear (CPSC 9.1). • Ropes, chains and cables have not frayed or worn out (CPSC 7.2). • Equipment has not shifted or become bent (CPSC 8.1). • There is no corrosion or visible rotting at points where equipment comes into contact with ground surface (CPSC 7.2, 8.1).	10 5 10 10 10 10		

© NRPA/NPSI/PDRMA

Specific Conditions	Possible Index Points	Index Points Given	Comments
Hardware, cont.			
• No components are missing. All parts of the equipment are present and in good working order with no loose play or excessive wear in moving parts (CPSC 7.2, 8.1).	20		
• Handgrips are between 0.95" and 1.55" in diameter (CPSC 10.2.1).	10		
• Footings for equipment are stable and buried below ground level or covered by surfacing materials (CPSC 9.7).	20		
• Equipment is free of any litter, debris and surfacing material (ASTM 7.1.2).	20		
• Equipment use zone is free of litter and debris (CPSC 7.2).	10		
Section Subtotal	**235**		

SEIP Form, cont.

© NRPA/NPSI/PDRMA

Audit Summary:

Audit Section Headings	Questions	Possible Index Points	Actual Index Pts.	Index Pts. Given	Audit %Rating

Section A: General Conditions

Audit Section Headings	Questions	Possible Index Points	Actual Index Pts.	Index Pts. Given	Audit %Rating
Playground Border Factors	3	70	70		
General Environment	4-14	103	103		
Age/Size Appropriateness Design	15-17	140	140		
Playground Protective Surface	18-22	150	150		
Use Zone	23-28	110	110		
Accessibility Design	29-43	171	171		
Section A Subtotal:		**744**	**744**		

Section B: Specific Conditions

Audit Section Headings	Questions	Possible Index Points	Actual Index Pts.	Index Pts. Given	Audit %Rating
Slides	44-62	395			
Climbing Equipment	63-77	365			
Upper Body Climbing Equipment	78-96	390			
Stairways and Ladders	97-108	320			
Decks and Platforms	109-120	325			
Swings	121-139	422			
Rotating and Rocking Equipment	140-159	385			
Sand Play Areas	160-169	271			
Section B Subtotal:		**2873**			

Section C: SEIP Forms **used for equipment not identified in specific conditions section

Audit Section Headings	Questions	Possible Index Points	Actual Index Pts.	Index Pts. Given	Audit %Rating
SEIP Form _____		235*			
SEIP Form _____		235*			
SEIP Form _____		235*			
Section C Subtotal:					
Site Total: totals for sections A,B,C					

*235 is the possible points for the Specific Equipment Index Points Form (SEIP Form).
Actual total may vary from playground site to playground site depending upon what type of equipment is present.

IMPORTANT
  This information is for internal use only and is not to be released or otherwise disseminated to anyone other than an agency official, or designated representative.

COMMENTS SUMMARY

Auditor:_____ Supervisor:_____Date:_____

_____

_____

_____

_____

_____

_____

_____

_____

_____

_____

_____

_____

_____

_____

_____

_____

_____

_____

_____

_____

_____

_____

_____

_____

_____

_____

_____

_____

_____

_____

_____

_____

_____

_____

_____

_____

© NRPA/NPSI/PDRMA

Interpreting the Results of Playground Safety Audits

By Final Audit Scores

The simplest means of interpreting multiple playground safety audit scores is to list them in descending numerical order. This list will provide a general ranking of your playground sites based on their index rating score. The higher the score, the greater the number of safety concerns that exists at an individual playground site

☞ **NOTE:** In general, you will find that larger playground sites will likely have higher point totals due to their having more play equipment and exposure to border hazards. Also, older playground equipment and park sites will likely have higher audit scores because of the changes that have taken place over the years in safer product design, layout philosophies, surfacing technologies, and installation guidelines.

The following is a sample list of audit index point totals for five individual park playground sites.

Ranking playground audits by index score totals can be helpful in establishing an agency's comprehensive replacement schedule for entire playground/park sites.

Ranking Playground Sites by Audit Score	
Park Location	**Final Score**
Grant Playfield	1610
Washington Field	1255
Tasha Park	1237
Presidents Park	1145
Northside Park	244

However, this method of analysis does not take into account any accident history by site or the frequency of use. Heavy use can accelerate the life cycle of play equipment, and over use by large numbers of children, such as an elementary school playground, can lead to an increase in frequency and severity of playground accidents.

Many factors should be evaluated beyond the final audit scores when determining which playgrounds should be replaced or what safety concerns should be eliminated first.

Comparison of Each Audit Subsection Point Total

Another means of interpreting the results of a group of safety audits is to compare the audit subsection scores against each other. This comparison can be helpful in identifying any safety concerns that are common among a group of playground sites.

This information can then be used to identify and respond to correctable safety concerns that can be eliminated on a uniform basis at all playground sites.

AUDIT SUMMARY		Audit Scores by Section				
Audit Section Heading	Possible Index Points	Presidents Park	Washington Field	Tasha Park	Grant Playfield	Northside Park
SECTION A: GENERAL CONDITIONS						
Border Factors	70	24	29	47	25	11
General Environment	103	29	7	10	26	6
Age/Size Design	140	110	90	100	95	0
Protective Surfacing	150	120	140	130	135	25
Use Zone	110	40	60	60	90	20
Accessibility Design	171	12	11	3	0	41
Section A: SUBTOTAL	744	335	337	350	371	103
SECTION B: SPECIFIC CONDITIONS						
Slides	395	120	185	135	165	45
Climbing Equipment	365	265	267	235	290	20
Upper Body Climbing Equipment	390	186	190	265	223	10
Stairways & Ladders	320	N/A	75	N/A	80	0
Decks & Platforms	325	36	125	30	120	20
Swings	422	55	40	80	85	0
Rotating & Rocking Equipment	385	N/A	N/A	N/A	130	25
Sand Play Areas	271	95	N/A	85	95	21
Section B: SUBTOTAL	2873	757	882	830	1188	141
SECTION C: SEIP FORMS – Used for equipment not identified in specific conditions section						
SEIP Form: Talk Tube	235*	24	29	47	25	N/A
SEIP Form: Ground Level Play Panel	235*	29	7	10	26	N/A
Section C: SUBTOTAL	470*	53	36	57	51	0
Site Total: totals for Sections A, B, & C	4037	1145	1255	1237	1610	244

*Audit site total subject to change based on the playground components and environment at each site.

© NRPA/NPSI/PDRMA

As each audit section subtotal is evaluated across (horizontally) the sample data chart provided on the previous page, the following inferences can be made:

1. All sites except Northside Park need review of age appropriate design because of the consistency of age/size design subsection scores.

2. Many of the playground sites are in need of improvements in the protective surfacing category. Surfacing problems are reflected in the consistently high protective surfacing sub-section scores at all park sites, but Northside Park.

3. The consistently high scores at most sites in the climbing equipment section should be further evaluated to see if any common safety concerns can be eliminated through retrofitting, repairs, or other means.

☞ **NOTE:** If the overall audit score of any type or specific piece of playground equipment is very high and cannot be corrected to a reasonably safe use level, consideration should be given to removing any dangerous equipment.

4. It is very likely that Northside Park is a newer park site with more contemporary equipment, yet still may need some accessibility design improvements.

Comparison of All Agency Sites Using Site Score Percentage Ratings

One of the best methods to comprehensively compare all agency playground sites regardless of their size is to use a percentage rating formula. As discussed in the previous section on interpreting by final audit scores, you will find that your larger playground sites will likely have higher audit scores than smaller sites due to their containing a greater number of playground components. Using the percentile score rating method in lieu of total audit point scores will help to more equitably compare large and small playground sites by evaluating the level of compliance that exists at each site based on the 1997 CPSC Handbook and the ASTM F1487-95 Standard.

Percentage Rating Formula:

$$\frac{\text{Index Points Given}}{\text{Actual Index Points}} = \text{Index \% Rating}$$

To rank all agency playground sites by percentage score ratings:

1. Complete the **Playground Audit Score Summary Form** with information from individual playground site audits (see page 58).

   IMPORTANT:

   - **Section A: General Conditions** has 744 total possible points available. In **Section B: Specific Conditions** and **Section C: Specific Equipment Index Points, SEIP** the total possible points may vary depending on the scoring of playground equipment *found or not found* at the playground site. Simply transfer your **Audit Summary results** (page 51) to the **Playground Audit Score Summary Form** (see page 58).

   - In **Section B: Specific Conditions** on the **Audit Summary Form** (page 58), it is very important to *only transfer* the **Possible Index Points** to the **Actual Index Points** column *for equipment that exists* at the playground site (page 57).

2. Divide the **Audit Score's Index Points Given** by the total possible points available **(Actual Index Points)**, which provides an Index Percentile Rating. Place the Percentile Rating in the boxes provided.

☞ **IMPORTANT:** The site score or index percentile ratings should be interpreted in the same fashion as golf scores. Higher scores are **not** positive. The higher the percentage, the higher its relative risk and non-compliance with the *1997 Consumer Products Safety Commission Playground Safety Guidelines* and the *ASTM F1487-95 Standard.* This information can be very useful in developing a long term playground replacement schedule.

© NRPA/NPSI/PDRMA

PLAYGROUND AUDIT SCORE SUMMARY FORM FOR ALL AGENCY SITES

AUDIT SUMMARY		Audit Scores by Section				
Audit Section Heading	Possible Index Points	Presidents Park Est. 1990	Washington Field Est. 1985	Tasha Park Est. 1980	Grant Playfield Est. 1990	Northside Park Est. 1995
SECTION A: GENERAL CONDITIONS						
Border Factors	70	24	29	47	25	11
General Environment	103	29	7	10	26	6
Age/Size Design	140	110	90	100	95	0
Protective Surfacing	150	120	140	130	135	25
Use Zone	110	40	60	60	90	20
Accessibility Design	171	12	11	3	0	41
Section A: SUBTOTAL	744	335	337	350	371	103
SECTION B: SPECIFIC CONDITIONS						
Slides	395	120	185	135	165	45
Climbing Equipment	365	265	267	235	190	20
Upper Body Climbing Equipment	390	186	190	223	127	10
Stairways & Ladders	320	N/A	75	N/A	80	0
Decks & Platforms	325	36	125	30	120	20
Swings	422	55	40	80	85	0
Rotating & Rocking Equipment	385	N/A	N/A	N/A	130	25
Sand Play Areas	271	95	N/A	85	95	21
Section B: SUBTOTAL	2873*	757	882	830	1188	141
SECTION C: SEIP FORMS – Used for equipment not identified in specific conditions section						
SEIP Form: Talk Tube	235	24	29	47	25	N/A
SEIP Form: Ground Level l Play Panel	235	29	7	10	26	N/A
Section C: SUBTOTAL	470	53	36	57	51	0
Site Total: totals for Sections A, B, & C	4087*	1145	1255	1237	1610	244
Index Points Given / Actual Index Points		1145 / 3382	1255 / 3431	1237 / 3382	1610 / 4087	244 / 3617
Index % Rating		34%	37%	37%	40%	7%

*The "Actual Index Points" total is the sum of all Possible Index Points for specific equipment types *found or not found* in Section B or C at each site.

© NRPA/NPSI/PDRMA

PLAYGROUND AUDIT SCORE SUMMARY FORM FOR ALL AGENCY SITES

Scores by Section for Each Playground Site

Audit Section Heading	Possible Index Points						
SECTION A: GENERAL CONDITIONS							
Playground Border Factors	70						
General Environment	103						
Age/Size Appropriate Design	140						
Playground Protective Surfacing	150						
Use Zone	110						
Accessibility Design	171						
SECTION A SUBTOTAL	**744**						
SECTION B: SPECIFIC CONDITIONS							
Slides	395						
Climbing Equipment	365						
Upper Body Climbing Equipment	390						
Stairways and Ladders	320						
Decks and Platforms	325						
Swings	422						
Rotating and Rocking Equipment	385						
Sand Play Areas	271						
SECTION B SUBTOTAL	**2873**						
SECTION C: SEIP FORMS							
SEIP Form _____	235*						
SEIP Form _____	235*						
SEIP Form _____	235*						
SECTION C SUBTOTAL							
Site Total: totals for Sections A, B, & C	4087*						
Index Points Given							
Acutal Index Points							
Index % Rating							

*235 is the possible points for the Specific Equipment Index Points Form (SEIP Form).
Actual total may vary from playground site to playground site depending upon what type of equipment is present.

IMPORTANT: This information is for internal use only and is not to be released or otherwise disseminated to anyone other than an agency official, or designated representative.

© NRPA/NPSI/PDRMA

The Public Playground Equipment Replacement Dilemma

The overall responsibility for the maintenance, repair, retrofitting and replacement of your playground facilities can become a much more complicated issue without establishing a number of planning guidelines. The realities of attempting to do more, build more, and manage more than is within the reasonable limits of a community's resources may threaten the safety of the playground users and the financial stability of the community. The first day a new public playground opens for use is generally the last time that the playground owner/operator can feel somewhat confident that the entire area is safe and hazard free. The first day also marks the beginning of the playground's routine and preventive maintenance and repair history. This includes the documentation of timely inspections and repairs plus the continued compliance to current industry safety guidelines and standards.

This publication provides public playground owners and operators with the philosophies and sample policy statement supporting the maintenance of the playground equipment that will prolong its life. Beyond the need to prolong the life and function of a major capital expenditure such as playground equipment, a maintenance program will help avoid more costly repairs. The real dilemma facing all owner/operators of public playgrounds begins when inspections bring to our attention a major deficiency in the playground's ability to provide a safe and enjoyable play experience for children or when the playground no longer complies with current safety guidelines and standards.

Let's make a few assumptions regarding this replacement dilemma that will allow us to focus on the questions that will provide the answers to make calculated decisions for the ongoing financial support of a viable public playground or playgrounds.

Assumptions

❑ Most of us will have many if not all of our playground facilities that will be out of compliance with the new 1997 US CPSC Handbook for Public Playground Safety and/or the ASTM F1487-95 Standard.

❑ Most of us will not have anywhere near enough financial resources to address all of the safety concerns in a short time period.

❑ It is not a viable solution to remove all the equipment with safety concerns per the new guidelines and standards when there have been no reported accidents (unless mandated by state law or local authority).

❑ Let's assume that we have all addressed the safety concerns dealing with appropriate resilient surfacing, equipment layout, use zones and removal of all equipment identified as unsuitable for public playgrounds.

The Question

The only question left unanswered is, how do we deal with a playground when all the safety concerns are eliminated except those inherent in the playground manufacturer's product design and there are no means to eliminate or retrofit the problem?

The Challenge

How do we plan for the inevitable replacement of all our public playgrounds when they are in non-compliance with safety guidelines and standards or just plain worn out?

© NRPA/NPSI/PDRMA

The Plan

A plan to replace all existing and future playgrounds is developed by completing the following steps:

A. Identify the playground user groups by age and number of users within each group.

B. Define the carrying capacity of a playground.

C. Establish the service area standards (physical size of the neighborhood) by distance and/or time required to access the playground or school or day care population served.

D. Establish how many playgrounds are needed to serve the community by establishing or utilizing any existing local codes or facility standards and the most recent demographic information available.

E. Establish site design criteria including minimum size for a site, list of desirable play events and site amenities for each user group.

F. Establish the total costs to create a playground facility that meets current safety standards, agency design criteria and carrying capacity standards (i.e. cost per child).

G. Define the life expectancy of your playground.

H. Estimate the total replacement value for all of your playground sites per the agency's planning criteria.

I. Develop a priority listing for replacement of all your playgrounds based on a comparative analysis of all playground sites using tools such as comprehensive safety audit results. Other factors related to shortened life expectancy, high maintenance costs, etc. should also be considered in playground replacement schedules.

J. Evaluate the data, refine the planning and design criteria as needed and develop a written plan that will provide the financial resources to address the public playground needs of your community in a responsible, timely fashion.

The agency must be prepared to review this process from time to time and make the necessary changes that will complement the commitment of resources to the plan implementation. The economic realities of owning and maintaining a network of public playgrounds that provide a safe, enjoyable, and appropriate play experience for all children may be more than a community can afford. The total cost to maintain and operate a public playground system that meets all the proposed planning and design criteria can negatively effect the financial security of the entire community. Therefore it is up to the public playground agency to develop a plan that is within the limits of available community resources.

Once your agency has analyzed and developed a plan to establish and maintain a network of public playgrounds the remaining challenge which still remains is, which playground should be replaced first? A reasonable assumption might be to start with the oldest one. However, the age of a playground is not always representative of the inherent problems of a particular piece of playground equipment which can be affected by the primary materials used in the equipment's construction or the durability of one manufacturer's equipment to the next.

The selection process should evaluate, weigh, and rank the many factors that affect the need for playground equipment replacement. The simplest process might be to first evaluate all your playground surfacing for proper depth and fall zones, since almost 75% of all playground accidents are related to falls.

Next you should evaluate all your playgrounds for proper layout and spacing. A playground that has adequate spacing with proper resilient surfacing reduces the likelihood of overcrowding, pushing, shoving, and hopefully many falls.

© NRPA/NPSI/PDRMA

The next factor that should be analyzed is the manufacturer's equipment design. Most equipment designed prior to 1980 and before the release of the United States Consumer Product Safety Commission's Handbooks I and II on Public Playground Safety probably have many safety concerns. Equipment designed between 1981 and 1991 is likely to be safer than the earlier models, however, equipment that is being manufactured to comply with the (November 1991) US CPSC Handbook for Public Playground Safety will undoubtedly have fewer equipment design safety concerns than any of its predecessors. Playgrounds purchased between 1991 and 1993 will probably not be in total compliance with the first ASTM F1487 Standard published in 1993. Compliance may be verified through the assistance of a manufacturer's representative. Revisions to the ASTM Standard occurred again in 1995, and CPSC has released a revision to the CPSC Handbook in 1994 and lastly in October, 1997. These dates in American public playground history provide objective tools to measure every playground's compliance to voluntary safety guidelines and industry standards that were in effect when the playground was installed. However, the most recent ASTM Standard and CPSC Guidelines provides the most current analysis towards compliance to today's standard of care in playground safety.

These three factors (surfacing, layout, equipment design) are not always sufficient to establish clear priorities for playground equipment replacement. The owner/operator should look for additional criteria to assist in the decision making process. Additional factors might include rating the durability of materials used to make the equipment, the use or misuse the playground gets, or simply the age of the playground. A numerical weighting system must be developed to differentiate one site from another regardless of what factors you use to establish an equipment replacement schedule.

Refer to previous table (Site Score Percentage Rating Form, page 54 and 57) for the following discussion points.

This form presents a comprehensive look at all the pertinent information required to make an objective decision as to which playground should be replaced first.

If your replacement decision is based on the numerical index rating score from the Playground Safety Audit Form, then the playground with the highest total in the bottom column should be replaced first. In this case, Grant Playfield with a total of 1610 is first, Washington Field with 1255 is second, then Tasha Park, Presidents Park, and Northside Park.

If your replacement decision is based on the numerical rating results of the first six sections of the Audit Form Section A: General Conditions which deal with all the major playground site safety concerns except for those primarily related to the manufacturer's design, then Grant Playfield with 371 would be first, Tasha Park with 350 second, Washington Field with 337 third, Presidents Park with 335, and Northside Park with 103. Given the low score of the General Conditions Section for Northside Park suggests that it was installed in accordance with more recent playground standards and guidelines.

If your replacement decision is based solely on the age of the playground, then Tasha Park built in 1980 would be first, Washington Field built in 1985 would be next and so on. Which playground gets replaced third? This brings to light another problem when more than one playground was built in the same year. This situation requires more analysis of the criteria available such as the first two examples already discussed. Since Presidents Park and Grant Playfield were both built in 1990, it would seem logical that the playground with the highest index percentage rating would be replaced first.

A final option in developing your replacement schedule would be to use final index percentage ratings. This calculation will help to equitably evaluate both large and small playground sites in their compliance with standards and guidelines. As discussed, final percentage ratings should be interpreted the same as golf scores. Higher scores are not positive. Grant Playfield would be first at 40%. Further analysis would be needed to decide if Tasha Park or Washington Field would be next which both had a 37% rating. Presidents Park would be next at 34%, and the last would be Northside Park at 7%.

Any one of these examples or combination of all may be used to create your agency's replacement schedule. You have the ability to create your own process. Remember that you know most about the existing conditions of your playgrounds and how they are used. Whichever process you adopt, it is important that it be as objective as possible to eliminate the potential for politics and individual subjectivity interfering in this process.

The economic realities of owning and maintaining a network of public playgrounds may be more than a community can afford. The total cost of maintaining and operating a public playground system that meets the proposed planning and design criteria should not exceed the community's means. What are the limits of your community's resources? Only you will be able to assess and answer this question with the help and input of your community, your governing board, and the top down commitment and participation from your agency's staff. It is your responsibility to evaluate your playground needs and sell your requests for funding.

What effect does maintenance have on the life-cycle cost of your public playgrounds? This is an altogether different question, however, maintenance costs over the lifetime of a public playground, if known, could play a significant role in an agency's management decision to select and build future playgrounds.

We can easily establish the costs to design a playground, purchase the equipment, and install the equipment, but we still must work on a reasonable estimate of the total maintenance and repair costs over the life of the playground. Once owner/operators get a handle on this cost, we can establish the total life-cycle cost of a playground. This cost divided by the estimated life expectancy of the playground will provide the annual cost to own and operate a public playground.

Imagine what this concept might do to the current public bidding process of playground equipment if the play value, equipment design, and installation costs were constant for all qualified bidders. The owners/operators might then be able to base their final selection of playground equipment on a reasonably accurate annual maintenance cost projection.

(This information is based on a chapter in Play It Safe: Anthology for Public Playground Safety. Further explanation of the playground equipment replacement dilemma plan (primarily steps A through H) can be found in this NRPA publication.)

© NRPA/NPSI/PDRMA

Playground Inspections

It is estimated that 28 percent of all accidents on public playgrounds could have been avoided if a good preventive maintenance program were in place. A good program establishes a frequency of inspections that are commensurate with the use and environmental factors unique to each play area. Some playgrounds might require daily inspections while others in the same area may require only biweekly inspections. The deterioration and/or wear of various play components can be predicted when certain factors are known. On the other hand, vandalism has a major influence on the inspection frequency but is not as predictable.

Playground Site Inspection Frequency Statement and Rationale

Many persons have developed various park inspection forms with and without instructions for how they should be used. Adopting an inspection form is only addressing part of the solution. Determining how often it should be used appears to be more of a problem.

Almost everyone agrees that when it comes to safety and safety inspections, more is better. However, the resources available for ensuring public playground safety are not unlimited. The rationale for frequency of playground inspections should make efficient use of these resources by providing a timely, cost effective inspections to help ensure the safety of the children who use playgrounds.

Just providing resources to make timely safety inspections does not ensure a safe play environment. Park agencies must provide proper training for its personnel responsible for playground inspections.

In addition to the inspections by trained personnel, the agencies must be committed to the continuing education of the public and the playground users. Inspections can only ensure the on-site immediate safety of a park or playground. Vandals can create an unsafe condition minutes after an inspection is completed. Therefore, public agencies should develop an information sign covering some safety guidelines to use in public playgrounds that includes a statement encouraging user cooperation in reporting playground problems, use rules, use hours, age appropriateness of this equipment, etc. (see Playground Signage, page 95-97).

The frequency of documented public playground inspections should be based on factors such as playground size, age of the equipment, playground usage, frequency of repairs, vandalism, and frequency of reported incidents or accidents. Agency staff should evaluate these factors, and determine how often your playground should be inspected. This can be accomplished by using the Inspection Frequency Form first developed by Landscape Structures, Inc.* (See form page 66.)

Some experts suggest a higher frequency of inspections than others. Your agency might wish to compromise on this point by using two separate types of inspections. Using two types could facilitate more frequent short inspections of items that directly relate to usage and vandalism and can help reduce the frequency of accidents. This inspection process will be referred to as the **high frequency or routine inspection.** This process helps identify surfacing problems, vandalism, and debris, such as glass, that can lead to an accident. The high frequency inspection requires limited staff training and can be easily performed by personnel who are already in your playground areas performing other routine maintenance tasks such as garbage pick up or grass mowing or playground supervision.

Low frequency (or periodic) and high frequency (daily or routine) inspections will be made at different times. The **low frequency inspection** will be made less often than high frequency inspections. This inspection is more comprehensive and takes a greater amount of time to perform by more experienced and knowledgeable personnel, and most significantly, it evaluates equipment structural integrity. The low frequency inspection might be done on a weekly to seasonal basis, depending on the individual playground factors affecting each location.

If use factors such as vandalism, environmental conditions, equipment age, etc. are evaluated, and

---

*Footnote: Landscape Structures, Inc. Delano, MN

© NRPA/NPSI/PDRMA

reasonable judgment used in developing a plan of action, the problem of appropriate inspection frequency will be adequately addressed. No simple black or white answer exists as to what inspection frequency is appropriate or adequate. Public agencies should monitor and evaluate all playgrounds and the factors affecting each and every site.

Guide to the Inspection Frequency Form

To assist public agencies in more comprehensively determining the frequency of inspections necessary to provide reasonably safe playground environments for its patrons, the Inspection Frequency Form should be used at each playground site to evaluate its inspection needs. It should be completed by a supervisor or responsible employee who has received some type of formalized playground safety training and is familiar with the current CPSC Handbook for Public Playground Safety and ASTM standards for public playgrounds.

It is very important that a high level of consistency be maintained when an agency is using the Guide to the Inspection Frequency Form. It is recommended that one employee complete the form for all playground sites. If this is not possible, it is recommended that those staff who will be completing the form do at least two playground sites as a group so that consistent scores will be recorded for similar factors listed on the form.

The three elements affecting how often your playgrounds should be inspected are use factors, materials used in your playground, and environmental factors.

A. **Use Factors**

Three types of use factors may affect how often your playgrounds should be inspected. These factors are vandalism, user demand, and the age range of the users being served.

1. *Vandalism.* If a playground site requires recurring vandalism repairs upon almost every safety inspection, the rater should assign a high point total. If over a period of a year there has been little or no vandalism, then the lowest point total should be used. There is some room for interpretation in the high rating of 8 to a low of 2.

2. *Use level.* The sheer number of users who typically frequent the playground have a cumulative effect on the frequency of inspections and repairs. A community park with many other park amenities will attract many more users than a neighborhood tot lot, as will a playground located adjacent to a recreation program center that runs many pre-school and youth programs. School playgrounds will have heavy use during the school hours but might have limited use after school or during the summer. Evening activities in the area also affect the number of users served in a given day. Personnel may not be aware of evening use levels, but garbage and litter pick up is a direct indicator of the site use, including misuse, if there is an unusually high amount of glass and other debris.

3. *Age Design.* Playground areas that are designed and used only by pre-school age children (ages 2–5) are typically smaller and have lower height equipment with fewer moving parts that can wear or strike a small child during play. This type of site would get the lowest point rating in this category.

    If a site was designed for school age children only (ages 5-12), it would receive a moderate rating if the play area was primarily used by the appropriate school age group for which it was designed. The highest rating would go to a playground site that was designed for both age groups (2-5 and 5-12) or was being used by both age groups. The main concern here is the height of equipment, the amount of moving equipment, the challenge level of the equipment for older children, and the likelihood of conflict between the two user groups.

B. **Materials**

1. *Resilient surfacing.* Loose fill materials get the highest rating because they are kicked or moved from areas under or around playground equipment that it is most needed to elimi-

© NRPA/NPSI/PDRMA

nate injuries from falls. Loose fill surfacing requires routine maintenance. Synthetic matting materials are easier to maintain in regards to their being kicked out or moved away from play equipment fall zones during normal play activities. Approximately seventy percent of all playground injuries are attributed to falls to the surface.

2. *Materials (major components).* Wood play structures, especially those with wood supports which extend below grade, tend to weather, split, check, splinter, and rot faster than other materials. A variety of environmental factors will affect this decomposition process and fewer points are given to materials with greater durability and less demand for routine maintenance, such as painted steel and plastics.

3. *Equipment.* Moving equipment is more likely to cause an accident than static equipment. Moving equipment also requires more preventive maintenance and repairs, such as the lubrication of moving parts and closer inspection for wear.

4. *Age of equipment.* Playground equipment eventually wears out. Components begin to degrade to a point where they need increased preventive maintenance, more frequent repairs, or even replacement. New equipment should require little or no major repairs during the first two years, however, as equipment starts to reach five to ten years of age, many things can begin to affect the structural integrity of your playground equipment. Plastic can begin to become brittle, metals begin to rust, wood surfaces can check and splinter badly, and excessive use of a playground can shorten the life expectancy of a playground before funds can be secured to replace it. Most older playgrounds need timely maintenance just like an older car or house.

C. Environmental Factors

1. Acid and Ph levels contained in soils and rain water can affect the rate of decomposition of playground equipment structures. This will vary in different parts of the country. The more extreme the Ph is from the neutral point (7), the higher the point total given.

2. The level of salt contained in the atmosphere in coastal regions can affect the rate of oxidation that affects metal surfaces. The higher the salt level, the higher the point total given.

3. The ultraviolet rays and heat generated by the sun can affect the life span and safety of playground equipment. Ultraviolet rays can fade and shorten the life of many plastics. Heat from the sun can heat metals that may cause burns to users. Shade trees in the playground environment can reduce some of these negative effects of the sun. Evaluate the level of sun exposure that affects your playground equipment and choose the point total that best reflects this level.

4. Drainage can have a dramatic effect on the long term structural integrity of your playground support members and the effectiveness and life expectancy of your surfacing material.

   Inadequate drainage under playground equipment can allow excessive amounts of moisture to accumulate around structure footings, which can cause heaving in freezing conditions and rapid decomposition of wood members.

   Excessive moisture or standing water tends to settle loose surfacing materials, making them less effective when submerged and hard packed when dried.

   When temperatures drop below 30 degrees in many parts of the country, the moisture that remains in and around loose surfacing materials will freeze and eliminate its ability to provide an acceptable landing surface.

   The drainage below playground equipment should be evaluated for its ability to move water away from the fall zone of the equipment and the appropriate point levels given.

Inspection Frequency Form

Playground Name/ID Number_____ Form Completed By _____Date _____

The following guide weighs the most common use, materials, and environmental factors that will influence your playground inspection scheduling. Each factor has been weighted as to its importance and influence on the schedule. Put one of the factor numbers in the right hand column that best describes the conditions at the playground site.

Factors		Possible Points	Points Given
A.	**Use Factors**		
1.	Vandalism (Misuse/Abuse)		
	High	10	
	Moderate	5	
	Low	2	
2.	Use Level (Community Use, Litter, Etc.)		
	High	10	
	Moderate	5	
	Low	2	
3.	Age Design		
	Preschool age (2-5 years)	2	
	School age (6-12 years)	4	
	All ages (2-12 years)	10	
	Use Factors Total	30	
B.	**Materials**		
1.	Resilient Surfacing		
	Loose Materials	12	
	Synthetic Material	2	
2.	Material (Major Components)		
	Wood, Painted Steel	4	
	Stabilized Plastics, Aluminum, Gal.Steel	2	
	Stainless Steel	0	
3.	Equipment		
	Moving (swing, spin around, spring rider, etc.)	6	
	Static (Non-moving climbers)	2	
	Both	6	

© NRPA/NPSI/PDRMA

Factors	Possible Points	Points Given
4.　Age of Equipment		
1-2 years old	0	
3-4 years old	3	
5-9 years old	6	
10-14 years old	9	
15 years old and over	12	
Materials Factors Total	34	
C.　Environmental Factors		
1.　Acid Soils/Rain/PH		
None (6-9)	0	
Moderate (10, 11, 4, 5)	4	
High (Acid 1-3, Basic 12-14)	8	
2.　Salt Air (Coastal Exposure)		
None	0	
Moderate	4	
High	8	
3.　Sun Exposure		
None	0	
Moderate	4	
High	8	
4.　Drainage		
Functioning underground drainage system	0	
Moist Surface	4	
Seasonal Flooding	8	
Routine Standing Water	12	
Environmental Factors Total	36	
Total Points for Site	100	

IMPORTANT This information has been prepared to assist the Playground owners attorney in defending potential litigation. **Do not** release to any person except an agency official or designated claim representative or an investigating police officer.

© NRPA/NPSI/PDRMA

Inspection Frequency Summary Form for all Agency Sites

Key to Inspection Frequency Chart		
Points	**High Frequency Inspections**	**Low Frequency Inspections**
71 or more	2 or more times per week	2-3 times per month
56-70	Weekly	Monthly
41-55	Biweekly	Bimonthly
40 & Below	Monthly	Seasonal

Once the inspection frequency form has been completed for each playground site, the results can be transferred to the blank inspection frequency summary form (Appendix A) so that all of your sites can be evaluated collectively. The total points for each site can then be compared to the key to inspection frequency chart (above) which will assist you in determining your most appropriate high and low frequency inspection schedule.

Local conditions may include other factors and in some cases affect seasonal adjustments to the schedule. Experience is your best guide.

Frequency of Inspection Summary Form (Sample)

Playground Site Name	Factors Evaluated					
	Use Factors	**Material**	**Environ-mental**	**Points Given**	**High Freq. Inspection**	**Low Freq. Inspection**
1.						
2.						
3.						
4.						
5.						
6.						
7.						
8.						
9.						
10.						

© NRPA/NPSI/PDRMA

High Frequency Playground Inspection

High frequency or routine inspections are usually conducted on a daily to weekly basis and take less time to complete than a low frequency or periodic inspection. High frequency playground inspections are typically performed by assigned work crews or personnel who are responsible for repetitive work tasks performed in and around the vicinity of the public playground area. In a public park environment, the inspector may be the trash pick-up or mowing crew, but at an elementary school or day care center the inspector might be the playground supervisor. The completed inspection forms should be returned to the person assigned to supervise and monitor all playground operations at the end of each day. This person is typically the facility manager, department head, or maintenance supervisor.

Any playground component determined to be unsafe or other identified safety concern must be corrected as soon as possible. If for some reason the problem cannot be corrected immediately, then whatever measures necessary should be taken to render the equipment safe or unusable until other measures can be taken (see page 87). Do not fix with inferior or temporary devices, such as wiring a broken chain or putting a small bolt in a large hole of a missing bolt. Some examples of making the equipment temporarily unusable include enclosing with snow fencing, removing the broken equipment, using warning signage, leaving an employee at the site, or calling the maintenance supervisor, facility supervisor, or local police.

When conducting a high frequency inspection, the playground should first be inspected for any obvious hazards such as vandalism, glass, trash, and the need for raking wood surfacing material back under the fall zones of the play equipment, sweeping walkways free of debris and loose surfacing that might create a slippery condition.

Next, a brief inspection of each piece of play equipment should be conducted for hazards such as vandalism, twisted swing chains, swing seats that are cut or cracked, exposed concrete footers, loose rails or bolts, etc. When major problems are identified and cannot be corrected on site, the parks superintendent or playground operator should be notified immediately so that actions can be taken quickly to eliminate or reduce the hazard.

Example

Problem: Badly cracked child's swing seat. There is no other seat available.

Possible Corrective Action: The employee should remove the entire swing chain and seat in question until a replacement seat is available.

Example

Problem: The depth level of surfacing materials below a climber is inadequate due to children removing it to a nearby play area.

Possible Corrective Action: The removed surfacing materials should be shoveled or raked back under the climber. If the depth of the surfacing material is still not sufficient, the parks maintenance supervisor should be notified so that another crew can deliver the needed surfacing material to the site.

Example

Problem: A composite structure has been severely vandalized with many component parts being disassembled and damaged.

Possible Corrective Action: One employee should stay with the damaged equipment to prevent any patrons from using the vandalized playground equipment while another contacts the parks maintenance supervisor for additional assistance. The local police should also be contacted to help keep patrons of off the equipment and investigate the criminal actions committed.

High Frequency Inspection Form (Daily or Routine)

Site Name/ID Number: _____ *1*_____

Inspector Name: _____ *2* _____ Date:____ *3* ____ Start/Finish Times: _____ *4* _____

Repairer Name: _____ *5* _____ Date:____ *6* ____ Start/Finish Times: _____ *7* _____

<u>8</u>

> Use the following codes: 1 = Okay   2 = Needs Maintenance   3 = Request for Repair
> O = Supervisor notified and work order written   X = Corrective Action Complete

General Inspection Items		Code	Inspection Comments	Repairs Comments
<u>9</u>	**Vandalism:** Damage, graffiti, glass, trash, needles, etc.	<u>22</u>	<u>23</u>	<u>24</u>
<u>10</u>	Loose or missing hardware			
<u>11</u>	Chains (kinked, twisted, broken)			
<u>12</u>	Guardrails/handrails secure			
<u>13</u>	Seats (cut, cracked, missing)			
<u>14</u>	Wood (rotten, cracked, missing)			
<u>15</u>	Remove foreign objects (ropes, chains, wood, etc.)			
<u>16</u>	Sweep walkways, platforms, steps			
<u>17</u>	Footers (concrete) exposed			
<u>18</u>	Standing water			
<u>19</u>	Objects in surfacing material			
<u>20</u>	Rake level surfacing material			
<u>21</u>	**Need Surfacing Material For:**			
	Swings			
	Climbers			
	Fire Pole			
	Slide			
	Others			
	Others			

<u>For office use only</u>
<u>25</u> Reviewed by Assistant Superintendent of Parks _____ Date_____
<u>26</u> Reviewed by Superintendent of Parks and Planning _____ Date_____

<u>27</u> **IMPORTANT** – This information has been prepared to assist the Playground owners attorney in defending potential litigation. *Do not* release to any person except an agency official or designated claim representative or an investigating police officer.

<u>28</u> USE BACK OF FORM FOR ADDITIONAL COMMENTS
<u>29</u> REPORT ALL VANDALISM TO ASSISTANT SUPERINTENDENT OF PARKS OR YOUR MAINTENANCE SUPERVISOR

© NRPA/NPSI/PDRMA

User's Guide for High Frequency Inspection Form

1. The playground site name or ID number should be clearly printed at the top of each form used.

2. The inspector's name should be clearly printed on each form used.

3. The inspector should correctly date each form used.

4. The inspector should record the start and finish times for the inspection.

5. The person who conducts any follow-up repairs must clearly print their name on the original inspection form.

6. The person who conducts a follow-up repair must date the form on the day repairs are conducted.

7. The repairer should record the start and finish times related to the equipment repair.

8. The inspection codes located near the top of the form should be used by the initial person conducting the high frequency playground inspection, and any person conducting follow-up repairs. These codes should be placed in the Code column as necessary.

   The first code (1=OK) should be used by the initial inspector to indicate that the equipment inspected is in satisfactory condition.

   The second code (2=Needs Maintenance) should be used by the initial inspector to indicate that some type of maintenance is needed that can be corrected on site. (Examples include raking loose surfacing materials back into use zones, removing litter, or unwrapping a swing that has been wrapped around its top beam.)

   The third code (3=Request for Repair) should be used by the initial inspector to indicate that additional assistance is needed to complete a repair that does not create an immediate safety concern. (Examples include minor paint chipping, graffiti vandalism, or a loose playground border timber.)

   The fourth code (O=Supervisor notified and work order requested) should be used to indicate that a repair is needed that cannot be corrected on site or that is a safety concern. The O code should be placed around a 3 code (i.e. code 3 should be circled), and the playground supervisor should be notified immediately if a significant safety concern exists. Examples include broken equipment, missing parts, or if the structural integrity of equipment is in question. Steps should also be taken to secure the equipment from use in certain cases. (For additional information, see Procedures for Playground Area Corrective Action, page .)

   The fifth code (X=Corrective Action Complete) should be used to indicate that a repair has been completed by the initial inspector or a follow-up repair person. The X code should be placed directly over the 2, 3, or O codes.

   ☞ **NOTE:** The general inspection items denoted by numbers 9-20 are a listing of common playground equipment problems that should be evaluated while conducting a high frequency inspection. In no way is this a complete listing of all potential problems that could occur on playground equipment. Persons performing high frequency inspections must be alert to identify other types of hazards that could exist.

9. Any vandalism noted in the playground area, which could include broken equipment, glass, trash, feces, needles, etc., should be evaluated.

10. Briefly inspect all equipment for any loose or missing hardware.

11. Briefly inspect all swing and chain climbers for any kinks, twists, or broken links.

12. Briefly inspect platforms and stairway guardrails to determine if they are secure.

13. Briefly inspect all swing seats for missing components, cracks, or cuts.

14. Briefly inspect wooden equipment and structures for missing components, rotting, or severe cracking.

15. Briefly inspect for any foreign objects that may be brought into the playground area such as ropes, chains, wood boards, toys, etc. Remove these materials from the site.

16. Briefly inspect all walkways, stairways, platforms, and steps and sweep any loose surfacing materials or related substances.

17. Briefly inspect all surface level areas where playground equipment is secured into the ground for any exposed concrete footings that exist.

18. Briefly inspect any areas under playground equipment in their use zones that have any standing water or excessive amounts of moisture.

19. Briefly inspect loose surfacing materials for any foreign objects located in the surfacing material such as glass, metal, or toys.

20. Briefly inspect below playground components that experience a "kick out" of loose surfacing materials and rake back the surfacing materials as needed.

21. List all those areas that experience regular surfacing "kick out" such as under swings and at the bottoms of slides. Briefly inspect below playground components that experience a "kick out" of loose surfacing materials and rake or replace loose surfacing materials as needed.

22. The Code column is used by the initial inspector and follow-up repair person to indicate the appropriate code or status of the playground components or area being inspected.

23. Inspection Comments should be made to indicate the actual problem noted during the high frequency inspection. The inspection comments should indicate the specific piece of equipment concerned, and briefly explain the potential safety concern and its location. This section must be completed whenever codes 2, 3, or O are used.

24. The Repair Comments should reflect the actions taken by the inspector or repairer to correct a playground problem. This section must be completed whenever codes 2, 3, or O are used by the inspector. These codes which require corrective action should be marked by an X when repaired.

25. This section should be completed by the assistant superintendent of parks or a comparable position. It should be initialed and dated. This person will typically first receive the results of the high frequency inspections, and be responsible for generating work orders for follow-up repairs. In the event that a serious playground hazard is noted, this person should be radioed or phoned immediately for instructions.

26. This section should be completed by the superintendent of parks and planning or equivalent position. It should be initialed and dated by the person responsible for the overall playground safety program and returned to the person responsible for follow-up action or permanent filing.

27. This important information is designed to prevent any person in your agency from releasing the high frequency inspection form(s) to any outside sources without the consent of your agency's attorney.

28. The playground inspector should use the back of the form to describe in depth any hazards or problems noted during the high frequency inspection. Do not limit your comments to the boxes provided on the front of the form when additional explanation is necessary.

29. All vandalism or other serious playground hazards noted during a high frequency inspection must be reported immediately to the maintenance supervisor responsible for the playground safety program.

   ☞ **NOTE:** This user's guide should be used during initial inspector training and photocopied and carried into the field as a reference guide for the inspector in completing the form.

© NRPA/NPSI/PDRMA

Low Frequency Playground Inspections

Low frequency (periodic) playground inspections should be conducted on a scheduled basis by a trained employee to evaluate the structural integrity and wear concerns of each individual piece of playground equipment at a park site. The scheduling of low frequency inspections may range from weekly to monthly, depending on existing conditions, environmental conditions, age, use factors, etc., which are brought together in the Inspection Frequency Form (see page 66 and 67). This form provides low frequency inspection scheduling recommendations.

Two types of low frequency forms will be discussed and provided.

Whichever you choose, it is best to make a low frequency inspection form that is customized to each of your individual park sites. To do this you should begin by compiling an itemized list of all playground components that exist at each individual playground site (see page 74).

Itemizing Park/Playground Components

One of the most important steps in the initial development of your low frequency inspection forms is the complete listing of all play equipment, play components, and site amenities that exist at each park. If this list can be coupled with a site plan of the play area, it can be an invaluable aid to playground safety inspectors in identifying a specific piece of equipment, especially if multiple types of the same exist (i.e., multi slides, swings, etc.). Many times this list has already been completed by the playground equipment manufacturer. If this information is missing from the playground file, a phone call to the equipment manufacturer may produce a copy of this information from their records. A visit to the site should also be done to identify any site components that may have been added or removed.

Remember the old saying, a picture is worth a thousand words? A site plan or black and white photographs can reduce the inspection time by clearly identifying the equipment you are inspecting by numbering or coding each piece of playground equipment. Inspections must be as simple as possible, and these tools will help reduce inspection time while eliminating some human errors and thereby increasing the degree of consistency from one inspector to another.

If a site plan cannot be re-created, black and white photographs can be taken to create a visual reference for each area within the playground. These photographs can be reproduced or photocopied for easy duplication of records.

Manufacturers may sell similar equipment and components using different names, which can confuse safety inspectors. If a site plan is available, it should be compared to the itemized list of play equipment to ensure accuracy (see page 74 and 76). The plan can then be alphabetically or numerically cross referenced to the itemized list and labeled. The itemized list must be completed before a low frequency playground inspection form can be developed for each playground site. (see page 78).

Itemized List of Playground Equipment

Site Name/ID Number: _Berens Play Area_

Inspector Name: _Steve Plumb_ Date: _4/20/85_

Play Area	Play Component	Description of Play Area or Component	Comments
A	Wood Structure		
	Balance Beam		
	Horizontal Ladder		
	Catwalk		
	Net		
	Slide		
	Slide Rope		
	Tire Swing		
B	Tot Swings (4)		
	Horse Swings (6)		Replace Metal Horse Swings
	Spiral Slide		
	Merry-Go-Round		
	Log-Roll		
	Spring Board		
	Playground Boarder	6"x6" CCA Treated 8' Timbers	
	Playground Surfacing	10" Pea Gravel	

© NRPA/NPSI/PDRMA

Itemized List of Playground Equipment

Site Name/ID Number:_____

Inspector Name:_____ Date:_____

Play Area	Play Component	Description of Play Area or Component	Comments

© NRPA/NPSI/PDRMA

Low Frequency Site Plan Inspection Method

Once a comprehensive listing of playground components by site is completed, they can be transferred to the low frequency/periodic playground inspection form (see page 78).

Site plans (see below) should be combined with the low frequency inspection form or re-created with black and white photographs to document the location of park components to be inspected.

A trained low frequency playground inspector can then systematically inspect each component in the playground for damage, wear, and other safety concerns. It is very important that the inspector have a substantial level of experience in playground repair methods and current playground safety guidelines. Also, manufacturer maintenance instructions should be closely followed to ensure proper repairs.

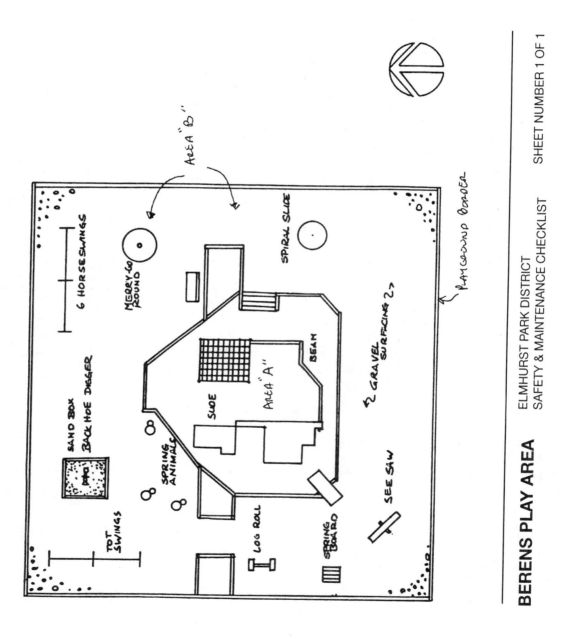

BERENS PLAY AREA

ELMHURST PARK DISTRICT
SAFETY & MAINTENANCE CHECKLIST

SHEET NUMBER 1 OF 1

© NRPA/NPSI/PDRMA

Low Frequency Site Plan Playground Inspection Form

Site Name/ID Number: _____ *1*

Inspector Name: _____ *2* _____ Date: _____ *3* _____ Start/Finish Times: _____ *4* _____

Repairer Name: _____ *5* _____ Date: _____ *6* _____ Start/Finish Times: _____ *7* _____

8

> Use the following codes: 1 = Okay   2 = Needs Maintenance   3 = Request for Repair
> O = Supervisor notified and work order written   X = Corrective Action Complete

Area	#	Play Component	Code	Problem (if any)	Action Taken
9	*10*	*11*	*12*	*13*	*14*
15 Playground surfacing material and draining					
16 Playground border/edger (if applicable)					

Directions: *17*
1. List each piece of playground equipment in the "Play Components" column.
2. As each component is inspected, indicate the appropriate codes in the Code column.
3. Describe the nature of any maintenance or follow-up repairs.
4. File each inspection report with your permanent records.

18 Work Order Numbers (list all that apply): _____

19 Supervisor _____ Signature _____ Date _____

> **20** This form has been prepared to assist the Playground owners Attorney in defending potential litigation. DO NOT release to any person except an agency official, designated claim representative, or an investigating officer.

© NRPA/NPSI/PDRMA

User's Guide for Low Frequency Site Plan Inspection Form

1. The playground site name or ID number should be clearly printed at the top of each form used.

2. The inspector's name should be clearly printed on each form used.

3. The inspector should correctly date each form used.

4. The inspector should record the start and finish times for the inspection.

5. The person who conducts any follow-up repairs must clearly print their name on the original inspection form.

6. The person who conducts a follow-up repair must date the form on the day repairs are conducted.

7. The repairer should record the start and finish times related to the equipment repair.

8. The first code (1=OK) should be used by the playground inspector to indicate that the equipment inspected is in satisfactory condition.

   The second code (2=Needs Maintenance) should be used by the inspector to indicate that some form of maintenance is needed and can be corrected on site.

   The third code (3=Request for Repair) should be used when a maintenance concern has been noted, but repairs cannot be completed while on site and additional follow-up is necessary.

   The fourth code (O=Supervisor Notified and Work Order Written) should be used to indicate that a serious maintenance or safety consideration exists, and that a supervisor will be notified and work order completed to correct or minimize the concern. The 3 code should be circled by this code.

   The fifth code (X=Corrective Action Completed) should be used to indicate that a repair has been completed by the inspector or repair person. The X code should be placed directly over the 2, 3, or O codes.

9. The playground components should be grouped into a number of areas on the site plan drawings to assist in identification of each component to be inspected. (If available, indicate the appropriate area number in the first column.)

10. Specific playground components to be inspected should be numbered to assist in their identification.

11. A description of the playground component should be typed or printed.

12. The Code column is used by the initial inspector and follow-up repair person to indicate the appropriate code which relates to the status of the playground components being inspected.

13. The inspector should indicate the nature of a maintenance concern noted during the low frequency inspection.

14. The inspector or follow-up repair person should indicate what actions were taken to correct a maintenance concern.

15. The low frequency inspector should evaluate the need for surfacing materials so that adequate levels are available to meet the critical fall height criteria (see page 3).

16. The inspector should evaluate the condition of any playground borders or edges for maintenance concerns or trip hazards.

17. Four directions are listed to assist the inspector in completing the form.

18. All work orders that are developed to correct a playground maintenance concern should be listed when completed.

19. The playground maintenance supervisor or other manager should print their name, and sign and date the form.

20. This important information is designed to prevent any person in your agency from releasing the high frequency inspection form(s) to any outside sources without the consent of your agency's attorney.

© NRPA/NPSI/PDRMA

Low Frequency Matrix Inspection Method

The low frequency matrix inspection method involves the construction of a customized matrix grid that may speed up the low frequency inspection process by directing the inspector to only those maintenance concerns that exist on each component at the park site.

Along the right side of the form (see page 82) is a listing of the many common playground equipment maintenance needs or concerns that should be evaluated during a low frequency inspection.

The next step is to list the site playground components on the vertical lines at the top of the form. Next, blacken or block out squares that correspond to the equipment listed on the vertical lines where the corresponding maintenance is **not** needed. When completed, the form will have available squares below each playground component listed at the top of the form that must be evaluated and marked during each low frequency inspection.

This method may make the low frequency inspections easier for your staff since they will only have to check the indicated maintenance concerns listed on the right side of the form for each white square available below the playground equipment. This system should speed up the low frequency inspection process by more quickly identifying specific maintenance needs for specific playground equipment, while not compromising the integrity of the inspection process.

Any park site plans, drawings, or photographs that are available should be attached to or reduced and copied onto the back of each park site low frequency inspection form. The individual playground components that are to be inspected can be numbered on the site plans so that they can be identified by the inspector.

© NRPA/NPSI/PDRMA

Low Frequency Matrix Playground Inspection Form

1999 by NRPA

Agency: _____ (1)

Playground Site Name: _____ (2)

Inspector: _____ (3)

Signature: _____ (4)

Date: _____ (5)

Start/Finish Times: _____ (6)

Supervisor: _____ (11)

Signature: _____ (12)

Date: _____ (13)

Use following codes throughout checklist:
1 = OK
2 = Needs Maintenance
3 = Request for Repair (14)
0 = Supervisor notified/Work order written
X = Corrective Action Complete

Use back of form to indicate action taken.

(15) **Site Condition**

_____ Vandalism, broken glass/trash

_____ Poor drainage areas

_____ Surface material worn/scattered

_____ Deterioration: borders, landscaping

_____ Tripping hazards: roots/rocks/obstacles

_____ Accessible sharp edges/corners

_____ Hazardous visual barriers

_____ Physical barriers

Additional Comments: (Use back as necessary.) (16)

Work Order #s (list all that apply): (17)

Repairer: _____ (7)

Signature: _____ (8)

Date: _____ (9)

Start/Finish Times: _____ (10)

This form has been prepared to assist the District Attorney in defending potential litigation. DO NOT release to any person except a district official, designated claim representative, or an investigating officer. (20)

(18) ... (19)

Logs: cracking/warping/decay
Endcaps: exposed tubing
Bolts: uncapped/loose/missing
Bedway: damage/protruding objects
Paint: chipping/rust
Support Posts: loose/exposed footing
Tire: damage/mounting
Boards: cracking/warping/decay/paint
Fittings: need grease
Handrails: loose/missing
Steps: loose/surface
Footings: loose/exposed/cracked
Welds: damage/decay
Bars & Pipes: loose/missing
S-Hooks: need replacement 25% wear
Support Rods: loose/need replacement
Foot Holds: loose/need replacement
Chains: damage/rust/pinch points
Seats: damage/needs replacement
Mountings: loose/need replacement
Wood Slats: cracking/warping/decay
Ladders: support/rungs
Ropes: damage/need replacement
Turnbolts & Turnbuckles: loose/replace
Cables: support/damage/need replacement
Springs: support/damage/need replacement
Handgrips: loose/need replacement
Poles: support/damage/need replacement
Handholds: loose/missing/need replacement
Bearings: grease/replace
Panels: loose/damage/need replacement
Other:

© NRPA/NPSI/PDRMA

User Guide for Low Frequency Matrix Playground Inspection Form

1.   The name of the public agency or organization should be typed or printed.

2.   The playground site name should be typed or printed.

3.   The name of the person conducting the low frequency inspection should print his or her name clearly.

4.   The inspector should sign the form when completed.

5.   The inspector should indicate the date of the inspection.

6.   The starting and finishing times for the low frequency inspection should be documented.

7.   The repairer should clearly print his or her name.

8.   The repairer should sign the form when completed.

9.   The repairer should indicate the date of the repair.

10.   The starting and finishing times for the repairs should be documented.

11.   The supervisor should clearly print his or her name on the form when received.

12.   The supervisor should sign the form when completed.

13.   The supervisor should date the form when received.

14.   The following codes should be placed into the appropriate white squares to indicate the condition of the playground equipment being inspected.

The first code (1=OK) should be used by the playground inspector to indicate that the equipment inspected is in satisfactory condition.

The second code (2=Needs Maintenance) should be used by the inspector to indicate that some form of maintenance is needed and can be corrected on site.

The third code (3=Request for Repair) should be used when a maintenance concern has been noted, but repairs cannot be completed while on site and additional follow-up is necessary.

The fourth code (O=Supervisor Notified and Work Order Written) should be used to indicate that a serious maintenance or safety consideration exists, and that a supervisor will be notified and work order completed to correct or minimize the concern. The 3 code should be circled by this code.

The fifth code (X=Corrective Action Completed) should be used to indicate that a repair has been completed by the inspector or repair person. The X code should be placed directly over the 2, 3, or O codes.

15.   The playground condition should be evaluated for:

   •   Any vandalism damage, glass, or water

   •   Poor drainage on playground surface areas

   •   Surfacing materials of adequate depth in accordance with CPSC playground safety guidelines and for excessive wear in unitary surfacing products

   •   Deterioration of playground borders and landscaping.

   •   Any tripping hazards on playground surface areas such as rocks, roots, and related problems

- Any sharp edges or corners that are accessible on playground components

- Any hazardous landscaping in and around the playground environment such as low hanging branches (< 7 feet), signs, bushes, or trees that may cause eye injuries or limit the vision of users near roadways

- Physical barriers such as fencing for damage. Also, the inspector should evaluate the need for physical barriers to minimize the potential effects of nearby border concerns such as open water, roadways, railroad tracks, or recreational activities that may conflict with playground activity.

16. Additional comments pertaining to the site condition and playground components being inspected should be made to describe any identified maintenance concerns such as over-grown landscaping, eye level branches, trip hazards, vandalism, loose surfacing, and litter on walkways, etc. Use the back of the form for these comments.

17. All work orders that pertain to the repair of a playground component for the inspection should be listed.

18. The names of the playground equipment to be inspected should be typed or printed on the vertical lines at the top of the form.

19. The list along the right side of the form contains common maintenance needs or concerns that should be evaluated during the low frequency inspection.

   NOTE: Blacken in or block out the squares that correspond to the playground components listed on the vertical lines where the corresponding maintenance is not needed. When completed, the form will have available squares below each playground component listed at the top of the form that must be evaluated and marked during the inspection process.

20. This important information is designed to prevent any person in your agency from releasing the high frequency inspection form(s) to any outside sources without the consent of your agency's attorney.

© NRPA/NPSI/PDRMA

Low Frequency Matrix Playground Inspection Form

Playground Site Name: Berens Park Playground

Agency: Elmhurst Park District

Inspector: Phil Milano
Signature: *P. Milano*
Date: 7/8/99
Start/Finish Times: 7:15 / 8:00 am

Supervisor: S. Plumb
Signature: *S. Plumb*
Date: 7/9/99

© 1999 by NRPA

Use following codes throughout checklist:

1 = OK
2 = Needs Maintenance
3 = Request for Repair
0 = Supervisor notified/Work order written
X = Corrective Action Complete

Use back of form to indicate action taken.

Site Condition

2 — Vandalism, broken glass/trash
___ — Poor drainage areas
2 — Surface material worn/scattered
___ — Deterioration; borders, landscaping
___ — Tripping hazards; roots/rocks/obstacles
___ — Accessible sharp edges/corners
___ — Hazardous visual barriers
___ — Physical barriers

Additional Comments: (Use back as necessary.)
Picked up trash, raked surfacing slide handrail broken, log roll bearing needs repair

Work Order #s (list all that apply):
Slide handrail #231, Log roll #232

Repairer: Russ Cole
Signature: ___
Date: ___
Start/Finish Times: ___

This form has been prepared to assist the District Attorney in defending potential litigation. DO NOT release to any person except a district official, designated claim representative, or an investigating officer.

Inspection Item	Wood Structure Area A	Balance Beam	Horizontal Ladder	Chain Bridge	Net	Slide	Tire Swing	Tot Swings	Spiral Slide	Log Roll
Logs: cracking/warping/decay	1	1	1	1			1	1		1
Endcaps: exposed tubing	1	1	1	1			1	1		1
Bolts: uncapped/loose/missing	1	1	1	1	1	1	1	1	1	1
Bedway: damage/protruding objects				1		②			1	
Paint: chipping/rust	1			1					1	1
Support Posts: loose/exposed footing			1	1		1	1	1		
Tire: damage/mounting				1			1			
Boards: cracking/warping/decay/paint				1						
Fittings: need grease	1			1		③	1		1	
Handrails: loose/missing				1					1	
Steps: loose/surface	1	1		1		②			1	1
Footings: loose/exposed/cracked	1	1		1					1	1
Welds: damage/decay				1	1					
Bars & Pipes: loose/missing			1	1						
S-Hooks: need replacement 25% wear				1			1	1		
Support Rods: loose/need replacement				1						
Foot Holds: loose/need replacement										
Chains: damage/rust/pinch points				1	1					
Seats: damage/needs replacement				1			1	1		
Mountings: loose/need replacement				1			1	1		
Wood Slats: cracking/warping/decay				1			1			
Ladders: support/rungs				1						
Ropes: damage/need replacement			1	1						
Turnbolts & Turnbuckles: loose/replace				1						
Cables: support/damage/need replacement				1						
Springs: support/damage/need replacement				1						
Handgrips: loose/need replacement	1			1						1
Poles: support/damage/need replacement				1						
Handholds: loose/missing/need replacement			1	1						3
Bearings: grease/replace	1	1	1	1		1	1		1	1
Panels: loose/damage/need replacement	1	1	1	1	1	1	1		1	1
Other:										

© NRPA/NPSI/PDRMA

Important Notes on Low Frequency Inspections

1. All provided playground equipment manufacturer installation and maintenance manuals provided by the manufacturer should be carefully reviewed for any specific maintenance procedures. These specific maintenance procedures should be listed on a separate form and attached to the low frequency inspection forms.

2. **Specific Note:** To protect your agency from voiding any product's liability protection provided through the equipment manufacturer, always closely follow the manufacturer's maintenance instructions, and never modify any playground parts in-house without the written permission of the manufacturer.

3. It is recommended that only replacement parts provided by original manufacturers be used in maintaining your playground components. If not, the agency risks voiding product's liability protection through the manufacturer.

4. In some cases, manufacturer's maintenance checklists are not sufficient for use in a long term comprehensive playground maintenance program.

© NRPA/NPSI/PDRMA

Procedures for Playground Area Corrective Action

Once we have designed, purchased, and installed a public playground, our work as a playground manager has just begun. The maintenance and repair costs over the life of a playground far exceed the initial acquisition and installation costs yet they are essential to preserving the function of the playground and extending the life of the play equipment. Proper maintenance of playgrounds can be easily documented and learned. However, the ability to identify safety problems and to take the necessary actions to eliminate a problem before an accident occurs requires quite a bit more training. Once an employee has mastered the skill of properly analyzing and identifying playground safety problems, it is imperative that the employee select the proper approach to correcting the problem in a timely and reasonable fashion.

The following are five situations that require staff to make an initial investigation, evaluation of a playground concern, and implement some type of appropriate corrective action. They must understand each procedure, and communicate their actions with supervisors while documenting the course of action that was taken.

1. **Immediate Repair**

   These corrective actions are made immediately during the time of a high or low frequency inspection or initial audit when a definite unsafe condition is detected. These actions may include the removal of litter, broken glass, or filling in low spots under equipment when surfacing material has been kicked out. If an unsafe condition cannot be corrected immediately, the situation must be reported to a supervisor, and the play equipment should be secured or removed to help manage the unsafe condition to prevent an injury.

2. **Play Equipment Removal**

   If any play equipment is broken and/or poses a serious potential hazard to the public, it must be immediately reported to a supervisor and removed from public use in a timely fashion. The repair or replacement of playground equipment may require that additional monies be available to replace equipment that is removed for safety reasons. This situation should be handled in an agency's annual budgetary process.

3. **Work Orders**

   Public agencies should have some type of written work order system to handle all work requests efficiently while providing a tracking mechanism to assure timely follow through. Each playground work order should be evaluated individually, and if a public safety situation appears to exist, it should be acted on immediately. Work orders are used most often to schedule repairs which require securing replacement parts and/or scheduling trained personnel and equipment.

4. **Phone Complaints**

   Agency administration offices receive many calls from concerned citizens about the conditions of its parks and facilities. The calls should be logged in message books by secretarial staff, and immediately passed on to the appropriate person or department for investigation. These phone messages should be treated as work orders and potential safety problems. They should be immediately investigated and actions should be taken if repairs are warranted.

5. **Annual Budgetary Consideration**

   When playground equipment is no longer determined to be safe or in compliance with current safety guidelines, it may be necessary to expend large sums of money to replace or retrofit the equipment in question. This action can only be accomplished through a timely budget request. Agencies must budget money for scheduled playground replacements and unpredictable repairs due to public safety concerns.

Employee Requirements Related to Public Playground Safety Program

The success of a Comprehensive Public Playground Safety Program is directly related to cooperation and commitment from both the public policy and financial decision makers to the operations personnel who are directly responsible for maintaining playground safety.

The term "operations personnel" ranges from the person in charge of the park, recreation facility, school, or daycare center to the full-time maintenance staff person who is in the playground areas on a daily, or at least weekly, basis. This program will never meet its objectives unless all members of the organization communicate well, and maintain an acceptable level of consistency in all phases of the playground safety program implementation.

Management must select, orient, train, and supervise the personnel involved in playground safety in order to implement this program and guarantee its success.

Playground Safety Team

An agency or organization might consider forming a comprehensive public playground safety team to help ensure that all aspects of the program are understood and being carried out effectively. The creation of this team will foster the desired bottom up and top down exchange of information.

In most cases, the team is headed by the top administrator responsible for overseeing the operation, safety, and repair of your public playgrounds. Other team members may include the department heads and their assistants, the park planner/landscape architect who might design or oversee the playground design, purchasing, and installation, facility supervisor, consultant, teacher, and a member of the operations personnel who best represents the field personnel who typically inspect, maintain, and repair the playground areas.

Suggested Public Playground Safety Team Members

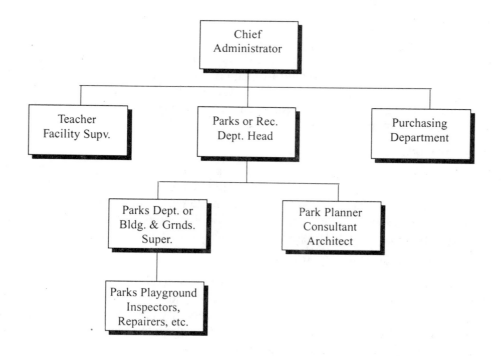

© NRPA/NPSI/PDRMA

The responsibility for the success of the comprehensive public playground safety program does not stop with this team. The responsibility to observe and report unsafe conditions in your public playgrounds rests with all personnel. To ensure this responsibility is understood, communicate to all departments and staff their role in the success of the public playground safety program. You can accomplish this through your agency job descriptions, playground safety policy, and staff meetings.

In summary, your public playground safety team should meet at least annually to review any reported accidents, discuss the results and specific comments documented through the playground area inspection process, and review current practices that are related to public playgrounds such as:

❑ Staff training

❑ Purchasing requirements

❑ Installation requirements

❑ Future equipment selection

❑ Prioritizing capital expenditures

❑ Recurring problem areas including vandalism, repeated product failures, high maintenance concerns, etc.

The effectiveness of your public playground safety team is ultimately up to each agency and it will only be as successful as the level of importance everyone places on safety playground safety. Once your team has been established, they should develop their own agenda within the guidelines they are given using the resources available to them. The evolutionary process should be flexible enough to address the most pressing safety issues realizing that priorities change, and so do playground safety guidelines and standards.

Their most important goal is to provide as safe and enjoyable public playground experience as possible within the resources available. A sample of Wheaton Park District's Annual Playground Safety Committee meeting minutes can be found in Appendix B.

Job Descriptions for Playground Staff

Job descriptions of the principle members of the playground safety team should include specific work tasks regarding their role in the playground safety program.

Included in the job descriptions should be a number of specific skills, traits, or qualifications that an employee must possess in order to perform the work tasks required to maintain safe public playgrounds.

It is important that public agencies make every effort to comply with the Americans With Disabilities Act by including the essential functions necessary to perform a particular job function in your job descriptions. Consult your attorney for specific recommendations.

Auditors and Low Frequency Inspectors

It is important that agencies consider those staff members directly responsible for inspecting and repairing playground equipment as trades level persons. The existing in-depth playground safety standards and the technical knowledge necessary to interpret them, combined with the technological advances in playground equipment structures, require a high level of ability. It is also strongly recommended that auditors and low frequency inspectors attain a playground safety inspector certification (CPSI) to measure their technical abilities in maintaining playgrounds. This level of technical ability and the important responsibility of maintaining the physical integrity and safety of playgrounds warrant trades level pay.

Listed below are some sample basic physical and cognitive traits that should exist in the job descriptions of a person responsible for auditors and low frequency playground inspections and repairs are:

❑ The ability to read and write

❑ The ability to work without direct supervision

❑ The ability to perform clerical duties

❑ The ability to climb onto playground equipment

❑ The ability to use various measurement tools to evaluate compliance

❑ The ability to climb a ladder, stand, walk, bend, crouch, and kneel for extended periods of time

❑ Some agencies are responsible for several playground sites and the ability to drive from site to site will become imperative

High Frequency Inspectors and Repair Personnel

Those persons who will be conducting high frequency playground inspections such as mowing crews, trash pick-up crews, ballfield maintenance crews, etc. will need less technical abilities than low frequency inspectors. In some cases, specific essential physical or cognitive abilities may need to be listed in the job descriptions depending on their job functions in the playground safety program and organizations as a whole.

Staff Training

The only way to help ensure the consistent implementation of an agency's comprehensive playground safety program is to conduct staff training sessions.

All staff involved in the development of new park, school and daycare facilities, installation of new playgrounds, inspection of existing playgrounds, staff responsible for supervising field personnel who inspect, repair and maintain playgrounds should receive some type of formal training in current playground safety guidelines and agency playground program policies.

Recommended Staff Training Levels

The level of training that should be provided to those staff participating in the agency's playground safety program should be in accordance with the knowledge and technical ability required for each job position. The supervisor responsible for the on-going playground safety program should be knowledgeable in all aspects of the program and have an in-depth understanding of current playground safety standards and guidelines. An important role of the supervisor responsible for overseeing the playground safety program is to review field inspections, repairs, and installations on a regular basis to ensure compliance with written procedures.

The following three sections discuss the suggested level of training that should be provided to playground designers and auditors, low frequency inspectors, and high frequency inspectors, including playground supervisors.

☞ **NOTE:** The numbers used in sections A, B, and C correspond to training resources listed on page 92.

© NRPA/NPSI/PDRMA

A. The staff member responsible for conducting the agency's **initial playground safety audits** or responsible for **designing public playgrounds** should:

- ❏ Be trained and tested in all current playground safety standards and guidelines. **It is recommended that this staff member become a Certified Playground Safety Inspector (CPSI) through the National Recreation and Park Association's National Playground Safety Institute's National Certification Program and exam. The CPSI program requires retesting every three years in an effort to update inspectors on the latest changes in playground safety standards.**

- ❏ Be trained in the policies and procedures used by the agency to maintain a comprehensive public playground maintenance safety program.

- ❏ Be trained in many of the playground safety training resources numbers 1-7 in the list on the following page.

- ❏ Attend outside playground safety instructional seminars.

- ❏ Be instructed in the use of all probes, gauges, and other tools needed to complete the play ground safety audit.

- ❏ Have previous experience in playground inspections, repairs, design, and installation.

- ❏ Be trained in the use of the agency's playground safety audit form, the guide to frequency of inspection form, and the high and low frequency inspection forms.

B. The staff member responsible for conducting the **low frequency inspections** should:

- ❏ Be trained and tested in all current playground safety standards and guidelines by attending an NRPA National Playground Safety Institute and become a Certified Playground Safety Inspector (CPSI).

- ❏ Be trained in the policies and procedures used by the agency to maintain a comprehensive public playground maintenance safety program.

- ❏ Be trained in playground safety training resources numbers 1, 5, 6, 7 and parts of 2, 3 and 4 in the following list of available training materials.

- ❏ Attend outside playground safety instructional seminars.

- ❏ Be instructed in agency playground repair procedures.

- ❏ Be instructed in playground equipment manufacturer maintenance instructions.

- ❏ Be trained and tested at a playground site to ensure adequate skill level and decision making ability.

- ❏ Be trained in the use of the agency's high and low frequency inspection forms and procedures.

C. The staff member who will be conducting **high frequency inspections** should:

- ❏ Be trained in the process used by the agency to maintain a comprehensive public playground maintenance safety program.

- ❏ Be trained in the use of the agency's high frequency (routine) inspection forms and procedures.

- ❏ Be trained in playground safety training resources numbers 1, 5, and 6 and parts of 2 in the following list of available training materials.

- ❏ Be instructed in agency playground repair procedures.

- ❏ Be trained in specific maintenance duties such as raking surface materials, sweeping loose materials from walking areas, removing trash, identifying vandalism, evaluating the general condition of each playground component, etc.

- ❏ Be audited by the supervisor responsible for the playground safety program to ensure that all aspects of the high frequency inspection process are conducted.

Playground Safety Training Materials Available

A variety of training materials are available to instruct agency staff in current playground safety practices. These include:

1. *Handbook for Public Playground Safety.* 1997 Consumer Products Safety Commission, Publication Number 325.

2. Kutska K. and Hoffman K. and Malkusak T. (1998) *Playground Safety Is No Accident: Developing a Public Playground Safety and Maintenance Program.* Second Edition. National Recreation and Park Association.

3. Christiansen, Monty L. (Ed.) and Vogelsong, Hans (1996). *Play It Safe: Anthology of Playground Safety.* Second Edition. Alexandria, VA: National Recreation and Park Association.

4. Christiansen, Monty L. *Points About Playgrounds.* Third Edition (1993) Compiled & edited

5. American Society For Testing and Materials ASTMF1487-95, Avaialable through National Recreation and Park Association, Professional Services, 22377 Belmont Ridge Rd., Ashburn, VA 20148, 703-858-0784.

6. *Safe Active Play, A Guide to Avoiding Play Area Hazards,* © 1997 Video, by Video Active Production

7. MacIntyre, S., Goltsman, S.M., (1997) *Safety First Checklist: Audit and Inspection Program for Children's Play Areas.* MIG Communication, Berkeley, CA, 94710.

Using Playground Safety Exercises

Although it is important that public agencies provide appropriate levels of training to those staff members who will actively be conducting audits, inspections, and repairs, it is even more important that these employees fully understand the information presented to them so they can correctly perform their playground safety assignments.

Quality playground safety training begins by having the most current playground safety written materials and videos available for your training sessions. These training sessions should be presented in a comfortable setting, be documented in a roster form, and be followed by some type of understanding exercises that should indicate that the presented information is absorbed.

One of the best ways to help ensure that your staff understands current playground safety guidelines and related agency procedures is to take them out into the playgrounds, present a variety of situations and scenarios, and ask them how they would respond. If their understanding of important playground safety concepts is not acceptable, further training will be necessary.

All playground safety training should be documented and include the names of attendees, date, topics covered, and the instructor's name. A sample training roster can be found in Appendix A.

Sample playground understanding questions are also provided in Appendix A to assist agencies in determining if your staff has absorbed some of the necessary information needed for conducting audits, and low/high frequency inspections.

Level I questions can be answered by those staff who will be conducting high frequency inspections.

Level II questions are for those staff members who will be conducting low frequency inspections. **NOTE:** Level II staff must also understand Level I questions.

Level III questions are for those staff members who are responsible for designing playgrounds and conducting initial playground audits. **NOTE:** Level III staff must have an understanding of all previous levels.

© NRPA/NPSI/PDRMA

The provided sample questions and answers (in Appendix A) are not a guarantee that a particular employee will fully understand all necessary playground concepts at any level. Managers must evaluate other factors such as maturity level, past work history, education level, and related traits in determining the specific responsibilities assigned to staff involved in a playground safety program and modify the understanding exercises to meet each agency's specific needs.

Managers and supervisors also must regularly audit performance levels in the field to help ensure that the playground safety program is functioning as designed.

© NRPA/NPSI/PDRMA

Playground Signage

Signage and user education are another component of your playground safety program.

The question of whether signage is effective in reducing accidents on public playgrounds has been debated over and over. Signage alone has not been proven to reduce accidents, but it has helped to reduce awards in some public playground liability cases.

Since the *1991 CPSC Handbook for Public Playground Safety,* it has been recommended that playground areas be designed for separate age groups (2-5 and 5-12) due to the significant developmental and physical differences that exist between these groups. Because of this recommendation, public playgrounds should be signed in accordance with the age group for which they were designed. The CPSC Handbook also recognizes that pre-school age children require more attentive supervision on playgrounds.

User education and supervision on school playgrounds has been documented to reduce the frequency of accidents. It is also documented that once supervision is stopped, the frequency of accidents will again increase.

Almost all public playgrounds other than schools' and day care centers' play areas are typically not supervised because of the significant costs that would be generated by the hours they remain open. Since supervision cannot be provided by most public agencies, signage can be used to educate users and denote the appropriate age group for which the play area was designed.

Another major purpose for playground signage is to gain the support and respect of those users who are concerned about playground safety, and to encourage them to help report safety problems immediately so they can be corrected.

Placement of Playground Signage

Playground signage should be placed at the defined entrance to the play area. If several defined access points exist, the agency should consider placing signage at each location.

Where no distinct entry point to the play area exists, the sign should be placed in a conspicuous location near the playground equipment.

Language on Playground Signage

At a minimum, per 1997 CPSC playground safety guidelines, your signage should indicate the age group for which the play area was designed.

The playground equipment in this area is for use by children ages _____ to _____.

Other playground signage language should include use rules, hours of operation, safety warnings and related issues specific to your playground area. The following sample playground signage issues should be considered:

❑ Welcome. For your play enjoyment, please obey the following rules or you may cause injury to yourself or others.

❑ Children under age 7 should be accompanied by an adult.

❑ This area is to be used only with adult supervision.

❑ Inspect play area before starting play.

❑ If you notice any broken equipment or anything that requires immediate attention, please call _____.

❑ No running, pushing, or shoving.

❑ Do not use equipment when wet.

- ❑ Bare feet may cause injury. Proper footwear is required.
- ❑ No bicycles, roller blades, or skateboard use in the playground area.
- ❑ No pets allowed.
- ❑ We appreciate your cooperation.
- ❑ There is a $_____ fine for damage or defacing public property.

Construction of Playground Signage

Playground signage should be placed on a yellow background with a text of contrasting colors such as black. The color yellow is the universally recognized color for caution which is the level of warning likely appropriate for most typical public playgrounds.

Vinyl adhesive construction can easily be mass produced at a reasonable cost. This low cost factor assists those public agencies that experience a higher degree of signage vandalism.

Signage Sample

The following sample playground sign was designed by Ken Kutska, CLP, CPSI, Superintendent of Parks and Planning, Wheaton Park District, Wheaton, Illinois.

Work with your legal department and risk manager to develop the most appropriate wording for your specific needs.

© NRPA/NPSI/PDRMA

PUBLIC PLAYGROUND SAFETY GUIDELINES

Welcome. For your play enjoyment, please obey the following or you may cause injury to yourself or others around you.

No pets allowed.

No bicycles, roller skates, or skateboard use within play area.

Inspect play area before starting to play and remove litter.

Children 7 and under should be accompanied by an adult.

This playground is designed for ages ___ to ___.

CAUTION

Bare feet may cause injury.

Throwing sand or any other objects within play area may cause injury.

Playing on this equipment when wet may cause injury.

SWINGS

Hold on with both hands.

Standing on swings cause injury.

Stop swinging before getting off.

Never swing or twist empty seats.

Stand clear of moving swing to avoid contact and possible injury.

SLIDES

Slide feet first only.

No running or walking up slide.

CLIMBERS

No pushing, running, or shoving.

Play safely and be courteous of others.

If you notice broken equipment or anything that requires immediate attention, call 665-4710. We appreciate your cooperation.

THE WHEATON PARK DISTRICT
$500.00 fine for damaging or defacing public property.

*NOTE: Actual Sign is 11"x17"

© NRPA/NPSI/PDRMA

Storage of Playground Documentation

The average playground equipment purchased today may last between 15-20 years and generate a sizable amount of paper and computer documentation. This documentation should be stored in an organized manner so that it can be retrieved for purposes such as contacting the manufacturer for replacement parts, evaluating the maintenance level for a site, or to locate maintenance inspection records and manufacturer's product's liability certificate of insurance following a serious accident.

To help organize the many forms of documentation that should be kept by public agencies after installing a playground, the site history checklist (sample form following) is provided. This checklist can be placed in the front of each playground site file as a Table of Contents and be filled in as each piece as documentation is obtained. This form can also act as a prompt to obtain certain important documentation that should be included in a file.

Many public agencies are now relying more on computers to condense the paperwork that must be maintained. While computers are very efficient to use, they can easily be disrupted by a variety of factors such as lightning strikes, computer viruses, and human error, which can destroy thousands of hours of work in an instant. To avoid most of these potential problems, simply make a back-up of your computerized playground records on a weekly or monthly basis and store them off site at another safe facility. Never rely on fire proof safes or cabinets to protect electronic media. In the event you lose one set of computer records, the other will be available.

The following briefly explains suggested items for a Table of Contents of the Site History Checklist and playground site file (see page 101).

1. A copy of the playground bid specifications should be included in the site file.

2. A copy of the purchase order or invoice should be included to document the date the playground equipment was purchased from the vendor.

3. An insurance certificate that includes product's liability limits should be requested from the manufacturer in the bid specifications and be included in the file.

4. A letter from the manufacturer's representative or manufacturer should be obtained stating that the playground equipment **purchased** meets all current playground safety standards and guidelines. Verification of IPEMA a third party certification is another form of assurance of ASTM standard compliance.

5. All manufacturer installation drawings and instructions should be maintained to document the correct installation procedures as provided by the manufacturer.

6. A letter from the manufacturer's representative or manufacturer should be obtained stating that the playground equipment has been **installed** in accordance with manufacturer instructions.

7. A site plan drawing of the playground/park should be included in the file.

8. An itemized list of the types and quantity of playground equipment components should be included in the file.

9. The parts lists for all playground equipment located at the park site should be included in the file.

9. The parts lists for all playground equipment located at the park site should be included in the file.

10. The completed initial playground safety audit should be included in the file.

11. The completed inspection frequency form should be kept in the file.

12. All completed high and low frequency playground inspection records should be maintained in the file.

13. All remedial maintenance history and safety repair records should be maintained. These records include work orders and telephone complaints that relate to the site.

NOTE: The date each item was placed in the individual site history file should be marked in the appropriate corresponding box. Site histories will change over time. Having the date and staff initials of the person filling out or modifying the checklist for each item placed in the file will help staff review the files for accuracy.

© NRPA/NPSI/PDRMA

Playground Site History Checklist

Site name, locations and identification number:

_____

Date equipment installed:_____

Date site history checklist completed:_____

Staff member completing history checklist:_____

Item on File		Item
Yes	**No**	
		① Playground bid specifications
		② Copy of P.O. or invoice
		③ Insurance certificate including product's liability limits
		④ Manufacturer's letter stating that playground equipment meets all current playground safety standards and guidelines
		⑤ Manufacturer's installation drawings and instructions
		⑥ Manufacturer's installation verification
		⑦ Site plans
		⑧ Itemized list and quantity of play components
		⑨ Parts list
		⑩ Initial playground safety audit
		⑪ Recommended inspection frequency checklist
		⑫ Inspection history and checklist copies
		⑬ Remedial action history:
		a. Telephone complaints
		b. Work orders

IMPORTANT
This information has been prepared to assist the agency's attorney in defending potential litigation. *Do not* release to any person except an agency official or designated claim representative or an investigating police officer.

© NRPA/NPSI/PDRMA

Playground Accidents and Investigations

No matter how well a public agency audits, inspects, and maintains its facilities and playgrounds, accidents will occur. They will occur because as children develop physically and socially, they will progressively take risks on the playground as a normal part of this development. As some children test their physical abilities, they may not complete a skill and be injured.

Playground Accident Investigations

After playground injuries occur, it is vitally important that they be immediately investigated to determine the specific causes of the accident. This investigation should include a visit to the site to inspect the play equipment to determine if any repairs are needed, photograph the accident site, document the names of any witnesses, and gather all other pertinent information.

In the event of a serious injury, the agency's attorney and insurance carrier should be notified immediately so that they can direct the investigation process and preserve your agency's defense to a claim. In some cases, the equipment may be removed or temporarily taken out of use to eliminate the potential for another injury if a repair is not immediately possible.

It is recommended that agencies designate at least two supervisory level persons to conduct immediate accident investigations following an incident. These individuals should be trained in proper questioning of witnesses and completing the accident investigation form.

☞ **NOTE:** It is extremely important that agency staff never admit any liability immediately following a playground accident regardless of the circumstances. Laws in your state may provide you with legal immunities to certain types of accidents that caused an injury. All questions pertaining to liability and payment of medical bills should be directed to your agency manager or attorney. Also, photographs should be taken to document the condition of the equipment.

Accident Report Forms

It is recommend that agencies develop some type of accident report form to document accident information. The following list of questions should be included in your playground accident and investigation form. A sample Accident/Incident Report Form can be found in Appendix A-54 and A-55.

- ❏ Date and time of the accident
- ❏ Exact location of the accident
- ❏ Name, address, and phone number of injured person
- ❏ Names, addresses, and phone numbers of any witnesses
- ❏ Explanation of events that led to accident by injured person or witnesses
- ❏ Nature of injury (list specific body part and type of injury)
- ❏ Level of medical assistance provided (first aid, paramedics, etc.)
- ❏ Description of the condition of the equipment at the time of accident
- ❏ Verification that photographs have been taken
- ❏ Name and signature of person completing the report
- ❏ Date of the report

Following Up on the Results of Your Accident Investigations

All playground accident reports should be closely evaluated to identify any trends that may point to equipment that is being misused, a need for adjustments in maintenance schedules, or other safety concerns. Your playground safety team or safety committee should review accident reports on a scheduled basis to identify and correct any safety concerns.

It is vitally important that agencies identify specific playground equipment safety concerns or general trends in accident frequency so that actions can be taken to prevent future accidents. In many states, remedial safety-related actions taken following an accident to prevent future accidents are not admissible as proof of liability. Consult your agency's attorney for specific actions. Once the site has been secured and the accident investigation complete, obtain supervisory approval for repair, retrofit or removal of any defective equipment, especially if not in compliance with the current standard of care, i.e. 1997 CPSC Handbook for Public Playgrounds and current ASTM F1487 Standard.

© NRPA/NPSI/PDRMA

Appendix A

Blank Playground

Inspection Forms

© NRPA/NPSI/PDRMA

Playground Safety Audit Form
(revised March, 1998)

Injuries to children may occur from many types of playground equipment and environmental conditions. The checklist on the following pages will help you to assess and correct safety concerns that may be present on or near your playground. While it does not cover every potential safety concern in a children's environment, it is an overview of most known playground safety concerns. The checklist does not apply to home playground equipment, amusement park equipment, or to equipment normally intended for sports use. The checklist also does not address the many important issues of child development that pertain to play.

The playground audit form is not a regulatory standard, but a compilation of suggested guidelines based upon the *Handbook for Public Playground Safety* written by the Consumer Product Safety Commission (CPSC) (Revised 1997), *American Society for Testing and Materials* (ASTM) F1487-95 Standard, and expert opinions from consultants in the field of playground safety.

Acknowledgments

From the "Statewide Comprehensive Injury Prevention Program" (SCIPP), Department of Public Health, 150 Trecost Street, Boston, MA 02111

Adapted as Wheaton Park District's "Initial Playground Safety Audit" September, 1989, Revised December 20, 1990 and November, 1991, Ken Kutska.

Edited and updated June, 1992, by Ken Kutska, CLP, and Kevin Hoffman, ARM, Park District Risk Management Agency.

Edited and updated March, 1998, by Ken Kutska, CLP, CPSI; Kevin Hoffman, ARM, CPSI, and Tony Malkusak, CLP, CPSI.

ASTM
American Society for Testing and Materials
100 Barr Harbor Drive
West Conshohocken, Pennsylvania 19428
(610)832-9585

U.S. CPSC
Consumer Product Safety Commission
Washington, DC 20207
(1-800-638-CPSC)

National Playground Safety Institute, NPSI
22377 Belmont Ridge Road
Ashburn, VA 20148
(703) 858-0784
www.nrpa.org

Background Information:

Playground/Park:_____ Date of Audit: _____

Site Location: _____ Agency: _____

Equipment Type: _____ Surfacing: _____

Inspected By: _____ Ages of Intended Users:_____

General Environment:

1.   **Category of playground (circle all that apply):**

- Public School
- Private School
- Day Care

- Community Park
- Neighborhood Park/Tot Lot
- Other (please specify)_____

2.   **Equipment Inventory. Indicate the number of equipment pieces that exist.**

A. Composite play structure	B. Free standing equipment	C. Site amenities
• Stairways and Step Ladders _____	• Swings (to-fro) _____	• Benches _____
• Vertical Rung Ladders _____	• Tire Swings _____	• Tables _____
• Ridgid Climber _____	• Seesaws _____	• Fountains _____
• Flexible Climber _____	• Slides _____	• Bike Rack _____
• Decks and Platforms _____	• Rigid Climbers _____	• Wheelchair Parking _____
• Play Panel _____	• Flexible Climbers _____	
• Slides _____	• Upper Body Equipment _____	• Signs _____
• Sliding Pole _____	• Rocking Equipment _____	• Trash Receptacles _____
• Horizontal Ladder _____	• Whirl _____	• Fencing _____
• Horizontal Rings _____	• Sand Play Area _____	• Other _____
• Track Ride _____	• Blackhoe Digger _____	• Other _____
• Crawl Tunnel _____	• Play Panels _____	
• Clatter Bridge/Bridges _____	• Other _____	
• Ramps _____	• Other _____	
• Transfer Stations _____	• Other _____	
• Roofs _____		
• Other _____		

© NRPA/NPSI/PDRMA

3. Playground Border Factors:

Directions: Determine which playground border concerns exist and circle them. In the second column, indicate the actual distance the item is from the playground border. In the third column, assign index points based on the distance each potential border concern is from the nearest playground border (see Key to Border Concern Points).

Key to Border Concern Points:
Within 100 feet   (5 points)
101-199 feet   (2 points)
200 feet or more (0 points)

Playground Border Concerns Measurements or Distances	Distance from Play Edge	Index Points Given	Comments
1st public street			
2nd public street			
3rd public street			
4th public street			
Streets with heavy traffic			
Water (ponds/stream/drainage ditch)			
Soccer/football field			
Baseball/softball field from home plate			
Basketball court			
Parking lots			
Railroad tracks			
Trees (not pruned up at least 7')			
Golf course			
Other (specify) _____			
Point Total for Question 3:			

General Conditions	Possible Index Points	Index Points Given	Comments

General Environment Concerns

	General Conditions	Possible Index Points	Index Points Given	Comments
4.	The playground can be accessed safely by a sidewalk that is free of standing water, sand, pea gravel & low hanging branches.	5		
5.	If needed, a suitable barrier (fence) is provided for border concerns within 100' of playground edge. See question 3 for list of possible border concerns (CPSC 6.1).	20		
6.	Seating (benches, outdoor tables) is in good condition (free of splinters, missing hardware or slats, protruding bolts, etc.).	1		
7.	Signs give information about: • regulations on the use of the playground (hours, pets, specific rules, etc.). • name and phone number of playground owner (to report problems). • age appropriateness of equipment. (CPSC 6.3)	15		
8.	Signs on all bordering roads advise motorists that a playground is nearby.	5		
9.	Trash receptacles are provided and located outside of the play area.	1		
10.	Poisonous plants are removed from play area.	10		
11.	Shaded area is provided.	1		
12.	The play area is visible to deter inappropriate behavior (CPSC 6.2).	5		
13.	The play area is free from lead in paint (maximum 0.06% lead by dry weight) (CPSC 8.1).	20		
14.	The play area is free from toxic materials and preservatives (CPSC 8.1).	20		
Section Subtotal		103		

© NRPA/NPSI/PDRMA

General Conditions	Possible Index Points	Index Points Given	Comments

Age/Size Appropriateness Design

		Possible Index Points	Index Points Given	Comments
15.	Net, chain, arch or tire climbers are not the sole means to access play equipment for 2-5 yr. old users (ASTM 7.2.2.1).	10		
16.	Play equipment not recommended for 2-5 yr. old users: chain or cable walks, free standing arch climbers, free standing climbing events with flexible components, fulcrum seesaws, log rolls, long spiral slides, overhead rings, parallel bars, swinging gates, track rides and vertical sliding poles (CPSC 6.3).	10 pts. for each item found (Possible 110 pts.)		
17.	The play area has signs that inform users of intended user age group (CPSC 6.3).	20		
	Section Subtotal	**140**		

Playground Protective Surface

		Possible Index Points	Index Points Given	Comments
18.	All elevated play equipment (slides, swings, bridges, seesaws, climbing apparatus, etc.) has proper depth of impact-absorbing material underneath the structure. Refer to CPSC and ASTM F1487-95 and ASTM 1292 for specifications on conforming protective surface type, critical fall heights and how far surfacing should extend from structure (CPSC Section 4).	20		
19.	Surfaces are inspected at least weekly and raked to prevent them from becoming packed down and to remove hidden hazards (e.g. litter, sharp objects, animal feces). (Daily=0 points, weekly=5 pts, monthly=10 pts, seasonally=20 pts, annually=40 pts) (CPSC 7.2).	40 20 10 5 0		
20.	Loose materials are replenished as recommended to maintain adequate depth and coverage (annually=10, seasonally=5, monthly or less=0) (CPSC 7.2).	10 5 0		
21.	Standing water is not found within any of the use zones (CPSC 6.1).	20		

© NRPA/NPSI/PDRMA

General Conditions	Possible Index Points	Index Points Given	Comments

Playground Protective Surface, cont.

	General Conditions	Possible Index Points	Index Points Given	Comments
22.	For equipment installed after 1995, manufacturer's sign attached to equipment stating equipment must be installed over impact absorbing surface (ASTM 14.3).	10		
	Section Subtotal	**150**		

<u>Note</u>: If playground protective surface inspections are not documented in writing; <u>add 50 points</u> to section subtotal.

Use Zone

	General Conditions	Possible Index Points	Index Points Given	Comments
23.	There is a minimum use zone of 6' in all directions for all equipment. Use zones for adjacent pieces of play equipment may overlap if the adjacent designated play surfaces are less than 30" above the protective surface. If either adjacent structure exceed 30", the minimum distance between the structures should be 9'. Rocking/springing equipment intended for users to stand upon is no less than 7'. Swings, slide exits, and moving equipment other than less than 30" high rocking equipment shall not overlap use zones. (CPSC 5.1.1, ASTM 9.2.1, 9.5.2.1).	20		
24.	Swings with enclosed swing seat or bucket, use zone to the front and to therear shall be a minimum distance of 2W, where W equals the distance from the top of the occupant's sitting surface to the pivot-point on the swing (CPSC 5.1.3, ASTM 9.4.1.2).	20		
25.	Belt swings' use zone to the front and to the rear shall be a minimum distance of 2X, where X equals the distance from the top of the protective surface to the pivot-point on the swing (CPSC 5.1.3, ASTM 9.4.1.1).	20		
26.	Slides have adequate space from other equipment at the bottom (height of slide plus 4' from the reduced gradient, or 6' from edge of slide; whichever is greater, but not more than 14'). (CPSC 5.1.2, ASTM 9.6.2, 9.6.2.1, Fig. A1.32).	20		

© NRPA/NPSI/PDRMA

General Conditions	Possible Index Points	Index Points Given	Comments

Use Zone, cont.

	General Conditions	Possible Index Points	Index Points Given	Comments
27.	The use zone for a rotating swing (tire swing) shall be a minimum of 6' in all directions of the support structure plus a minimum horizontal distance in all directions equal to the distance between the pivot point to the top of seat plus 6' (CPSC 5.1.3, 5.1.4, ASTM 9.4.2).	20		
28.	Barriers between equipment are installed so as not to create a trip hazard and are free of protrusions, splinters, sharp edges, etc. and are outside equipment use zone (CPSC 9.7).	10		
	Section Subtotal	**110**		

Accessibility

NOTE: The purpose of this audit form, with regard to accessibility, is to allow the audit inspector to determine compliance of the play area with ASTM F 1487-95. The goal of the inspector is to determine if a person with a disability has access to, on and through the equipment and play area. This audit form is not intended to assess design compliance with the soon to be released access board report.

The auditor shall indicate in the comments column and audit summary report, in your opinion, whether or not the playground is accessible per this simple three part question. Does the user have access to, through, and onto the playground equipment?

	General Conditions	Possible Index Points	Index Points Given	Comments
29.	The playground has an accessible route with a maximum horizontal slope of 1:20 (greater than 1:20 would be considered a ramp) and a maximum cross-slope of 1:50 (access to and around the playground area is at least 60" wide) (ASTM 10.1.3).	10		
30.	Ramps are 36" wide minimum; with a slope between 1:20 and 1:12 and maximum horizontal run of 12 feet (ASTM 10.2.2.1, 10.2.2.2).	10		
31.	Landings are 60" minimum diameter at bottom and top of each run; landings with play components shall have area 30" x 48" to park wheelchair while not reducing adjacent circulation path to less than 36" (ASTM 10.2.2.4).	10		
32.	For ramps, either the barrier extends to within 1 inch of the ramp surface or a curb stop exists that projects a minimum of 2" above the ramp. (ASTM 10.2.2.8).	20		
33.	For ramps higher than 30" (designed for 2-5 yr. olds) or higher than 48" (designed for 5-12 yr. olds) barriers are provided (ASTM 7.4.4, 10.2.2.5).	20		

© NRPA/NPSI/PDRMA

General Conditions	Possible Index Points	Index Points Given	Comments
Accessibility, cont.			
34. For ramps > 30" H (designed for 2-5 yr. olds) or > 48" H (designed for 5-12 yr. olds) handrails are provided on each side of a ramp at a height between 26-28". For ramps less than or equal to 30" H and 48" H (for 2-5 and 5-12 yr. olds, respectively) two handrails are provided on each side that are between 12-16" H and 26-28" H (ASTM 7.4.3, 10.2.2.6, 10.2.2.7).	20		
35. Transfer point height is between 14-18" with a clear width of minimum 24" and depth of no less than 14". Transfer point steps are a maximum of 8" high with handholds (ASTM 10.2.3.1-10.2.3.3, 10.3.1).	10		
36. Transfer pts. have; wheelchair turning space at base of transfer point; a clear space area of 60" minimum. T-shaped area in accordance with ASTM Fig. A1-39a (ASTM 10.2.4.1).	10		
37. The playground use zone has an accessible safety surface (ASTM 10.1.2).	10		
38. Accessible restroom facilities, accessible seating, accessible drinking fountain and shade are located in or near the play area.	1		
39. Wheelchair accessible platforms: single wheelchair passage 36"; two wheelchair passage 60"; single wheelchair and 1 able-bodied user 44"; openings between deck not greater than 0.50" (ASTM 10.2.5.1-10.2.5.4).	10		
40. Accessible play opportunities designed with different access and egress points, such as slides, allow the user to return unassisted to access the original transfer point (ASTM 10.3.2.1).	10		
41. Vertical leg clearance is not less than 24" for equipment that requires a wheelchair user to pull partially under, such as sand tables, with a top playing surface of no greater than 30" (ASTM 10.3.2.2).	10		

© NRPA/NPSI/PDRMA

General Conditions	Possible Index Points	Index Points Given	Comments
Accessibility, cont.			
42. Wheelchair accessible upper body equipment, such as horizontal ladders and rings, are less than or equal to 54" high (ASTM 10.3.2.3).	10		
43. Wheelchair accessible manipulative equipment, such as interactive panels, are between 9"-48" H for side reach and 20"-36" H for front reach from the accessible surface (ASTM 10.3.2.4, 10.3.2.5).	10		
Section Subtotal	**171**		

© NRPA/NPSI/PDRMA

Specific Conditions	Possible Index Points	Index Points Given	Comments

- **Important:** For the following audit sections, if multiple types of the same equipment exists (such as two swing sets), you can apply the questions to all multiple pieces of equipment as a whole. However, no more than full index points should be applied if a negative response exists on more than one piece of the same equipment. Also, deficiencies on a specific piece of equipment should be noted in the comments section for repair or future consideration.

Slides

	Specific Conditions	Possible Index Points	Index Points Given	Comments
44.	Slides are accessed by stairs, step ladders, or platforms which are evenly spaced, less than 12" apart, and pass the entrapment test. Refer to ASTM F 1487 Table 2 (CPSC 12.4.2).	10		
45.	There is a flat surface the width of the slide bed at the top of the slide to help position the child for sliding (min. 22" deep going back from the slide bedway and min. 12" wide for 2-5 yr. old users and a min. 16" for 5-12 yr. old users) (CPSC 12.4.3, ASTM 8.5.2.2, 8.5.2.3, 8.5.4.3).	10		
46.	There are sufficient safety barriers at the top of the slide to prevent falls, with hand holds to assist standing to sitting transition and a means to channel the user to the sitting position before slide entry (CPSC 12.4.3, ASTM 7.4, 8.5.3).	15		
47.	Sides of bedways are at least 4" high (CPSC 12.4.4, ASTM 8.5.4.4).	15		
48.	No portion of the angle of the sliding surface exceeds 50 degrees with the average angle of 30 degrees or less (CPSC 12.4.4, ASTM 8.5.4.2).	10		
49.	A flat sliding surface (run out zone) at the bottom of the slide is a min. of 11" long at transition point and angle is less than 5 degrees from the horizontal plane (CPSC 12.4.5, ASTM 8.5.5.1, 8.5.5.2).	10		
50.	For slides greater than 4' high, designed for 5-12 yr. olds, the slide exit height is between 7" and 15" above the protective surfacing material (CPSC 12.4.5, ASTM 8.5.5.3).	10		

© NRPA/NPSI/PDRMA

Specific Conditions	Possible Index Points	Index Points Given	Comments

Slides cont.

Specific Conditions	Possible Index Points	Index Points Given	Comments
51. For slides 4' high or less and designed for 2-5 yr. olds, the slide exit height does not exceed 11" above the protective surfacing material (CPSC 12.4.5, ASTM 8.5.5.3).	10		
52. Tube slides have a minimum diameter equal to or greater than 23" (CPSC 12.4.8, (ASTM 8.5.4.7).	5		
53. Only short spiral slides, with one turn or less, are recommended for 2-5 yr. old users (CPSC 12.4.7).	5		
54. A clear area, height of 60" along slide chute and width of 21" from inside edge of siderail including the transition platform. No obstacles or protrusions project more than 1/8" perpendicular to the plane of the initial surface. Underside of slide bedway is exempt (ASTM 8.5.6.1, figures A1.16 and A1.22).	20		
55. On roller slides, no opening allows a 3/16" rod to enter (ASTM 8.9.2.1).	10		
56. If the slide is made in several pieces, the sliding surface has no gaps or rough edges at the top of the slide or at section seams which could entangle clothing or trap foreign material (CPSC 12.4.3, 12.4.4).	20		
57. The sliding surface faces away from sun or is located in the shade and isn't made of wood or fiberglass (CPSC 12.4.4).	10		
58. Pinch, Crush and Shear Points (CPSC 9.5, ASTM 6.4): • Equipment is free of sharp edges. • There are no open holes in the equipment forming traps (e.g. at the ends of the tubes). • There are no pinch, crush or shear points.	10 10 10		
59. Protrusions (CPSC 9.2, ASTM 6.2): • No components fail protrusion test. • Nuts, bolts and screws are recessed, covered or sanded smooth and level.	10 10		

© NRPA/NPSI/PDRMA

Specific Conditions	Possible Index Points	Index Points Given	Comments

Slides cont.

Specific Conditions	Possible Index Points	Index Points Given	Comments
60. Entanglements/Entrapment Angles (CPSC 9.4, 9.6, ASTM 6.3):			
• No more than two threads of the fastener protrude through any nut.	10		
• No obstacles or protrusions project upwards from a horizontal plane extending more than 1/8" perpendicular to the plane of the initial surface.	10		
• There are no open "V" entrapment angles on any part of the equipment. See Figs. A1.3-4 in ASTM F 1487.	10		
61. Head Entrapments (CPSC 9.6, ASTM 6.1):			
• No components fail the entrapment test.	10		
• There are no partially bounded openings. See Figs. A1.6a-A1.10 in ASTM F 1487.	10		
62. Hardware:			
• Nuts and bolts are tight and not able to be loosened without tools. Upon close inspection, they show no loose play or excessive wear (CPSC 8.2).	10		
• Equipment is free of rust and chipping paint (CPSC 8.1).	5		
• Equipment is free of sharp edges, splinters or rough surfaces and shows no excessive wear (CPSC 9.1).	10		
• Ropes, chains and cables have not frayed or worn out (CPSC 7.2).	10		
• Equipment has not shifted or become bent (CPSC 8.1).	10		
• There is no corrosion or visible rotting at points where equipment comes into contact with ground surface (CPSC 7.2, 8.1).	10		
• No components are missing. All parts of the equipment are present and in good working order with no loose play or excessive wear in moving parts (CPSC 7.2, 8.1).	20		
• Handgrips are between 0.95" and 1.55" in diameter (CPSC 10.2.1).	10		
• Footings for equipment are stable and buried below ground level or covered by surfacing materials (CPSC 9.7).	20		
• Equipment is free of any litter, debris and surfacing material (ASTM 7.1.2).	20		
• Equipment use zone is free of litter and debris (CPSC 7.2).	10		
Section Subtotal			

© NRPA/NPSI/PDRMA

Specific Conditions	Possible Index Points	Index Points Given	Comments
Climbing Equipment			
63. Handholds stay in place when grasped (CPSC 10.4).	20		
64. Climbing bars and handrails are between 0.95"-1.55" in diameter (CPSC 10.2.1, ASTM 8.2.1).	10		
65. Flexible access equipment anchoring devices are below level of playing surface (CPSC 12.1.3, ASTM 7.2.2.2).	10		
66. Flexible climbing devices used as access for use by 2-5 yr. olds, readily allows users to bring feet to the same level before ascending to the next level (ASTM 7.2.2.4).	5		
67. Climbers don't have climbing bars or other structural components in the interior of the structure onto which a child may fall from a height of greater than 18" (CPSC 12.1.2).	20		
68. Accesses which don't have side handrails, such as rung ladders, arch or flexible climbers, are to have alternate hand-gripping support at transition (CPSC 10.4, ASTM 7.3.2).	10		
69. Rung ladders, arch and flexible climbers used as access, are not above the designated play surface it serves (no trip hazard) (ASTM 7.3.3).	10		
70. Balance beam maximum height from the playing surface is 12" for 2-5 yr. old users and 16" for 5-12 yr. old users (CPSC 12.1.8, ASTM 8.1.1).	5		
71. No obstacles or protrusions project upwards from a horizontal plane extending more than a 1/8" perpendicular to the plane of the initial surface. See ASTM F1487 fig. A1.13 (CPSC 9.3, ASTM 6.3.2.1).	20		

© NRPA/NPSI/PDRMA

Specific Conditions	Possible Index Points	Index Points Given	Comments
Climbing Equipment, cont.			
72. All components of crawl through tunnels are secure and firmly fixed. The tunnel has two safe, clear exits and is designed to drain freely.	20		
73. Pinch, Crush and Shear Points (CPSC 9.5, ASTM 6.4): • Equipment is free of sharp edges. • There are no open holes in the equipment forming traps (e.g. at the ends of the tubes). • There are no pinch, crush or shear points.	10 10 10		
74. Protrusions (CPSC 9.2, ASTM 6.2): • No components fail protrusion test. • Nuts, bolts and screws are recessed, covered or sanded smooth and level.	10 10		
75. Entanglements/Entrapment Angles (CPSC 9.4, 9.6, ASTM 6.3): • No more than two threads of the fastener protrude through any nut. • No obstacles or protrusions project upwards from a horizontal plane extending more than 1/8" perpendicular to the plane of the initial surface. • There are no open "V" entrapment angles on any part of the equipment. See Figs. A1.3-4 in ASTM F 1487.	10 10 10		
76. Head Entrapments (CPSC 9.6, ASTM 6.1): • No components fail the entrapment test. • There are no partially bounded openings. See Figs. A1.6a-A1.10 ASTM F 1487.	10 10		
77. Hardware: • Nuts and bolts are tight and not able to be loosened without tools. Upon close inspection, they show no loose play or excessive wear (CPSC 8.2). • Equipment is free of rust and chipping paint (CPSC 8.1). • Equipment is free of sharp edges, splinters or rough surfaces and shows no excessive wear (CPSC 9.1). • Ropes, chains and cables have not frayed or worn out (CPSC 7.2). • Equipment has not shifted or become bent (CPSC 8.1).	10 5 10 10 10		

© NRPA/NPSI/PDRMA

Specific Conditions	Possible Index Points	Index Points Given	Comments

Climbing Equipment, cont.

Specific Conditions	Possible Index Points	Index Points Given	Comments
77. Hardware, cont.			
• There is no corrosion or visible rotting at points where equipment comes into contact with ground surface (CPSC 7.2, 8.1).	10		
• No components are missing. All parts of the equipment are present and in good working order with no loose play or excessive wear in moving parts (CPSC 7.2, 8.1).	20		
• Handgrips are between 0.95" and 1.55" in diameter (CPSC 10.2.1).	10		
• Footings for equipment are stable and buried below ground level or covered by surfacing materials (CPSC 9.7).	20		
• Equipment is free of any litter, debris and surfacing material (ASTM 7.1.2).	20		
• Equipment use zone is free of litter and debris (CPSC 7.2).	10		
Section Subtotal	**365**		

Upper Body Climbing Equipment

Specific Conditions	Possible Index Points	Index Points Given	Comments
78. Upper body climbing equipment, other than turning bars, not recommended for 2-5 yr. old users (CPSC 6.3, ASTM 8.3.1).	10		
79. Upper body climbing equipment maximum height is 84" for 5-12 yr. old users (CPSC 12.1.5, ASTM 8.3.4).	10		
80. Maximum distance between rungs for upper body equipment is 15" and openings pass the entrapment test (CPSC 9.6, 12.1.5, ASTM 8.3.2).	10		
81. Overhead swinging rings pass the entrapment test and chain is maximum length of 12" (CPSC 9.6, 12.1.5).	10		
82. Climbing ropes are secured at both ends and are not capable of being looped back on itself creating a loop with an inside perimeter of greater than 5" (CPSC 12.1.7, ASTM 6.5.1).	20		

© NRPA/NPSI/PDRMA

Specific Conditions	Possible Index Points	Index Points Given	Comments

Upper Body Climbing Equipment, cont.

	Specific Conditions	Possible Index Points	Index Points Given	Comments
83.	Horizontal take-off distance from landing structure to first handhold of upper body equipment is no greater than 10"; if access and egress is by rungs, horizontal distance to first rung is at least 8", but no greater than 10" (ASTM 8.3.3).	10		
84.	Maximum ht. of take off/landing for upper body equipment is 36" for 5-12 yr. old users (ASTM 8.3.5).	10		
85.	There are no single non-rigid components (cable, rope, wire, or similar component) suspended between play units or from the ground to the play unit within 45 degrees of horizontal, unless it is above 7 ft. from the playground surface and is a minimum of 1" at its widest cross-section dimension. It is recommended that the suspended components be brightly colored or contrast with surrounding equipment (CPSC 9.8, ASTM 6.5).	10		
86.	Sliding pole clearance from structures is between 18" and 20" (CPSC 12.1.6, ASTM 8.4.1).	10		
87.	Sliding pole is a minimum of 38" above the access structure, 60" min., recommended (CPSC 12.1.6, ASTM 8.4.3).	10		
88.	Sliding pole is a maximum 1.9" in diameter and continuous with no protruding welds or joints within sliding area (CPSC 12.1.6, ASTM 8.4.4, 8.4.5).	10		
89.	Track rides not recommended for 2-5 yr. old users (CPSC 6.3, ASTM 8.13.5).	20		
90.	Track rides; the lowest portion of the hand gripping component is a minimum 64" above protective surface with maximum height of 78" (ASTM 8.13.1).	10		
91.	Underside of track beam is a minimum of 78" above the protective surfacing (ASTM 8.13.2).	5		

© NRPA/NPSI/PDRMA

Specific Conditions	Possible Index Points	Index Points Given	Comments

Upper Body Climbing Equipment, cont.

Specific Conditions	Possible Index Points	Index Points Given	Comments
92. Pinch, Crush and Shear Points (CPSC 9.5, ASTM 6.4): • Equipment is free of sharp edges. • There are no open holes in the equipment forming traps (e.g. at the ends of the tubes). • There are no pinch, crush or shear points.	10 10 10		
93. Protrusions (CPSC 9.2, ASTM 6.2): • No components fail protrusion test. • Nuts, bolts and screws are recessed, covered or sanded smooth and level.	10 10		
94. Entanglements/Entrapment Angles (CPSC 9.4, 9.6, ASTM 6.3): • No more than two threads of the fastener protrude through any nut. • No obstacles or protrusions project upwards from a horizontal plane extending more than 1/8" perpendicular to the plane of the initial surface. • There are no open "V" entrapment angles on any part of the equipment. See Figs. A1.3-4 in ASTM F 1487.	10 10 10		
95. Head Entrapments (CPSC 9.6, ASTM 6.1): • No components fail the entrapment test. • There are no partially bounded openings. See Figs. A1.6a-A1.10 in ASTM F 1487.	10 10		
96. Hardware: • Nuts and bolts are tight and not able to be loosened without tools. Upon close inspection, they show no loose play or excessive wear (CPSC 8.2). • Equipment is free of rust and chipping paint (CPSC 8.1). • Equipment is free of sharp edges, splinters or rough surfaces and shows no excessive wear (CPSC 9.1). • Ropes, chains and cables have not frayed or worn out (CPSC 7.2). • Equipment has not shifted or become bent (CPSC 8.1). • There is no corrosion or visible rotting at points where equipment comes into contact with ground surface (CPSC 7.2, 8.1).	10 5 10 10 10 10		

Specific Conditions	Possible Index Points	Index Points Given	Comments

Upper Body Climbing Equipment, cont.

Specific Conditions	Possible Index Points	Index Points Given	Comments
96. Hardware, cont. • No components are missing. All parts of the equipment are present and in good working order with no loose play or excessive wear in moving parts (CPSC 7.2, 8.1).	20		
• Handgrips are between 0.95" and 1.55" in diameter (CPSC 10.2.1).	10		
• Footings for equipment are stable and buried below ground level or covered by surfacing materials (CPSC 9.7).	20		
• Equipment is free of any litter, debris and surfacing material (ASTM 7.1.2).	20		
• Equipment use zone is free of litter and debris (CPSC 7.2).	10		
Section Subtotal	**390**		

Stairways and Ladders

Specific Conditions	Possible Index Points	Index Points Given	Comments
97. Continuous handrails on both sides for stairways >1 tread; on those with only 1 tread, an alternate means of hand support or handrail present. Handrail height is between 22" and 38" (CPSC 10.3.1, ASTM 7.1.4).	10		
98. Children have an easy, safe way to descend equipment when they reach the top. (via platform, stairway, or step ladder) (CPSC 12.1.2).	20		
99. Steps and rungs do not allow for accumulation of water and debris (CPSC 10.2, ASTM 7.1.2).	5		
100. Net, chain, arch or tire climbers not the sole means to access equipment for play areas for 2-5 yr. old users (CPSC 12.1.3, ASTM 7.2.2.1).	10		
101. Steps and rungs are evenly spaced within a tolerance of ±0.25 inches and horizontal within a tolerance of ±2 degrees. This includes the spacing between the top step or rung and the surface of the platform (ASTM 7.1.1).	10		

© NRPA/NPSI/PDRMA

Specific Conditions	Possible Index Points	Index Points Given	Comments

Stairways and Ladders, cont.

Specific Conditions	Possible Index Points	Index Points Given	Comments
102. Openings between steps or rungs and between the top step or rung and underside of a platform pass the testing requirements for head entrapment (CPSC 9.6.1, 10.2, ASTM 6.1)	20		
103. All stairways, step ladders and rung ladders, as it relates to the intended users, conform with access slope; tread, rung, and ramp width; tread depth; rung diameter; and vertical rise specifications as per ASTM F1487 Table 2 (CPSC 10.2).	10		
104. Pinch, Crush and Shear Points (CPSC 9.5, ASTM 6.4): • Equipment is free of sharp edges. • There are no open holes in the equipment forming traps (e.g. at ends of the tubes). • There are no pinch, crush or shear points.	10 10 10		
105. Protrusions (CPSC 9.2, ASTM 6.2): • No components fail protrusion test. • Nuts, bolts and screws are recessed, covered or sanded smooth and level.	10 10		
106. Entanglements/Entrapment Angles (CPSC 9.4, 9.6, ASTM 6.3): • No more than two threads of the fastener protrude through any nut. • No obstacles or protrusions project upwards from a horizontal plane extending more than 1/8" perpendicular to the plane of the initial surface. • There are no open "V" entrapment angles on any part of the equipment. See Figs. A1.3-4 in ASTM F1487.	10 10 10		
107. Head Entrapments (CPSC 9.6, ASTM 6.1): • No components fail the entrapment test. • There are no partially bounded openings. See Figs. A1.6a-A1.10 in ASTM F 1487.	10 10		
108. Hardware: • Nuts and bolts are tight and not able to be loosened without tools. Upon close inspection, they show no loose play or excessive wear (CPSC 8.2). • Equipment is free of rust and chipping paint (CPSC 8.1).	10 5		

© NRPA/NPSI/PDRMA

Specific Conditions	Possible Index Points	Index Points Given	Comments

Stairways and Ladders, cont.

Specific Conditions	Possible Index Points	Index Points Given	Comments
108. Hardware, cont.:			
• Equipment is free of sharp edges, splinters or rough surfaces and shows no excessive wear (CPSC 9.1).	10		
• Ropes, chains and cables have not frayed or worn out (CPSC 7.2).	10		
• Equipment has not shifted or become bent (CPSC 8.1).	10		
• There is no corrosion or visible rotting at points where equipment comes into contact with ground surface (CPSC 7.2, 8.1).	10		
• No components are missing. All parts of the equipment are present and in good working order with no loose play or excessive wear in moving parts (CPSC 7.2, 8.1).	20		
• Handgrips are between 0.95" and 1.55" in diameter (CPSC 10.2.1).	10		
• Footings for equipment are stable and buried below ground level or covered by surfacing materials (CPSC 9.7).	20		
• Equipment is free of any litter, debris and surfacing material (ASTM 7.1.2).	20		
• Equipment use zone is free of litter and debris (CPSC 7.2).	10		
Section Subtotal	**320**		

Decks and Platforms

Specific Conditions	Possible Index Points	Index Points Given	Comments
109. Unless an alternate means of access is provided, the maximum difference in height between stepped platforms for 2-5 yr. olds is 12" and for 5-12 yr. olds is 18" (CPSC 11.7, ASTM 7.4.5.1).	20		
110. There is a 29" high (min.) protective perimeter barrier around 2-5 yr. old users' equipment that is more than 30" above the underlying surface (CPSC 11.5, ASTM 7.4.4.1, 7.4.4.3).	10		
111. There is a 38" high (min.) protective perimeter barrier on all elevated surfaces 48" above the underlying surface for 5-12 yr. old users' equipment (CPSC 11.5, ASTM 7.4.4.1, 7.4.4.3).	10		

© NRPA/NPSI/PDRMA

Specific Conditions	Possible Index Points	Index Points Given	Comments
Decks and Platforms, cont.			
112. The space between slats of protective barriers and guardrails is not between 3-1/2" and 9" and passes the entrapment test (CPSC 9.6, ASTM 6.1).	10		
113. Guardrails or protective barriers are present on all elevated surfaces greaterthan 20" above the underlying surface for 2-5 yr. old users' equipment (29" top edge, 23" lower edge) (CPSC 11.4, ASTM 7.4.3.1-7.4.3.4).	10		
114. Guardrails or protective barriers are present for all elevated surfaces 30" above the underlying surface for 5-12 yr. old users' equipment (38" top edge, 24" high lower edge) (CPSC 11.4, ASTM 7.4.3.1-7.4.3.4).	10		
115. No partially bounded openings are projecting upwards from the horizontal plane that are greater than 1 7/8" or less than 9" and fail the test method for partially bounded openings. See ASTM F1487 Figures A1.6a-A1.10 (CPSC Fig. 8, ASTM 6.1.4).	20		
116. Pinch, Crush and Shear Points (CPSC 9.5, ASTM 6.4): • Equipment is free of sharp edges. • There are no open holes in the equipment forming traps (e.g. at ends of the tubes). • There are no pinch, crush or shear points.	10 10 10		
117. Protrusions (CPSC 9.2, ASTM 6.2): • No components fail protrusion test. • Nuts, bolts and screws are recessed, covered or sanded smooth and level.	10 10		
118. Entanglements/Entrapment Angles (CPSC 9.4, 9.6, ASTM 6.3): • No more than two threads of the fastener protrude through any nut. • No obstacles or protrusions project upwards from a horizontal plane extending more than 1/8" perpendicular to the plane of the initial surface.	10 10		

© NRPA/NPSI/PDRMA

Specific Conditions	Possible Index Points	Index Points Given	Comments
Decks and Platforms, cont.			
118. Entanglements/Entrapment Angles (CPSC 9.4, 9.6, ASTM 6.3): • There are no open "V" entrapment angles on any part of the equipment. See Figs. A1.3-4 in ASTM F 1487.	10		
119. Head Entrapments (CPSC 9.6, ASTM 6.1): • No components fail the entrapment test. • There are no partially bounded openings. See Figs. A1.6a-A1.10 in ASTM F1487.	10 10		
120. Hardware: • Nuts and bolts are tight and not able to be loosened without tools. Upon close inspection, they show no loose play or excessive wear (CPSC 8.2).	10		
• Equipment is free of rust and chipping paint (CPSC 8.1).	5		
• Equipment is free of sharp edges, splinters or rough surfaces and shows no excessive wear (CPSC 9.1).	10		
• Ropes, chains and cables have not frayed or worn out (CPSC 7.2).	10		
• Equipment has not shifted or become bent (CPSC 8.1).	10		
• There is no corrosion or visible rotting at points where equipment comes into contact with ground surface (CPSC 7.2, 8.1).	10		
• No components are missing. All parts of the equipment are present and in good working order with no loose play or excessive wear in moving parts (CPSC 7.2, 8.1).	20		
• Handgrips are between 0.95" and 1.55" in diameter (CPSC 10.2.1).	10		
• Footings for equipment are stable and buried below ground level or covered by surfacing materials (CPSC 9.7).	20		
• Equipment is free of any litter, debris and surfacing material.	20		
• Equipment use zone is free of litter and debris.	10		
Section Subtotal	**325**		

© NRPA/NPSI/PDRMA

Specific Conditions	Possible Index Points	Index Points Given	Comments
Swings			
121. All swings, to and fro and rotating swings are not attached to main structure (CPSC 12.6.2, ASTM 8.6.1.1).	20		
122. All flying animal figure swings, multiple occupancy swings (except tire swings), rope swings, and trapeze bars are removed from public playgrounds (CPSC 12.6.4, ASTM 8.7.1).	40		
123. Lightweight enclosed swing seats, are used and all openings meet entrapment criteria (CPSC 12.6.3).	10		
124. All swing seats are made of canvas, rubber, or other lightweight material (CPSC 12.6.2, ASTM 8.6.1.3).	20		
125. There are no open "S" hooks (openings greater than or equal to 0.04") (CPSC 12.6.1).	10		
126. When stationary, all seats same type are level.	1		
127. There are no more than two swings, evenly spaced, in any individual swing bay (CPSC 12.6.2, ASTM 8.6.1.3). Swing seat shall be of the same type in each bay. (CPSC 12.6.3)	20		
128. Swings are at least 24" from each other and 30" away from the frame. See ASTM Figs. A1.23, A1.24 (CPSC Fig. 22, ASTM 8.6.1.5).	20		
129. Vertical distance is at least 12" between underside of occupied seat and protective surface (CPSC 12.6.2, ASTM 8.6.1.5).	1		
130. Swing hangers are spaced wider than seats, not less than 20" (CPSC 12.6.2, ASTM 8.6.1.5).	10		
131. For tire swings, there is at least a 30" safety zone from the crossbeam support structure and the farthest extensions of the swing, and each must have a minimum clearance of 12" from the bottom of the tire to the protective surface (CPSC 12.6.4, ASTM 8.6.1.5).	10		
132. Swing tires have adequate drainage (CPSC 12.6.4).	5		

© NRPA/NPSI/PDRMA

Specific Conditions	Possible Index Points	Index Points Given	Comments

Swings, cont.

Specific Conditions	Possible Index Points	Index Points Given	Comments
133. Tire swings are not made of steel belted radial tires (CPSC 12.6.2, ASTM 8.6.2.3).	10		
134. To and fro swings and tire swings are located away from circulation paths (a distance at least equal to the equipment use zone and an additional safety factor for circulation, with this area free of any obstructions) and near the periphery of the playground (CPSC 6.2, ASTM 8.6.1.1, 8.6.2.1).	10		
135. Pinch, Crush and Shear Points (CPSC 9.5, ASTM 6.4): • Equipment is free of sharp edges. • There are no open holes in the equipment forming traps (e.g. at the ends of the tubes). • There are no pinch, crush or shear points.	10 10 10		
136. Protrusions (CPSC 9.2, ASTM 6.2): • No components fail protrusion test. • Nuts, bolts and screws are recessed, covered or sanded smooth and level.	10 10		
137. Entanglements/Entrapment Angles (CPSC 9.4, 9.6, ASTM 6.3): • No more than two threads of the fastener protrude through any nut. • No obstacles or protrusions project upwards from a horizontal plane extending more than 1/8" perpendicular to the plane of the initial surface. • There are no open "V" entrapment angles on any part of the equipment. See Figs. A1.3-4 in ASTM F 1487.	10 10 10		
138. Head Entrapments (CPSC 9.6, ASTM 6.1): • No components fail the entrapment test. • There are no partially bounded openings. See Figs. A1.6a-A1.10 in ASTM F 1487.	10 10		
139. Hardware: • Nuts and bolts are tight and not able to be loosened without tools. Upon close inspection, they show no loose play or excessive wear (CPSC 8.2).	10		

© NRPA/NPSI/PDRMA

Specific Conditions	Possible Index Points	Index Points Given	Comments

Swings, cont.

Specific Conditions	Possible Index Points	Index Points Given	Comments
139. Hardware, cont.: • Equipment is free of rust and chipping paint (CPSC 8.1).	5		
• Equipment is free of sharp edges, splinters or rough surfaces and shows no excessive wear (CPSC 9.1).	10		
• Ropes, chains and cables have not frayed or worn out (CPSC 7.2).	10		
• Equipment has not shifted or become bent (CPSC 8.1).	10		
• There is no corrosion or visible rotting at points where equipment comes into contact with ground surface (CPSC 7.2, 8.1).	10		
• No components are missing. All parts of the equipment are present and in good working order with no loose play or excessive wear in moving parts (CPSC 7.2, 8.1).	20		
• Handgrips are between 0.95" and 1.55" in diameter (CPSC 10.2.1).	10		
• Footings for equipment are stable and buried below ground level or covered by surfacing materials (CPSC 9.7).	20		
• Equipment is free of any litter, debris and surfacing material (ASTM 7.1.2).	20		
• Equipment use zone is free of litter and debris (CPSC 7.2).	10		
Section Subtotal	**422**		

Rotating and Rocking Equipment

Specific Conditions	Possible Index Points	Index Points Given	Comments
140. The seesaws seating surface does not reach more than 5' above the underlying surface ASTM 8.10.6).	10		
141. The seesaw fulcrum is fixed, enclosed or designed to prevent pinching (CPSC 12.3, ASTM 8.10.3).	10		
142. Seesaw handgrips intended to be gripped by one hand have a minimum length of 3" and 2-hands a minimum of 6" and pass the protrusion test (CPSC 12.3, ASTM 8.10.4.1).	10		

© NRPA/NPSI/PDRMA

Specific Conditions	Possible Index Points	Index Points Given	Comments

Rotating and Rocking Equipment, cont.

	Specific Conditions	Possible Index Points	Index Points Given	Comments
143.	A rubber segment is buried in the surfacing under the seesaw seats unless seesaw uses a spring centering device (CPSC 12.3, ASTM 8.10.2).	10		
144.	Log rolls (not recommended for 2-5yr. old users) have maximum ht. of 18" above the protective surface for 5-12 yr. old users (ASTM 8.12.2, 8.12.3).	20		
145.	Spring rocking equipment seat height is between 14" and 28" (ASTM 8.11.5).	5		
146.	There are no equipment parts that could cause a pinching or crushing injury on spring rocking equipment. Exemption is the attachment area of heavy duty coil springs to the body and base of spring rocking equipment (CPSC 12.5, ASTM 6.4.1.3 [2], 8.11.4).	10		
147.	Handholds stay in place when grasped and pass the protrusion test (CPSC 12.5, ASTM 8.11.2).	10		
148.	Footrests stay in place and pass the protrusion test (CPSC 12.5, ASTM 8.11.3).	5		
149.	Merry-go-rounds are approximately circular, and the distance between the minimum and maximum radii of a noncircular platform does not exceed 2". See Fig. A1.25 in ASTM F1487 (CPSC 12.2, ASTM 8.8.1.1, 8.8.1.2).	10		
150.	Components of the merry-go-round do not extend beyond the platform perimeter (CPSC 12.2, ASTM 8.8.1.2).	10		
151.	There are no openings in the surface of the platform that permit the penetration of 5/16" rod through the surface of the merry-go-round (CPSC 12.2, ASTM 8.8.1.4).	10		
152.	There are no accessible shearing or crushing mechanisms in the undercarriage of the equipment, and the platform does not provide an oscillatory (up and down) motion (CPSC 12.2, ASTM 8.8.1.5).	10		

© NRPA/NPSI/PDRMA

Specific Conditions	Possible Index Points	Index Points Given	Comments

Rotating Equipment, cont.

Specific Conditions	Possible Index Points	Index Points Given	Comments
153. The peripheral speed of the platform does not exceed 13 feet per second (CPSC 12.2, ASTM 8.8.1.6).	10		
154. There is a minimum of 9" between the protective surface and the underside of a merry-go-round platform with a max. ht. of 14" for the platform surface (CPSC 12.2, ASTM 8.8.1.2, 8.8.1.4).	10		
155. Pinch, Crush and Shear Points (CPSC 9.5, ASTM 6.4): • Equipment is free of sharp edges. • There are no open holes in the equipment forming traps (e.g. at the ends of the tubes). • There are no pinch, crush or shear points.	10 10 10		
156. Protrusions (CPSC 9.2, ASTM 6.2): • No components fail protrusion test. • Nuts, bolts and screws are recessed, covered or sanded smooth and level.	10 10		
157. Entanglements/Entrapment Angles (CPSC 9.4, 9.6, ASTM 6.3): • No more than two threads of the fastener protrude through any nut. • No obstacles or protrusions project upwards from a horizontal plane extending more than 1/8" perpendicular to the plane of the initial surface. • There are no open "V" entrapment angles on any part of the equipment. See Figs. A1.3-4 in ASTM F 1487.	10 10 10		
158. Head Entrapments (CPSC 9.6, ASTM 6.1): • No components fail the entrapment test. • There are no partially bounded openings. See Figs. A1.6a-A1.10 in ASTM F 1487.	10 10		
159. Hardware: • Nuts and bolts are tight and not able to be loosened without tools. Upon close inspection, they show no loose play or excessive wear (CPSC 8.2). • Equipment is free of rust and chipping paint (CPSC 8.1).	10 5		

Specific Conditions	Possible Index Points	Index Points Given	Comments

Rotating Equipment, cont.

Specific Conditions	Possible Index Points	Index Points Given	Comments
159. Hardware, cont.			
• Equipment is free of sharp edges, splinters or rough surfaces and shows no excessive wear (CPSC 9.1).	10		
• Ropes, chains and cables have not frayed or worn out (CPSC 7.2).	10		
• Equipment has not shifted or become bent (CPSC 8.1).	10		
• There is no corrosion or visible rotting at points where equipment comes into contact with ground surface (CPSC 7.2, 8.1).	10		
• No components are missing. All parts of the equipment are present and in good working order with no loose play or excessive wear in moving parts (CPSC 7.2, 8.1).	20		
• Handgrips are between 0.95" and 1.55" in diameter (CPSC 10.2.1).	10		
• Footings for equipment are stable and buried below ground level or covered by surfacing materials (CPSC 9.7).	20		
• Equipment is free of any litter, debris and surfacing material (ASTM 7.1.2).	20		
• Equipment use zone is free of litter and debris (CPSC 7.2).	10		
Section Subtotal	**385**		

Sand Play Area

<u>Note:</u>   This section is only applicable to sand box areas designated for play. Ground level sand boxes and activity walls require a child to be at ground level. Such ground level activities are excluded from the recommendations for protective surfacing under and around playground equipment. Refer to CPSC revised handbook May, 1997.

Specific Conditions	Possible Index Points	Index Points Given	Comments
160. Sand play is located in a shaded area.	1		
161. The sand play area is inspected and raked at least every week for debris and to provide exposure to air and sun.	5		
162. If the sand play area is in a box, it is covered at night to prevent animal excrement contamination.	5		
163. The sand play area does not have standing water 24 hours after a rainfall.	5		

© NRPA/NPSI/PDRMA

Specific Conditions	Possible Index Points	Index Points Given	Comments

Sand Play Area cont.

Specific Conditions	Possible Index Points	Index Points Given	Comments
164. Elevated sand boxes have appropriate use zone with proper impact absorbing material (CPSC 4.4).	20		
165. Pinch, Crush and Shear Points (CPSC 9.5, ASTM 6.4): • Equipment is free of sharp edges. • There are no open holes in the equipment forming traps (e.g. at ends of the tubes). • There are no pinch, crush or shear points.	10 10 10		
166. Protrusions (CPSC 9.2, ASTM 6.2): • No components fail protrusion test. • Nuts, bolts and screws are recessed, covered or sanded smooth and level.	10 10		
167. Entanglements/Entrapment Angles (CPSC 9.4, 9.6, ASTM 6.3): • No more than two threads of the fastener protrude through any nut. • No obstacles or protrusions project upwards from a horizontal plane extending more than 1/8" perpendicular to the plane of the initial surface. • There are no open "V" entrapment angles on any part of the equipment. See Figs. A1.3-4 in ASTM F 1487.	10 10 10		
168. Head Entrapments (CPSC 9.6, ASTM 6.1): • No components fail the entrapment test. • There are no partially bounded openings. See Figs. A1.6a-A1.10 in ASTM F 1487.	10 10		
169. Hardware: • Nuts and bolts are tight and not able to be loosened without tools. Upon close inspection, they show no loose play or excessive wear (CPSC 8.2). • Equipment is free of rust and chipping paint (CPSC 8.1). • Equipment is free of sharp edges, splinters or rough surfaces and shows no excessive wear (CPSC 9.1). • Ropes, chains and cables have not frayed or worn out (CPSC 7.2). • Equipment has not shifted or become bent (CPSC 8.1). • There is no corrosion or visible rotting at points where equipment comes into contact with ground surface (CPSC 7.2, 8.1).	10 5 10 10 10 10		

Specific Conditions	Possible Index Points	Index Points Given	Comments

Sand Play Area, cont.

Specific Conditions	Possible Index Points	Index Points Given	Comments
169. Hardware, cont.			
• No components are missing. All parts of the equipment are present and in good working order with no loose play or excessive wear in moving parts (CPSC 7.2, 8.1).	20		
• Handgrips are between 0.95" and 1.55" in diameter (CPSC 10.2.1).	10		
• Footings for equipment are stable and buried below ground level or covered by surfacing materials (CPSC 9.7).	20		
• Equipment is free of any litter, debris and surfacing material (ASTM 7.1.2).	20		
• Equipment use zone is free of litter and debris (CPSC 7.2).	10		
Section Subtotal	**271**		

© NRPA/NPSI/PDRMA

Specific Conditions	Possible Index Points	Index Points Given	Comments

Specific Equipment Index Points Form (SEIP Form)
Equipment/Component Name: _____

Specific Conditions	Possible Index Points	Index Points Given	Comments
Pinch, Crush and Shear Points (CPSC 9.5, ASTM 6.4): • Equipment is free of sharp edges. • There are no open holes in the equipment forming traps (e.g. at the ends of the tubes). • There are no pinch, crush or shear points.	10 10 10		
Protrusions (CPSC 9.2, ASTM 6.2): • No components fail protrusion test. • Nuts, bolts and screws are recessed, covered or sanded smooth and level.	10 10		
Entanglements/Entrapment Angles (CPSC 9.4, 9.6, ASTM 6.3: • No more than two threads of the fastener protrude through any nut. • No obstacles or protrusions project upwards from a horizontal plane extending more than 1/8" perpendicular to the plane of the initial surface. • There are no open "V" entrapment angles on any part of the equipment. See Figs. A1.3-4 in ASTM F 1487.	10 10 10		
Head Entrapments (CPSC 9.6, ASTM 6.1): • No components fail the entrapment test. • There are no partially bounded openings. See Figs. A1.6a-A1.10 in ASTM F 1487.	10 10		
Hardware: • Nuts and bolts are tight and not able to be loosened without tools. Upon close inspection, they show no loose play or excessive wear (CPSC 8.2). • Equipment is free of rust and chipping paint (CPSC 8.1). • Equipment is free of sharp edges, splinters or rough surfaces and shows no excessive wear (CPSC 9.1). • Ropes, chains and cables have not frayed or worn out (CPSC 7.2). • Equipment has not shifted or become bent (CPSC 8.1). • There is no corrosion or visible rotting at points where equipment comes into contact with ground surface (CPSC 7.2, 8.1).	10 5 10 10 10 10		

Specific Conditions	Possible Index Points	Index Points Given	Comments

SEIP Form, cont.

Specific Conditions	Possible Index Points	Index Points Given	Comments
Hardware, cont.			
• No components are missing. All parts of the equipment are present and in good working order with no loose play or excessive wear in moving parts (CPSC 7.2, 8.1).	20		
• Handgrips are between 0.95" and 1.55" in diameter (CPSC 10.2.1).	10		
• Footings for equipment are stable and buried below ground level or covered by surfacing materials (CPSC 9.7).	20		
• Equipment is free of any litter, debris and surfacing material (ASTM 7.1.2).	20		
• Equipment use zone is free of litter and debris (CPSC 7.2).	10		
Section Subtotal	**235**		

© NRPA/NPSI/PDRMA

Audit Summary:

Audit Section Headings	Questions	Possible Index Points	Actual Index Pts.	Index Pts. Given	Audit %Rating
Section A: General Conditions					
Playground Border Factors	3	70	70		
General Environment	4-14	103	103		
Age/Size Appropriateness Design	15-17	140	140		
Playground Protective Surface	18-22	150	150		
Use Zone	23-28	110	110		
Accessibility Design	29-43	171	171		
Section A Subtotal:		**744**	**744**		
Section B: Specific Conditions					
Slides	44-62	395			
Climbing Equipment	63-77	365			
Upper Body Climbing Equipment	78-96	390			
Stairways and Ladders	97-108	320			
Decks and Platforms	109-120	325			
Swings	121-139	422			
Rotating and Rocking Equipment	140-159	385			
Sand Play Areas	160-169	271			
Section B Subtotal:		**2873**			
Section C: SEIP Forms **used for equipment not identified in specific conditions section					
SEIP Form _____		235*			
SEIP Form _____		235*			
SEIP Form _____		235*			
Section C Subtotal:					
Site Total: totals for sections A,B,C					

*235 is the possible points for the Specific Equipment Index Points Form (SEIP Form).
Actual total may vary from playground site to playground site depending upon what type of equipment is present.

IMPORTANT

This information is for internal use only and is not to be released or otherwise diseminated to anyone other than an agency official, or designated representative.

© NRPA/NPSI/PDRMA

COMMENTS SUMMARY

Auditor:_____ Supervisor:_____ Date:_____

_____

_____

_____

_____

_____

_____

_____

_____

_____

_____

_____

_____

_____

_____

_____

_____

_____

_____

_____

_____

_____

_____

_____

_____

_____

_____

_____

_____

_____

_____

_____

_____

© NRPA/NPSI/PDRMA

PLAYGROUND AUDIT SCORE SUMMARY FORM FOR ALL AGENCY SITES

Scores by Section for Each Playground Site

Audit Section Heading	Possible Index Points						
SECTION A: GENERAL CONDITIONS							
Playground Border Factors	70						
General Environment	103						
Age/Size Appropriate Design	140						
Playground Protective Surfacing	150						
Use Zone	110						
Accessibility Design	171						
SECTION A SUBTOTAL	**744**						
SECTION B: SPECIFIC CONDITIONS							
Slides	395						
Climbing Equipment	365						
Upper Body Climbing Equipment	390						
Stairways and Ladders	320						
Decks and Platforms	325						
Swings	422						
Rotating and Rocking Equipment	385						
Sand Play Areas	271						
SECTION B SUBTOTAL	**2873**						
SECTION C: SEIP FORMS							
SEIP Form _____	235*						
SEIP Form _____	235*						
SEIP Form _____	235*						
SECTION C SUBTOTAL							
Site Total: totals for Sections A, B, & C	4087*						
Index Points Given							
Acutal Index Points							
Index % Rating							

*235 is the possible points for the Specific Equipment Index Points Form (SEIP Form).
Actual total may vary from playground site to playground site depending upon what type of equipment is present.

IMPORTANT: This information is for internal use only and is not to be released or otherwise disseminated to anyone other than an agency official, or designated representative.

© NRPA/NPSI/PDRMA

Inspection Frequency Form

Playground Name/ID Number_____ Form Completed By _____Date _____

The following guide weighs the most common use, materials, and environmental factors that will influence your playground inspection scheduling. Each factor has been weighted as to its importance and influence on the schedule. Put one of the factor numbers in the right hand column that best describes the conditions at the playground site.

Factors	Possible Points	Points Given
A. Use Factors		
1. Vandalism (Misuse/Abuse)		
High	10	
Moderate	5	
Low	2	
2. Use Level (Community Use, Litter, Etc.)		
High	10	
Moderate	5	
Low	2	
3. Age Design		
Preschool age (2-5 years)	2	
School age (6-12 years)	4	
All ages (2-12 years)	10	
Use Factors Total	30	
B. Materials		
1. Resilient Surfacing		
Loose Materials	12	
Synthetic Material	2	
2. Material (Major Components)		
Wood, Painted Steel	4	
Stabilized Plastics, Aluminum, Gal.Steel	2	
Stainless Steel	0	
3. Equipment		
Moving (swing, spin around, spring rider, etc.)	6	
Static (Non-moving climbers)	2	
Both	6	

© NRPA/NPSI/PDRMA

Factors	Possible Points	Points Given
4. Age of Equipment		
1-2 years old	0	
3-4 years old	3	
5-9 years old	6	
10-14 years old	9	
15 years old and over	12	
Materials Factors Total	34	
C. Environmental Factors		
1. Acid Soils/Rain/PH		
None (6-9)	0	
Moderate (10, 11, 4, 5)	4	
High (Acid 1-3, Basic 12-14)	8	
2. Salt Air (Coastal Exposure)		
None	0	
Moderate	4	
High	8	
3. Sun Exposure		
None	0	
Moderate	4	
High	8	
4. Drainage		
Functioning underground drainage system	0	
Moist Surface	4	
Seasonal Flooding	8	
Routine Standing Water	12	
Environmental Factors Total	36	
Total Points for Site	**100**	

IMPORTANT This information has been prepared to assist the Playground owners attorney in defending potential litigation. Do not release to any person except an agency official or designated claim representative or an investigating police officer.

© NRPA/NPSI/PDRMA

Inspection Frequency Summary Form for all Agency Sites

Key to Inspection Frequency Chart		
Points	High Frequency Inspections	Low Frequency Inspections
71 or more	2 or more times per week	2-3 times per month
56-70	Weekly	Monthly
41-55	Biweekly	Bimonthly
40 & Below	Monthly	Seasonal

Once the inspection frequency form has been completed for each playground site, the results can be transferred to the blank inspection frequency summary form (Appendix A) so that all of your sites can be evaluated collectively. The total points for each site can then be compared to the key to inspection frequency chart (above) which will assist you in determining your most appropriate high and low frequency inspection schedule.

Local conditions may include other factors and in some cases affect seasonal adjustments to the schedule. Experience is your best guide.

Frequency of Inspection Summary Form (Sample)

Playground Site Name	Factors Evaluated					
	Use Factors	Material	Environ-mental	Points Given	High Freq. Inspection	Low Freq. Inspection
1.						
2.						
3.						
4.						
5.						
6.						
7.						
8.						
9.						
10.						

© NRPA/NPSI/PDRMA

High Frequency Inspection Form (Daily or Routine)

Site Name/ID Number: _____

Inspector Name: _____ Date _____ Start/Finish Times _____

Repairer Name: _____ Date _____ Start/Finish Times _____

> Use the following codes: 1 = Okay 2 = Needs Maintenance 3 = Request for Repair
> O = Supervisor notified and work order written X = Corrective Action Complete

General Inspection Items	Code	Inspection Comments	Repairs Comments
Vandalism: Damage, graffiti, glass, trash, needles, etc.			
Loose or missing hardware			
Chains (kinked, twisted, broken)			
Guardrails/handrails secure			
Seats (cut, cracked, missing)			
Wood (rotten, cracked, missing)			
Remove foreign objects (ropes, chains, wood, etc.)			
Sweep walkways, platforms, steps			
Footers (concrete) exposed			
Standing water			
Objects in surfacing material			
Rake level surfacing material			
Need Surfacing Material For:			
Swings			
Climbers			
Fire Pole			
Slide			
Others			
Others			

For office use only
Reviewed by Assistant Superintendent of Parks _____ Date_____
Reviewed by Superintendent of Parks and Planning _____ Date_____

> **IMPORTANT** – This information has been prepared to assist the Playground owners attorney in defending potential litigation. *Do not* release to any person except an agency official or designated claim representative or an investigating police officer.

USE BACK OF FORM FOR ADDITIONAL COMMENTS
REPORT ALL VANDALISM TO ASSISTANT SUPERINTENDENT OF PARKS OR YOUR
MAINTENANCE SUPERVISOR

© NRPA/NPSI/PDRMA

Itemized List of Playground Equipment

Site Name/ID Number:_____

Inspector Name:_____ Date:_____

Play Area	Play Component	Description of Play Area or Component	Comments

© NRPA/NPSI/PDRMA

Low Frequency Site Plan Playground Inspection Form

Site Name/ID Number:_____

Inspector Name: _____ Date_____ Start/Finish Times _____

Repairer Name:_____ Date _____ Start/Finish Times _____

Use the following codes: 1 = Okay   2 = Needs Maintenance   3 = Request for Repair
O = Supervisor notified and work order written   X = Corrective Action Complete

Area	#	Play Component	Code	Problem (if any)	Action Taken
Playground surfacing material and draining					
Playground border/edger (if applicable)					

Directions:
1. List each piece of playground equipment in the "Play Components" column.
2. As each component is inspected, indicate the appropriate codes in the Code column.
3. Describe the nature of any maintenance or follow-up repairs.
4. File each inspection report with your permanent records.

Work Order Numbers (list all that apply):_____

Supervisor_____Signature_____Date_____

This form has been prepared to assist the Playground owners Attorney in defending potential litigation. DO NOT release to any person except an agency official, designated claim representative, or an investigating officer.

© NRPA/NPSI/PDRMA

Low Frequency Matrix Playground Inspection Form

Repairer:
Signature:
Date:
Start/Finish Times:

This form has been prepared to assist the District Attorney in defending potential litigation. DO NOT release to any person except a district official, designated claim representative, or an investigating officer.

Logs: cracking/warping/decay
Endcaps: exposed tubing
Bolts: uncapped/loose/missing
Bedway: damage/protruding objects
Paint: chipping/rust
Support Posts: loose/exposed footing
Tire: damage/mounting
Boards: cracking/warping/decay/paint
Fittings: need grease
Handrails: loose/missing
Steps: loose/surface
Footings: loose/exposed/cracked
Welds: damage/decay
Bars & Pipes: loose/missing
S-Hooks: need replacement 25% wear
Support Rods: loose/need replacement
Foot Holds: loose/need replacement
Chains: damage/rust/pinch points
Seats: damage/needs replacement
Mountings: loose/need replacement
Wood Slats: cracking/warping/decay
Ladders: support/rungs
Ropes: damage/need replacement
Turnbolts & Turnbuckles: loose/replace
Cables: support/damage/need replacement
Springs: support/damage/need replacement
Handgrips: loose/need replacement
Poles: support/damage/need replacement
Handholds: loose/missing/need replacement
Bearings: grease/replace
Panels: loose/damage/need replacement
Other:

Playground Site Name:
Agency:
Inspector:
Signature:
Date:
Start/Finish Times:
Supervisor:
Signature:
Date:

© 1999 by NRPA

Use following codes throughout checklist:
1 = OK
2 = Needs Maintenance
3 = Request for Repair
0 = Supervisor notified/Work order written
X = Corrective Action Complete
Use back of form to indicate action taken.

Site Condition

Vandalism, broken glass/trash

Poor drainage areas

Surface material worn/scattered

Deterioration; borders, landscaping

Tripping hazards; roots/rocks/obstacles

Accessible sharp edges/corners

Hazardous visual barriers

Physical barriers

Additional Comments: (Use back as necessary.)

Work Order #s (list all that apply):

© NRPA/NPSI/PDRMA

Playground Site History Checklist

Site name, locations and identification number:

_____

Date equipment installed: _____

Date site history checklist completed: _____

Staff member completing history checklist: _____

Item on File		Item
Yes	**No**	
		Playground bid specifications
		Copy of P.O. or invoice
		Insurance certificate including product's liability limits
		Manufacturer's letter stating that playground equipment meets all current playground safety standards and guidelines
		Manufacturer's installation drawings and instructions
		Manufacturer's installation verification
		Site plans
		Itemized list and quantity of play components
		Parts list
		Initial playground safety audit
		Recommended inspection frequency checklist
		Inspection history and checklist copies
		Remedial action history:
		a. Telephone complaints
		b. Work orders

IMPORTANT
This information has been prepared to assist the agency's attorney in defending potential litigation. Do not release to any person except an agency official or designated claim representative or an investigating police officer.

© NRPA/NPSI/PDRMA

Playground Safety Exercises

Level I (High Frequency Inspectors)

1. You discover that the slide on a composite structure has been vandalized and is in danger of falling if used. Do you:
   a. Place bolts found in your tool box in holes where a different size bolt was removed?
   b. Call the police from a pay phone located at the playground site?
   c. Wrap warning tape around the structure and continue your inspection?
   d. Radio your supervisor to report the incident while guarding the site?
   e. b and c
   f. c and d
   g. a and b

2. Most playground accidents are attributable to falls from equipment to the surface. True or false?

3. When a dangerous piece of broken, missing, or vandalized playground equipment is identified, the high frequency inspector should:
   a. Report it in writing to the supervisor at the end of the day.
   b. Temporarily fix it with whatever parts of hardware the inspector has on the truck.
   c. Remove the broken piece of equipment.
   d. Report the problem immediately to the supervisor and guard the area of concern until given further direction.

4. 99% of all accidents occur to children ages 5-12. True or false?

5. Whenever a playground area is inspected, the playground surfacing used throughout the use zone should be checked for:
   a. Litter and other debris
   b. Standing water
   c. Exposed footings or other trip hazards
   d. Proper depth in kick out areas
   e. Excessive compaction or decomposition
   f. All of the above

6. If an exposed footing, rock, or tree root is detected within the playground use zone it should be:
   a. Reported in writing to your supervisor.
   b. Covered with the proper depth of surfacing material.
   c. Removed.
   d. All of the above.

7. The entire playground area, including adjacent turf and landscaped areas, should be inspected for:
   a. Broken glass, litter, and other debris
   b. Poisonous plants
   c. Insect infestations such as bees' nests and evidence of undesirable pests and rodents

© NRPA/NPSI/PDRMA

d. Branches 7' high and lower

e. All of the above

8. The playground inspection form should be filled out in its entirety at the playground site and turned into the maintenance supervisor before the end of the day. True or false?

9. Place the following inspection form codes with the proper definition: 4, 7, 4, 3, 2, 1, 0, OK

    a. _____ Okay

    b. _____ Needs maintenance

    c. _____ Request for repair

    d. _____ Supervisor notified and work order written

    e. _____ Corrective action complete

10. A code number 2 or 3 on the inspection form means there is a problem found with the play ground. True or false?

11. It is not necessary to mark the time down when you complete your inspection of a park site. True or false?

12. If you pick up trash around a playground, it is not necessary to mark it as work done. True or false?

13. If serious vandalism is identified, the inspector should notify their supervisor, to secure the area and wait for further instructions. True or false?

14. The surfacing "kick-out" zone area for a swing is directly under the swing seat. True or false?

15. The inspection form is turned in to your immediate supervisor who forwards it to the manager of all agency public playgrounds. True or false?

16. A cut swing seat is probably vandalism. True or false?

© NRPA/NPSI/PDRMA

Level II (Low Frequency Inspectors)

1. Swing sets should be inspected regularly for:
   a. Twisted chain
   b. Open S-hooks
   c. Excessive wear of chain
   d. Proper depth of surfacing under swing seats
   e. Worn, cut, or damaged swing seats
   f. All of the above

2. If a nut placed on the end of a bolt fits within the 1.5 inch diameter protrusion gauge and exceeds the top surface of the gauge, is it considered a protrusion? Explain your answer.

3. What is the minimum distance allowed between two single axis swing seats?

4. What is the most serious injury that can occur from equipment protrusions?
   a. Clothing entanglement
   b. Cuts to arms and legs
   c. Broken arms and legs
   d. All of the above

5. Explain the term use zone.

6. Should common playground replacement parts be on hand during low frequency inspections?

7. It is okay to use replacement parts of equal size from another playground manufacturer if parts from the original manufacturer are not available?

8. Is a 1/4" gap when closing S-hooks acceptable?

9. When is the best time to conduct a low frequency inspection, 7:00 AM or 1:00 PM? Why?

10. Why is it important that low frequency inspectors describe in writing the nature of a maintenance concern and the actions taken to correct the problem?

© NRPA/NPSI/PDRMA

Level III (Auditors and Playground Designers)

1. The use zone of composite playground equipment is defined as any equipment surface on which a child can stand or sit. True or false.

2. At what height are protective barriers required on platforms for equipment designed for children ages 5-12.

3. What is the formula used in determining the size of the fall zone for a single axis (to-fro) belt swing in front and back bucket (infant)?

4. Using the formula in question 3, what would the length of the fall zone need to be for a to-fro belt swing if the pivot point was 11 feet above the ground level?

5. Why are only two swings recommended in a single swing bay?

6. What is the maximum height recommended for a balance beam for ages 2-3 and 5-12?

7. What is the formula for determining the fall zone at the bottom of a slide?

8. The inspector must use all four protrusion gauges to detect hazards on flexible and rigid climbers. True or false?

9. On slides, where do most fatal accidents occur?
   a. Top
   b. Bottom
   c. Going up stairway
   d. Going up slide bed

10. Describe some of the pros and cons for each of the following loose fill surfacing materials commonly used on public playgrounds.
    a. Fine sand
    b. Pea gravel
    c. Wood chip from forestry department
    d. Manufactured engineered wood mulch

11. Name four types of swings not recommended on public playgrounds.

12. What is the recommended fall zone distance that should exist around stationary playground equipment?

13. Name two modifications that can be made to an "accurate angle type" equipment hazard to minimize head entrapment.

14. What is the minimum clearance between the seat and supporting structure of a tire swing?

15. Flexible grid climbers need to meet head entrapment criteria. True or false? How is this tested?

© NRPA/NPSI/PDRMA

Playground Safety Exercises Answer Key

Level I

1. d
2. True
3. d
4. False
5. f
6. d
7. e
8. True
9a. 1
9b. 2
9c. 3
9d. 0
9e. x
10. True
11. False
12. False
13. True
14. True
15. True
16. True

Level II

1. f
2. Yes, any hardware that fits the inside of a protrusion gauge starting with the smallest to largest must not exceed the gauge height. (Presents a hazard to impailment to the eye socket and temporal region of the skull.)
3. 24 inches
4. a
5. An area under and around the equipment where protective surfacing is required.
6. True
7. False
8. False
9. 7:00 AM. Fewer patrons will be in the park site which will minimize safety concerns and speed inspection time.
10. To track future maintenance needs, legal reasons, to ensure that the work was completed.

Level III

1. False

2. Any platform that exceeds 48 inches

3. Belt swing two times the height of the pivot point of the swing chain to the underlying surface both in front and in back. (Bucket swing) two times the height of the pivot point of the swing chain to the bottom of the bucket.

4. 22 feet front and back

5. To give each user a wider exit area without having to cross the path of other swingers.

6. 12 inches (2-5) 16 inches (5-12)

7. Height of slide plus 4 feet or a minimum of 6 feet.

8. False, one of the four gauges is used only on swings.

9. a

10. See 1997 CPSC Handbook for Public Playground Safety for additional information.

    Pros

    a. Inexpensive, readily available good manipulative play value

    Needs regular maintenance, (kick out points) easily compacted, slip hazard on walkways, limited impact absorbation, not ADA accessible.

    b. Slow deterioration, low cost, readily available

    Can be thrown causing injuries, slip hazard on walkways, easily displaced from "kick-out" points, difficult to walk on, not ADA accessible, needs regular maintenance, stones can mix with sub-grade to create a hard surface.

    c. Cheap, free, readily available, less attractive to animals than sand

    May contain sharp points, bugs, fungus, and other foreign materials, rapidly decomposes, not ADA accessible, easily displaced, do not always know where it comes from?

    d. ADA accessible if properly maintained, free of foreign materials, readily available, less attractive to animals than sand, likely comes with products liability insurance.

    More costly, does deteriorate, must be replenished, easily displaced.

11. Multiple occupancy swings, animal figure swings, rope swings, swinging exercise rings, and trapeze bars.

12. 6 feet in all directions

13. Make angles more than 55 degrees, have lower leg of angle project downward below the horizontal plane, attach a rigid shield at vertex to prevent a 9 inch diameter circular template from simultaneously touching each side of the angle before it touches the shield.

14. 30 inches from the top of the seat to the supporting structure.

15. True, use the torso probe, if it penetrates more than 4" while applying at least 50 lbs. of pressure, then the head probe must also pass at least 4" with 50 lbs. of pressure.

                                            © NRPA/NPSI/PDRMA

Training Roster

Session Title_____

Date _____ Start Time _____ Finish Time _____

Instructor Name _____

Topics Covered _____

_____

_____

Materials Presented_____

_____

_____

Print names below.   Sign names below.

1. _____   _____

2. _____   _____

3. _____   _____

4. _____   _____

5. _____   _____

6. _____   _____

7. _____   _____

8. _____   _____

9. _____   _____

10. _____   _____

11. _____   _____

12. _____   _____

13. _____   _____

14. _____   _____

15. _____   _____

© NRPA/NPSI/PDRMA

Park District Risk Management Agency
Accident/Incident Report

[Name of Park District, SRA or Forest Preserve District]

```
┌ ─ ─ ─ ─ ─ ─ ─ ─ ─ ─ ─ ─ ─ ─ ─ ─ ─ ─ ─ ─ ┐
                  General Liability Claim
│                                          │
  _____ Bodily Injury      _____ Property Damange
└ ─ ─ ─ ─ ─ ─ ─ ─ ─ ─ ─ ─ ─ ─ ─ ─ ─ ─ ─ ─ ┘
```

Date of Accident

Time of Accident

Location
(name of park, pool community center, etc.)

Specific Area
(playground, parking lot, gym, etc.)

Bodily Injury			
Name of Injured Person:		Birth Date:	Sex:
Address:	City:	State:	Zip:
Home Phone: ( )		Business/Daytime Phone: ( )	
Occupation:		Employer:	
Part of body injured and to what extent:			
Explain in detail how accident happened: (Attach more pages if necessary):			
Was First Aid Administered? ❑ YES ❑ By By whom: _____ (name and position)			
Explain:_____			

Paramedics Called? ❑ Yes ❑ No*	Police Called? ❑ Yes ❑ No
	Police Dept. _____
*If no, signature required under "Paramedic Waiver" on next page	Officer:_____
	Report No._____

© NRPA/NPSI/PDRMA

Parents/Relatives Notified? ❑ Yes ❑ No   By whom: _____(___)_____
                                                     (name)   (day phone)

Who specifically:_____Their comments/reactions?_____

If sent to doctor or hospital, which one? _____

Witnesses:

(Attach more pages if necessary)

                                    Home   Daytime
                                    Phone   Phone
Name _____ _____ _____

Address _____
              (street)   (city)   (state)   (zip)

Relationship to injured party: _____ Relative/friend, specify: _____

                              _____ Another program participant or park user

                              _____ Passer-by

                              _____ District/SRA employee or volunteer

                              _____ Other, specify: _____

*Paramedic Waiver

I refused to have the paramedics called for myself or my minor child/ward and hereby

for myself, my minor child/ward heirs, executors and administrator fully release and

discharge the District and its officers, agents, servants and employees from any and

all claims for damages I or my minor child/ward may have.

_____   _____
Signature   Date

Property Damage

Name of Property Owner:				Sex:
Address:	City:		State:	Zip:
Home Phone: ( )		Business/Daytime Phone: ( )		
Propery damage was:				
Explain how damage occurred:				
Estimated Cost to Repair:		Estimates attached? ❑ Yes ❑ No		

© NRPA/NPSI/PDRMA

Appendix B

Case Study of

Northside Park

© NRPA/NPSI/PDRMA

WHEATON PARK DISTRICT

COMPREHENSIVE PUBLIC PLAYGROUND SAFETY PROGRAM

SITE HISTORY CHECKLIST

PARK: _____#026 Northside Cove_____

DATE EQUIPMENT INSTALLED: _____1986_____

DATE SITE HISTORY CHECKLIST COMPLETED: _____12-7-89_____

Item On File		Item
Yes	**No**	
X		Copy of P.O. or Invoice Site Plans
X		Installation Drawings
X		Itemized List and Quantity of Play Components
X		Parts List
	X	Insurance Certificate
X		Initial Playground Safety Audit
X		Inspection History and Checklist Copies
X		Recommended Inspection Frequency Checklist
X		Remedial Action History
		Additional Items:
	X	(Telephone Complaints)
	X	(Work Orders)
	X	(Playground Bid Specifications)
X		Pictures
X		Public Playground Safety Guideline Sign

PLAYGROUND SITE HISTORY CHECKLIST

Park: _____ **Northside (Revision of Area A only)** _____

Date equipment installed: _____ **Spring/Summer 1994** _____

Date site history checklist completed: _____ **12/94 Revision** _____

Staff member completing history checklist: _____ **Jerry Culp** _____

Item on File		Item
Yes	No	
X		1. Playground bid specifications
X		2. Copy of P.O. or invoice
X		3. Insurance certificate including product's liability limits
X		4. Manufacturer's letter stating that playground equipment meets all current playground safety standards and guidelines
X		5. Manufacturer's installation drawings and instructions
		6. Manufacturer's installation verification
X	Rev. 1994	7. Site plans
X	Rev. 1994	8. Itemized list and quantity of play components
X	Rev. 1994	9. Parts list
X	Area A Only	10. Initial playground safety audit
X	Rev. 1994	11. Recommended inspection frequency checklist
X		12. Inspection history and checklist copies
X		13. Remedial action history:
X		a. Telephone complaints
X		b. Work orders

IMPORTANT
This information has been prepared to assist the agency's attorney in defending potential litigation. Do not release to any person except an agency official or designated claim representative or an investigating police officer.

© NRPA/NPSI/PDRMA

Playground Safety Audit Form
(revised March, 1998)

Playground Name/ID Number _Northside Park #26_

Injuries to children may occur from many types of playground equipment and environmental conditions. The checklist on the following pages will help you to assess and correct safety concerns that may be present on or near your playground. While it does not cover every potential safety concern in a children's environment, it is an overview of most known playground safety concerns. The checklist does not apply to home playground equipment, amusement park equipment, or to equipment normally intended for sports use. The checklist also does not address the many important issues of child development that pertain to play.

The playground audit form is not a regulatory standard, but a compilation of suggested guidelines based upon the *Handbook for Public Playground Safety* written by the Consumer Product Safety Commission (CPSC) (Revised 1997), *American Society for Testing and Materials (ASTM) F1487-95 Standard,* and expert opinions from consultants in the field of playground safety.

Acknowledgments

From the "Statewide Comprehensive Injury Prevention Program" (SCIPP), Department of Public Health, 150 Trecost Street, Boston, MA 02111

Adapted as Wheaton Park District's "Initial Playground Safety Audit" September, 1989, Revised December 20, 1990 and November, 1991, Ken Kutska.

Edited and updated June, 1992, by Ken Kutska, CLP, and Kevin Hoffman, ARM, Park District Risk Management Agency.

Edited and updated March, 1998, by Ken Kutska, CLP, CPSI; Kevin Hoffman, ARM, CPSI, and Tony Malkusak, CLP, CPSI.

ASTM
American Society for Testing and Materials
100 Barr Harbor Drive
West Conshohocken, Pennsylvania 19428
(610)832-9585

U.S. CPSC
Consumer Product Safety Commission
Washington, DC 20207
(1-800-638-CPSC)

National Playground Safety Institute, NPSI
22377 Belmont Ridge Road
Ashburn, VA 20148
(703) 858-0784
www.nrpa.org

Background Information:

Playground/Park: Northside Park #26   Date of Audit: 2/20/98

Site Location: West Street (1300 N)   Agency: Wheaton Park District

Equipment Type: Composite (Plastic, Metal)   Surfacing: Wood Fiber Mulch/Sand

Inspected By: Cameron Bettin / Wendy Anderson   Ages of Intended Users: 2-5 and 5-12

General Environment:

1.   Category of playground (circle all that apply):

- Public School
- Private School
- Day Care

- (Community Park)
- Neighborhood Park/Tot Lot
- Other (please specify)_____

2.   Equipment Inventory. Indicate the number of equipment pieces that exist.

A. Composite play structure		B. Free standing equipment		C. Site amenities	
Stairways and Step Ladders	4	Swings (to-fro) 2 Belt 2 Bucket	4	Benches	12
Vertical Rung Ladders	0	Tire Swings	0	Tables 10 Under Shelter	26
Ridgid Climber	6	Seesaws	0	Fountains	1
Flexible Climber	1	Slides	0	Bike Rack	1
Decks and Platforms	13	Rigid Climbers	1	Wheelchair Parking	5
Play Panel	14	Flexible Climbers	0		
Slides	5	Upper Body Equipment	0	Signs	3
Sliding Pole	0	Rocking Equipment	3	Trash Receptacles	11
Horizontal Ladder	1	Whirl	0	Fencing Metal Ramp Gaurdrail and Splitrail	1
Horizontal Rings	1	Sand Play Area	2	Other Picnic Shelter	1
Track Ride	1	Blackhoe Digger	3	Other Hot Coal Container	2
Crawl Tunnel	0	Play Panels	0	Recycling Container	
Clatter Bridge/Bridges	1	Other Concrete Crawl Tunnel	1		
Ramps	2	Other			
Transfer Stations	2	Other			
Roofs	3				
Other	0				

B-6

© NRPA/NPSI/PDRMA

3. Playground Border Factors:

Directions: Determine which playground border concerns exist and circle them. In the second column, indicate the actual distance the item is from the playground border. In the third column, assign index points based on the distance each potential border concern is from the nearest playground border (see Key to Border Concern Points).

Key to Border Concern Points:
Within 100 feet (5 points)
101-199 feet (2 points)
200 feet or more (0 points)

Playground Border Concerns Measurements or Distances	Distance from Play Edge	Index Points Given	Comments
1st public street West Street	Approx. 225'	0	
2nd public street			
3rd public street			
4th public street			
Streets with heavy traffic			
Water (ponds/stream/drainage ditch)	Approx. 165'	2	
Soccer/football field	+200"	0	
Baseball/softball field from home plate	Approx. 160'	2	
Basketball court	+200'	0	
Parking lots	Approx. 170	2	
Railroad tracks			Comment #1
Trees (not pruned up at least 7')	In Play Area	5	2 of 10 Trees not pruned up to 7' above equip. or surface
Golf course			
Other (specify) _____			
Point Total for Question 3:		11	

General Conditions	Possible Index Points	Index Points Given	Comments

General Environment Concerns

	General Conditions	Possible Index Points	Index Points Given	Comments
4.	The playground can be accessed safely by a sidewalk that is free of standing water, sand, pea gravel & low hanging branches.	5	0	
5.	If needed, a suitable barrier (fence) is provided for border concerns within 100' of playground edge. See question 3 for list of possible border concerns (CPSC 6.1).	20	0	Splitrail fence and plantings are located between play area and park road
6.	Seating (benches, outdoor tables) is in good condition (free of splinters, missing hardware or slats, protruding bolts, etc.).	1	1	Comment #2 Protruding bolts are found under picnic tables and benches
7.	Signs give information about: • regulations on the use of the playground (hours, pets, specific rules, etc.). • name and phone number of playground owner (to report problems). • age appropriateness of equipment. (CPSC 6.3)	15	0	
8.	Signs on all bordering roads advise motorists that a playground is nearby.	5	0	
9.	Trash receptacles are provided and located outside of the play area.	1	0	
10.	Poisonous plants are removed from play area.	10	0	
11.	Shaded area is provided.	1	0	
12.	The play area is visible to deter inappropriate behavior (CPSC 6.2).	5	5	See Comment #3
13.	The play area is free from lead in paint(maximum 0.06% lead by dry weight) (CPSC 8.1).	20	0	
14.	The play area is free from toxic materials and preservatives (CPSC 8.1).	20	0	
	Section Subtotal	**103**	6	

© NRPA/NPSI/PDRMA

General Conditions	Possible Index Points	Index Points Given	Comments

Age/Size Appropriateness Design

	General Conditions	Possible Index Points	Index Points Given	Comments
15.	Net, chain, arch or tire climbers are not the sole means to access play equipment for 2-5 yr. old users (ASTM 7.2.2.1).	10	○	
16.	Play equipment not recommended for 2-5 yr. old users: chain or cable walks, free standing arch climbers, free standing climbing events with flexible components, fulcrum seesaws, log rolls, long spiral slides, overhead rings, parallel bars, swinging gates, track rides and vertical sliding poles (CPSC 6.3).	10 pts. for each item found (Possible 110 Pts.)	○	
17.	The play area has signs that inform users of intended user age group (CPSC 6.3).	20	○	
	Section Subtotal	**140**	○	

Playground Protective Surface

	General Conditions	Possible Index Points	Index Points Given	Comments
18.	All elevated play equipment (slides, swings, bridges, seesaws, climbing apparatus, etc.) has proper depth of impact-absorbing material underneath the structure. Refer to CPSC and ASTM F1487-95 and ASTM 1292 for specifications on conforming protective surface type, critical fall heights and how far surfacing should extend from structure (CPSC Section 4).	20	○	
19.	Surfaces are inspected at least weekly and raked to prevent them from becoming packed down and to remove hidden hazards (e.g. litter, sharp objects, animal feces). (Daily=0 points, weekly=5 pts, monthly=10 pts, seasonally=20 pts, annually=40 pts) (CPSC 7.2).	40 20 10 5 0	5	
20.	Loose materials are replenished as recommended to maintain adequate depth and coverage (annually=10, seasonally=5, monthly or less=0) (CPSC 7.2).	10 5 0	10	
21.	Standing water is not found within any of the use zones (CPSC 6.1).	20	○	

General Conditions	Possible Index Points	Index Points Given	Comments

Playground Protective Surface, cont.

General Conditions	Possible Index Points	Index Points Given	Comments
22. For equipment installed after 1995, manufacturer's sign attached to equipment stating equipment must be installed over impact absorbing surface (ASTM 14.3).	10	O	See Comment #4 Area A-1994 (None) Area E-1996 (One) Area F-1997 (One) In bad repair
Section Subtotal	**150**	25	

<u>Note</u>: **If playground protective surface inspections are not documented in writing; <u>add 50 points</u> to section subtotal.**

Use Zone

General Conditions	Possible Index Points	Index Points Given	Comments
23. There is a minimum use zone of 6' in all directions for all equipment. Use zones for adjacent pieces of play equipment may overlap if the adjacent designated play surfaces are less than 30" above the protective surface. If either adjacent structure exceed 30", the minimum distance between the structures should be 9'. Rocking/springing equipment intended for users to stand upon is no less than 7'. Swings, slide exits, and moving equipment other than less than 30" high rocking equipment shall not overlap use zones. (CPSC 5.1.1, ASTM 9.2.1, 9.5.2.1).	20	O	
24. Swings with enclosed swing seat or bucket, use zone to the front and to the rear shall be a minimum distance of 2W, where W equals the distance from the top of the occupant's sitting surface to the pivot-point on the swing (CPSC 5.1.3, ASTM 9.4.1.2).	20	O	
25. Belt swings' use zone to the front and to the rear shall be a minimum distance of 2X, where X equals the distance from the top of the protective surface to the pivot-point on the swing (CPSC 5.1.3, ASTM 9.4.1.1).	20	O	
26. Slides have adequate space from other equipment at the bottom (height of slide plus 4' from the reduced gradient, or 6' from edge of slide; whichever is greater, but not more than 14'). (CPSC 5.1.2, ASTM 9.6.2, 9.6.2.1, Fig. A1.32).	20	O	

© NRPA/NPSI/PDRMA

General Conditions	Possible Index Points	Index Points Given	Comments

Use Zone, cont.

	General Conditions	Possible Index Points	Index Points Given	Comments
27.	The use zone for a rotating swing (tire swing) shall be a minimum of 6' in all directions of the support structure plus a minimum horizontal distance in all directions equal to the distance between the pivot point to the top of seat plus 6' (CPSC 5.1.3, 5.1.4, ASTM 9.4.2).	20	20	_See Comment #5_ It appears use zone was measured from pivot point of digger
28.	Barriers between equipment are installed so as not to create a trip hazard and are free of protrusions, splinters, sharp edges, etc. and are outside equipment use zone (CPSC 9.7).	10	0	
	Section Subtotal	**110**	20	

Accessibility

NOTE: The purpose of this audit form, with regard to accessibility, is to allow the audit inspector to determine compliance of the play area with ASTM F 1487-95. The goal of the inspector is to determine if a person with a disability has access to, on and through the equipment and play area. This audit form is not intended to assess design compliance with the soon to be released access board report.

The auditor shall indicate in the comments column and audit summary report, in your opinion, whether or not the playground is accessible per this simple three part question. Does the user have access to, through, and onto the playground equipment?

	General Conditions	Possible Index Points	Index Points Given	Comments
29.	The playground has an accessible route with a maximum horizontal slope of 1:20 (greater than 1:20 would be considered a ramp) and a maximum cross-slope of 1:50 (access to and around the playground area is at least 60" wide) (ASTM 10.1.3).	10	10	_Comment #6_ All main access walks and ramps to play area and to 5-12 play area are >1:20.
30.	Ramps are 36" wide minimum; with a slope between 1:20 and 1:12 and maximum horizontal run of 12 feet (ASTM 10.2.2.1, 10.2.2.2).	10	0	
31.	Landings are 60" minimum diameter at bottom and top of each run; landings with play components shall have area 30" x 48" to park wheelchair while not reducing adjacent circulation path to less than 36" (ASTM 10.2.2.4).	10	0	
32.	For ramps, either the barrier extends to within 1 inch of the ramp surface or a curb stop exists that projects a minimum of 2" above the ramp. (ASTM 10.2.2.8).	20	0	
33.	For ramps higher than 30" (designed for 2-5 yr. olds) or higher than 48" (designed for 5-12 yr. olds) barriers are provided (ASTM 7.4.4, 10.2.2.5).	20	0	

© NRPA/NPSI/PDRMA

General Conditions	Possible Index Points	Index Points Given	Comments

Accessibility, cont.

	General Conditions	Possible Index Points	Index Points Given	Comments
34.	For ramps > 30" H (designed for 2-5 yr. olds) or > 48" H (designed for 5-12 yr. olds) handrails are provided on each side of a ramp at a height between 26-28". For ramps less than or equal to 30" H and 48" H (for 2-5 and 5-12 yr. olds, respectively) two handrails are provided on each side that are between 12-16" H and 26-28" H (ASTM 7.4.3, 10.2.2.6, 10.2.2.7).	20	20	Comment #7 Guardrails along ramps at entry to 5-12 yr. old play structre are 19" and 38"
35.	Transfer point ht. is between 14-18" with a clear width of minimum 24" and depth of no less than 14". Transfer point steps are a maximum of 8" high with handholds (ASTM 10.2.3.1-10.2.3.3, 10.3.1).	10	0	Comment #8 (4 stations) *One is 21" to platform and 10.5" to step * One is 18.5" to platform and 8.5" to step * One has 9" step height in sand area because trex has shifted * 2 transfer platforms are triangles no 24" w x 14" transition platform
36.	Transfer pts. have; wheelchair turning space at base of transfer pt.; a clear space area of 60" minimum. T-shaped area in accordance with ASTM Fig. A1-39a (ASTM 10.2.4.1).	10	0	
37.	The playground use zone has an accessible safety surface (ASTM 10.1.2).	10	0	
38.	Accessible restroom facilities, accessible seating, accessible drinking fountain and shade are located in or near the play area.	1	1	Comment #9 Restroom accessible but route is not because of 7% grade from 5-12 yr. old ramp to perimeter walkway.
39.	Wheelchair accessible platforms: single wheelchair passage 36"; two wheelchair passage 60"; single wheelchair and 1 able-bodied user 44"; openings between deck not greater than 0.50" (ASTM 10.2.5.1-10.2.5.4).	10	0	
40.	Accessible play opportunities designed with different access and egress points, such as slides, allow the user to return unassisted to access the original transfer point (ASTM 10.3.2.1).	10	0	
41.	Vertical leg clearance is not less than 24" for equipment that requires a wheelchair user to pull partially under, such as sand tables, with a top playing surface of no greater than 30" (ASTM 10.3.2.2).	10	NA	

© NRPA/NPSI/PDRMA

General Conditions	Possible Index Points	Index Points Given	Comments

Accessibility, cont.

	General Conditions	Possible Index Points	Index Points Given	Comments
42.	Wheelchair accessible upper body equipment, such as horizontal ladders and rings, are less than or equal to 54" high (ASTM 10.3.2.3).	10	N/A	
43.	Wheelchair accessible manipulative equipment, such as interactive panels, are between 9"-48" H for side reach and 20"-36" H for front reach from the accessible surface (ASTM 10.3.2.4, 10.3.2.5).	10	0	
	Section Subtotal	**171**	41	

© NRPA/NPSI/PDRMA

Specific Conditions	Possible Index Points	Index Points Given	Comments

• **Important:** For the following audit sections, if multiple types of the same equipment exists (such as two swing sets), you can apply the questions to all multiple pieces of equipment as a whole. However, no more than full index points should be applied if a negative response exists on more than one piece of the same equipment. Also, deficiencies on a specific piece of equipment should be noted in the comments section for repair or future consideration.

Slides

	Specific Conditions	Possible Index Points	Index Points Given	Comments
44.	Slides are accessed by stairs, step ladders, or platforms which are evenly spaced, less than 12" apart, and pass the entrapment test. Refer to ASTM F 1487 Table 2 (CPSC 12.4.2).	10	○	
45.	There is a flat surface the width of the slide bed at the top of the slide to help position the child for sliding (min. 22" deep going back from the slide bedway and min. 12" wide for 2-5 yr. old users and a min. 16" for 5-12 yr. old users) (CPSC 12.4.3, ASTM 8.5.2.2, 8.5.2.3, 8.5.4.3).	10	○	
46.	There are sufficient safety barriers at the top of the slide to prevent falls, with hand holds to assist standing to sitting transition and a means to channel the user to the sitting position before slide entry (CPSC 12.4.3, ASTM 7.4, 8.5.3).	15	○	
47.	Sides of bedways are at least 4" high (CPSC 12.4.4, ASTM 8.5.4.4).	15	○	
48.	No portion of the angle of the sliding surface exceeds 50 degrees with the average angle of 30 degrees or less (CPSC 12.4.4, ASTM 8.5.4.2).	10	○	
49.	A flat sliding surface (run out zone) at the bottom of the slide is a min. of 11" long at transition point and angle is less than 5 degrees from the horizontal plane (CPSC 12.4.5, ASTM 8.5.5.1, 8.5.5.2).	10	○	
50.	For slides greater than 4' high, designed for 5-12 yr. olds, the slide exit height is between 7" and 15" above the protective surfacing material (CPSC 12.4.5, ASTM 8.5.5.3).	10	○	

© NRPA/NPSI/PDRMA

Specific Conditions	Possible Index Points	Index Points Given	Comments

Slides cont.

51. For slides 4' high or less and designed for 2-5 yr. olds, the slide exit height does not exceed 11" above the protective surfacing material (CPSC 12.4.5, ASTM 8.5.5.3).	10	10	Comment #10 Double tot slide exit is at 14"
52. Tube slides have a minimum diameter equal to or greater than 23" (CPSC 12.4.8, (ASTM 8.5.4.7).	5	○	
53. Only short spiral slides, with one turn or less, are recommended for 2-5 yr. old users (CPSC 12.4.7).	5	○	
54. A clear area, height of 60" along slide chute and width of 21" from inside edge of siderail including the transition platform. No obstacles or protrusions project more than 1/8" perpendicular to the plane of the initial surface. Underside of slide bedway is exempt (ASTM 8.5.6.1, figures A1.16 and A1.22).	20	○	
55. On roller slides, no opening allows a 3/16" rod to enter (ASTM 8.9.2.1).	10	N/A	
56. If the slide is made in several pieces, the sliding surface has no gaps or rough edges at the top of the slide or at section seams which could entangle clothing or trap foreign material (CPSC 12.4.3, 12.4.4).	20	20	Comment #11 * Tot slide has gap between slides * Double slide on 5-12 yr. old structure apperas to have entanglement from dock posts to clamps to slide side rail.
57. The sliding surface faces away from sun or is located in the shade and isn't made of wood or fiberglass (CPSC 12.4.4).	10	10	Comment #12 Two slides face west
58. Pinch, Crush and Shear Points (CPSC 9.5, ASTM 6.4): • Equipment is free of sharp edges. • There are no open holes in the equipment forming traps (e.g. at the ends of the tubes). • There are no pinch, crush or shear points.	 10 10 10	 ○ ○ ○	
59. Protrusions (CPSC 9.2, ASTM 6.2): • No components fail protrusion test. • Nuts, bolts and screws are recessed, covered or sanded smooth and level.	 10 10	 ○ ○	

Specific Conditions	Possible Index Points	Index Points Given	Comments

Slides cont.

	Specific Conditions	Possible Index Points	Index Points Given	Comments
60.	Entanglements/Entrapment Angles (CPSC 9.4, 9.6, ASTM 6.3): • No more than two threads of the fastener protrude through any nut. • No obstacles or protrusions project upwards from a horizontal plane extending more than 1/8" perpendicular to the plane of the initial surface. • There are no open "V" entrapment angles on any part of the equipment. See Figs. A1.3-4 in ASTM F 1487.	10 10 10	○ ○ ○	
61.	Head Entrapments (CPSC 9.6, ASTM 6.1): • No components fail the entrapment test. • There are no partially bounded openings. See Figs. A1.6a-A1.10 in ASTM F 1487.	10 10	○ ○	
62.	Hardware: • Nuts and bolts are tight and not able to be loosened without tools. Upon close inspection, they show no loose play or excessive wear (CPSC 8.2). • Equipment is free of rust and chipping paint (CPSC 8.1). • Equipment is free of sharp edges, splinters or rough surfaces and shows no excessive wear (CPSC 9.1). • Ropes, chains and cables have not frayed or worn out (CPSC 7.2). • Equipment has not shifted or become bent (CPSC 8.1). • There is no corrosion or visible rotting at points where equipment comes into contact with ground surface (CPSC 7.2, 8.1). • No components are missing. All parts of the equipment are present and in good working order with no loose play or excessive wear in moving parts (CPSC 7.2, 8.1). • Handgrips are between 0.95" and 1.55" in diameter (CPSC 10.2.1). • Footings for equipment are stable and buried below ground level or covered by surfacing materials (CPSC 9.7). • Equipment is free of any litter, debris and surfacing material (ASTM 7.1.2). • Equipment use zone is free of litter and debris (CPSC 7.2).	10 5 10 10 10 10 20 10 20 20 10	○ 5 ○ ○ ○ ○ ○ ○ ○ ○ ○	Comment #13 Rusted bolts and screws on tunnel slide and tot double slide hardware.
	Section Subtotal		45	

© NRPA/NPSI/PDRMA

Specific Conditions	Possible Index Points	Index Points Given	Comments

Climbing Equipment

Specific Conditions	Possible Index Points	Index Points Given	Comments
63. Handholds stay in place when grasped (CPSC 10.4).	20	○	
64. Climbing bars and handrails are between 0.95"-1.55" in diameter (CPSC 10.2.1, ASTM 8.2.1).	10	○	
65. Flexible access equipment anchoring devices are below level of playing surface (CPSC 12.1.3, ASTM 7.2.2.2).	10	○	
66. Flexible climbing devices used as access for use by 2-5 yr. olds, readily allows users to bring feet to the same level before ascending to the next level (ASTM 7.2.2.4).	5	○	
67. Climbers don't have climbing bars or other structural components in the interior of the structure onto which a child may fall from a height of greater than 18" (CPSC 12.1.2).	20	○	
68. Accesses which don't have side handrails, such as rung ladders, arch or flexible climbers, are to have alternate hand-gripping support at transition (CPSC 10.4, ASTM 7.3.2).	10	○	
69. Rung ladders, arch and flexible climbers used as access, are not above the designated play surface it serves (no trip hazard) (ASTM 7.3.3).	10	○	
70. Balance beam maximum height from the playing surface is 12" for 2-5 yr. old users and 16" for 5-12 yr. old users (CPSC 12.1.8, ASTM 8.1.1).	5	N/A	
71. No obstacles or protrusions project upwards from a horizontal plane extending more than a 1/8" perpendicular to the plane of the initial surface. See ASTM F1487 fig. A1.13 (CPSC 9.3, ASTM 6.3.2.1).	20	○	

Specific Conditions	Possible Index Points	Index Points Given	Comments
Climbing Equipment, cont.			
72. All components of crawl through tunnels are secure and firmly fixed. The tunnel has two safe, clear exits and is designed to drain freely.	20	○	See question 77 for crawl through tunnel
73. Pinch, Crush and Shear Points (CPSC 9.5, ASTM 6.4):			
• Equipment is free of sharp edges.	10	○	
• There are no open holes in the equipment forming traps (e.g. at the ends of the tubes).	10	○	
• There are no pinch, crush or shear points.	10	○	
74. Protrusions (CPSC 9.2, ASTM 6.2):			
• No components fail protrusion test.	10	○	
• Nuts, bolts and screws are recessed, covered or sanded smooth and level.	10	○	
75. Entanglements/Entrapment Angles (CPSC 9.4, 9.6, ASTM 6.3):			
• No more than two threads of the fastener protrude through any nut.	10	○	
• No obstacles or protrusions project upwards from a horizontal plane extending more than 1/8" perpendicular to the plane of the initial surface.	10	○	
• There are no open "V" entrapment angles on any part of the equipment. See Figs. A1.3-4 in ASTM F 1487.	10	○	
76. Head Entrapments (CPSC 9.6, ASTM 6.1):			
• No components fail the entrapment test.	10	○	
• There are no partially bounded openings. See Figs. A1.6a-A1.10 ASTM F1487.	10	○	
77. Hardware:			
• Nuts and bolts are tight and not able to be loosened without tools. Upon close inspection, they show no loose play or excessive wear (CPSC 8.2).	10	○	
• Equipment is free of rust and chipping paint (CPSC 8.1).	5	○	
• Equipment is free of sharp edges, splinters or rough surfaces and shows no excessive wear (CPSC 9.1).	10	10	Comment #14 Concrete tunnel has rough edges
• Ropes, chains and cables have not frayed or worn out (CPSC 7.2).	10	10	Comment #15 Coating on chain cargo net is wearing off and showing rust.
• Equipment has not shifted or become bent (CPSC 8.1).	10	○	

© NRPA/NPSI/PDRMA

Specific Conditions	Possible Index Points	Index Points Given	Comments

Climbing Equipment, cont.

Specific Conditions	Possible Index Points	Index Points Given	Comments
77. Hardware, cont.			
• There is no corrosion or visible rotting at points where equipment comes into contact with ground surface (CPSC 7.2, 8.1).	10	○	
• No components are missing. All parts of the equipment are present and in good working order with no loose play or excessive wear in moving parts (CPSC 7.2, 8.1).	20	○	
• Handgrips are between 0.95" and 1.55" in diameter (CPSC 10.2.1).	10	○	
• Footings for equipment are stable and buried below ground level or covered by surfacing materials (CPSC 9.7).	20	○	
• Equipment is free of any litter, debris and surfacing material (ASTM 7.1.2).	20	○	
• Equipment use zone is free of litter and debris (CPSC 7.2).	10	○	
Section Subtotal	**365**	20	

Upper Body Climbing Equipment

Specific Conditions	Possible Index Points	Index Points Given	Comments
78. Upper body climbing equipment, other than turning bars, not recommended for 2-5 yr. old users (CPSC 6.3, ASTM 8.3.1).	10	○	
79. Upper body climbing equipment maximum height is 84" for 5-12 yr. old users (CPSC 12.1.5, ASTM 8.3.4).	10	○	
80. Maximum distance between rungs for upper body equipment is 15" and openings pass the entrapment test (CPSC 9.6, 12.1.5, ASTM 8.3.2).	10	○	
81. Overhead swinging rings pass the entrament test and chain is maximum length of 12" (CPSC 9.6, 12.1.5).	10	○	
82. Climbing ropes are secured at both ends and are not capable of being looped back on itself creating a loop with an inside perimeter of greater than 5" (CPSC 12.1.7, ASTM 6.5.1).	20	N/A	

Specific Conditions	Possible Index Points	Index Points Given	Comments

Upper Body Climbing Equipment, cont.

	Specific Conditions	Possible Index Points	Index Points Given	Comments
83.	Horizontal take-off distance from landing structure to first handhold of upper body equipment is no greater than 10"; if access and egress is by rungs, horizontal distance to first rung is at least 8", but no greater than 10" (ASTM 8.3.3).	10	10	Comment #16 Horizontal rungs - 1st rung is 12" from deck Ring trek - 1st ring is 9" from deck (OK)
84.	Maximum ht. of take off/landing for upper body equipment is 36" for 5-12 yr. old users (ASTM 8.3.5).	10	0	
85.	There are no single non-rigid components (cable, rope, wire, or similar component) suspended between play units or from the ground to the play unit within 45 degrees of horizontal, unless it is above 7 ft. from the playground surface and is a minimum of 1" at its widest cross-section dimension. It is recommended that the suspended components be brightly colored or contrast with surrounding equipment (CPSC 9.8, ASTM 6.5).	10	N/A	
86.	Sliding pole clearance from structures is between 18" and 20" (CPSC 12.1.6, ASTM 8.4.1).	10	N/A	
87.	Sliding pole is a minimum of 38" above the access structure, 60" min., recommended (CPSC 12.1.6, ASTM 8.4.3).	10	N/A	
88.	Sliding pole is a maximum 1.9" in diameter and continuous with no protruding welds or joints within sliding area (CPSC 12.1.6, ASTM 8.4.4, 8.4.5).	10	N/A	
89.	Track rides not recommended for 2-5 yr. old users (CPSC 6.3, ASTM 8.13.5).	20	0	
90.	Track rides; the lowest portion of the hand gripping component is a minimum 64" above protective surface with maximum height of 78" (ASTM 8.13.1).	10	0	
91.	Underside of track beam is a minimum of 78" above the protective surfacing (ASTM 8.13.2).	5	0	

© NRPA/NPSI/PDRMA

Specific Conditions	Possible Index Points	Index Points Given	Comments

Upper Body Climbing Equipment, cont.

Specific Conditions	Possible Index Points	Index Points Given	Comments
92. Pinch, Crush and Shear Points (CPSC 9.5, ASTM 6.4): • Equipment is free of sharp edges. • There are no open holes in the equipment forming traps (e.g. at the ends of the tubes). • There are no pinch, crush or shear points.	10 10 10	○ ○ ○	
93. Protrusions (CPSC 9.2, ASTM 6.2): • No components fail protrusion test. • Nuts, bolts and screws are recessed, covered or sanded smooth and level.	10 10	○ ○	
94. Entanglements/Entrapment Angles (CPSC 9.4, 9.6, ASTM 6.3): • No more than two threads of the fastener protrude through any nut. • No obstacles or protrusions project upwards from a horizontal plane extending more than 1/8" perpendicular to the plane of the initial surface. • There are no open "V" entrapment angles on any part of the equipment. See Figs. A1.3-4 in ASTM F 1487.	10 10 10	○ ○ ○	
95. Head Entrapments (CPSC 9.6, ASTM 6.1): • No components fail the entrapment test. • There are no partially bounded openings. See Figs. A1.6a-A1.10 in ASTM F 1487.	10 10	○ ○	
96. Hardware: • Nuts and bolts are tight and not able to be loosened without tools. Upon close inspection, they show no loose play or excessive wear (CPSC 8.2). • Equipment is free of rust and chipping paint (CPSC 8.1). • Equipment is free of sharp edges, splinters or rough surfaces and shows no excessive wear (CPSC 9.1). • Ropes, chains and cables have not frayed or worn out (CPSC 7.2). • Equipment has not shifted or become bent (CPSC 8.1). • There is no corrosion or visible rotting at points where equipment comes into contact with ground surface (CPSC 7.2, 8.1).	10 5 10 10 10 10	○ ○ ○ ○ ○ ○	

Specific Conditions	Possible Index Points	Index Points Given	Comments

Upper Body Climbing Equipment, cont.

Specific Conditions	Possible Index Points	Index Points Given	Comments
96. Hardware, cont. • No components are missing. All parts of the equipment are present and in good working order with no loose play or excessive wear in moving parts (CPSC 7.2, 8.1).	20	○	
• Handgrips are between 0.95" and 1.55" in diameter (CPSC 10.2.1).	10	○	
• Footings for equipment are stable and buried below ground level or covered by surfacing materials (CPSC 9.7).	20	○	
• Equipment is free of any litter, debris and surfacing material (ASTM 7.1.2).	20	○	
• Equipment use zone is free of litter and debris (CPSC 7.2).	10	○	
Section Subtotal	**390**	IO	

Stairways and Ladders

Specific Conditions	Possible Index Points	Index Points Given	Comments
97. Continuous handrails on both sides for stairways >1 tread; on those with only 1 tread, an alternate means of hand support or handrail present. Handrail height is between 22" and 38" (CPSC 10.3.1, ASTM 7.1.4).	10	○	
98. Children have an easy, safe way to descend equipment when they reach the top. (via platform, stairway, or step ladder) (CPSC 12.1.2).	20	○	
99. Steps and rungs do not allow for accumulation of water and debris (CPSC 10.2, ASTM 7.1.2).	5	○	
100. Net, chain, arch or tire climbers not the sole means to access equipment for play areas for 2-5 yr. old users (CPSC 12.1.3, ASTM 7.2.2.1).	10	○	
101. Steps and rungs are evenly spaced within a tolerance of ±0.25 inches and horizontal within a tolerance of ±2 degrees. This includes the spacing between the top step or rung and the surface of the platform (ASTM 7.1.1).	10	○	

© NRPA/NPSI/PDRMA

Specific Conditions	Possible Index Points	Index Points Given	Comments

Stairways and Ladders, cont.

Specific Conditions	Possible Index Points	Index Points Given	Comments
102. Openings between steps or rungs and between the top step or rung and underside of a platform pass the testing requirements for head entrapment (CPSC 9.6.1, 10.2, ASTM 6.1)	20	○	
103. All stairways, step ladders and rung ladders, as it relates to the intended users, conform with access slope; tread, rung, and ramp width; tread depth; rung diameter; and vertical rise specifications as per ASTM F1487 Table 2 (CPSC 10.2).	10	○	
104. Pinch, Crush and Shear Points (CPSC 9.5, ASTM 6.4): • Equipment is free of sharp edges. • There are no open holes in the equipment forming traps (e.g. at ends of the tubes). • There are no pinch, crush or shear points.	10 10 10	○ ○ ○	
105. Protrusions (CPSC 9.2, ASTM 6.2): • No components fail protrusion test. • Nuts, bolts and screws are recessed, covered or sanded smooth and level.	10 10	○ ○	
106. Entanglements/Entrapment Angles (CPSC 9.4, 9.6, ASTM 6.3): • No more than two threads of the fastener protrude through any nut. • No obstacles or protrusions project upwards from a horizontal plane extending more than 1/8" perpendicular to the plane of the initial surface. • There are no open "V" entrapment angles on any part of the equipment. See Figs. A1.3-4 in ASTM F1487.	10 10 10	○ ○ ○	
107. Head Entrapments (CPSC 9.6, ASTM 6.1): • No components fail the entrapment test. • There are no partially bounded openings. See Figs. A1.6a-A1.10 in ASTM F 1487.	10 10	○ ○	
108. Hardware: • Nuts and bolts are tight and not able to be loosened without tools. Upon close inspection, they show no loose play or excessive wear (CPSC 8.2). • Equipment is free of rust and chipping paint (CPSC 8.1).	10 5	○ ○	

Specific Conditions	Possible Index Points	Index Points Given	Comments

Stairways and Ladders, cont.

Specific Conditions	Possible Index Points	Index Points Given	Comments
108. Hardware, cont.: • Equipment is free of sharp edges, splinters or rough surfaces and shows no excessive wear (CPSC 9.1).	10	○	
• Ropes, chains and cables have not frayed or worn out (CPSC 7.2).	10	○	
• Equipment has not shifted or become bent (CPSC 8.1).	10	○	
• There is no corrosion or visible rotting at points where equipment comes into contact with ground surface (CPSC 7.2, 8.1).	10	○	
• No components are missing. All parts of the equipment are present and in good working order with no loose play or excessive wear in moving parts (CPSC 7.2, 8.1).	20	○	
• Handgrips are between 0.95" and 1.55" in diameter (CPSC 10.2.1).	10	○	
• Footings for equipment are stable and buried below ground level or covered by surfacing materials (CPSC 9.7).	20	○	
• Equipment is free of any litter, debris and surfacing material (ASTM 7.1.2).	20	○	
• Equipment use zone is free of litter and debris (CPSC 7.2).	10	○	
Section Subtotal	**320**	○	

Decks and Platforms

Specific Conditions	Possible Index Points	Index Points Given	Comments
109. Unless an alternate means of access is provided, the maximum difference in height between stepped platforms for 2-5 yr. olds is 12" and for 5-12 yr. olds is 18" (CPSC 11.7, ASTM 7.4.5.1).	20	○	
110. There is a 29" high (min.) protective perimeter barrier around 2-5 yr. old users' equipment that is more than 30" above the underlying surface (CPSC 11.5, ASTM 7.4.4.1, 7.4.4.3).	10	○	
111. There is a 38" high (min.) protective perimeter barrier on all elevated surfaces 48" above the underlying surface for 5-12 yr. old users' equipment (CPSC 11.5, ASTM 7.4.4.1, 7.4.4.3).	10	○	

© NRPA/NPSI/PDRMA

Decks and Platforms, cont.

Specific Conditions	Possible Index Points	Index Points Given	Comments
112. The space between slats of protective barriers and guardrails is not between 3-1/2" and 9" and passes the entrapment test (CPSC 9.6, ASTM 6.1).	10	○	
113. Guardrails or protective barriers are present on all elevated surfaces greaterthan 20" above the underlying surface for 2-5 yr. old users' equipment (29" top edge, 23" lower edge) (CPSC 11.4, ASTM 7.4.3.1-7.4.3.4).	10	○	
114. Guardrails or protective barriers are present for all elevated surfaces 30" above the underlying surface for 5-12 yr. old users' equipment (38" top edge, 24" high lower edge) (CPSC 11.4, ASTM 7.4.3.1-7.4.3.4).	10	10	Comment #17 Guardrail on ramp from sidesalk to play dock, the lower rail is 19.25" (See question #34) (See Comment #7)
115. No partially bounded openings are projecting upwards from the horizontal plane that are greater than 1 7/8" or less than 9" and fail the test method for partially bounded openings. See ASTM F1487 Figures A1.6a-A1.10 (CPSC Fig. 8, ASTM 6.1.4).	20	○	
116. Pinch, Crush and Shear Points (CPSC 9.5, ASTM 6.4): • Equipment is free of sharp edges. • There are no open holes in the equipment forming traps (e.g. at ends of the tubes). • There are no pinch, crush or shear points.	10 10 10	○ ○ ○	
117. Protrusions (CPSC 9.2, ASTM 6.2): • No components fail protrusion test. • Nuts, bolts and screws are recessed, covered or sanded smooth and level.	10 10	○ ○	
118. Entanglements/Entrapment Angles (CPSC 9.4, 9.6, ASTM 6.3): • No more than two threads of the fastener protrude through any nut. • No obstacles or protrusions project up wards from a horizontal plane extending more than 1/8" perpendicular to the plane of the initial surface.	10 10	○ ○	

Specific Conditions	Possible Index Points	Index Points Given	Comments
Decks and Platforms, cont.			
118. Entanglements/Entrapment Angles (CPSC 9.4, 9.6, ASTM 6.3): • There are no open "V" entrapment angles on any part of the equipment. See Figs. A1.3-4 in ASTM F 1487.	10	○	
119. Head Entrapments (CPSC 9.6, ASTM 6.1): • No components fail the entrapment test. • There are no partially bounded openings. See Figs. A1.6a-A1.10 in ASTM F1487.	10 10	○ ○	
120. Hardware: • Nuts and bolts are tight and not able to be loosened without tools. Upon close inspection, they show no loose play or excessive wear (CPSC 8.2).	10	○	
• Equipment is free of rust and chipping paint (CPSC 8.1).	5	○	
• Equipment is free of sharp edges, splinters or rough surfaces and shows no excessive wear (CPSC 9.1).	10	○	
• Ropes, chains and cables have not frayed or worn out (CPSC 7.2).	10	○	
• Equipment has not shifted or become bent (CPSC 8.1).	10	○	
• There is no corrosion or visible rotting at points where equipment comes into contact with ground surface (CPSC 7.2, 8.1).	10	○	
• No components are missing. All parts of the equipment are present and in good working order with no loose play or excessive wear in moving parts (CPSC 7.2, 8.1).	20	○	
• Handgrips are between 0.95" and 1.55" in diameter (CPSC 10.2.1).	10	○	Comment #18 Guardrails on ramp from side walk to deck, and suspension bridge rails on 2-5 yr. olds structure are greater than 1.55
• Footings for equipment are stable and buried below ground level or covered by surfacing materials (CPSC 9.7).	20	○	
• Equipment is free of any litter, debris and surfacing material.	20	○	
• Equipment use zone is free of litter and debris.	10	○	
Section Subtotal	**325**	20	

© NRPA/NPSI/PDRMA

Specific Conditions	Possible Index Points	Index Points Given	Comments

Swings

Specific Conditions	Possible Index Points	Index Points Given	Comments
121. All swings, to and fro and rotating swings are not attached to main structure (CPSC 12.6.2, ASTM 8.6.1.1).	20	○	
122. All flying animal figure swings, multiple occupancy swings (except tire swings), rope swings, and trapeze bars are removed from public playgrounds (CPSC 12.6.4, ASTM 8.7.1).	40	○	
123. Lightweight enclosed swing seats, are used and all openings meet entrapment criteria (CPSC 12.6.3).	10	○	
124. All swing seats are made of canvas, rubber, or other lightweight material (CPSC 12.6.2, ASTM 8.6.1.3).	20	○	
125. There are no open "S" hooks (openings greater than or equal to 0.04") (CPSC 12.6.1).	10	○	
126. When stationary, all seats same type are level.	1	○	
127. There are no more than two swings, evenly spaced, in any individual swing bay (CPSC 12.6.2, ASTM 8.6.1.3). Swing seat shall be of the same type in each bay. (CPSC 12.6.3)	20	○	
128. Swings are at least 24" from each other and 30" away from the frame. See ASTM Figs. A1.23, A1.24 (CPSC Fig. 22, ASTM 8.6.1.5).	20	○	
129. Vertical distance is at least 12" between underside of occupied seat and protective surface (CPSC 12.6.2, ASTM 8.6.1.5).	1	○	
130. Swing hangers are spaced wider than seats, not less than 20" (CPSC 12.6.2, ASTM 8.6.1.5).	10	○	
131. For tire swings, there is at least a 30" safety zone from the crossbeam support structure and the farthest extensions of the swing, and each must have a minimum clearance of 12" from the bottom of the tire to the protective surface (CPSC 12.6.4, ASTM 8.6.1.5).	10	N/A	
132. Swing tires have adequate drainage (CPSC 12.6.4).	5	N/A	

© NRPA/NPSI/PDRMA

Specific Conditions	Possible Index Points	Index Points Given	Comments
Swings, cont.			
133. Tire swings are not made of steel belted radial tires (CPSC 12.6.2, ASTM 8.6.2.3).	10	N/A	
134. To and fro swings and tire swings are located away from circulation paths (a distance at least equal to the equipment use zone and an additional safety factor for circulation, with this area free of any obstructions) and near the periphery of the playground (CPSC 6.2, ASTM 8.6.1.1, 8.6.2.1).	10	○	
135. Pinch, Crush and Shear Points (CPSC 9.5, ASTM 6.4): • Equipment is free of sharp edges. • There are no open holes in the equipment forming traps (e.g. at the ends of the tubes). • There are no pinch, crush or shear points.	10 10 10	○ ○ ○	
136. Protrusions (CPSC 9.2, ASTM 6.2): • No components fail protrusion test. • Nuts, bolts and screws are recessed, covered or sanded smooth and level.	10 10	○ ○	
137. Entanglements/Entrapment Angles (CPSC 9.4, 9.6, ASTM 6.3): • No more than two threads of the fastener protrude through any nut. • No obstacles or protrusions project upwards from a horizontal plane extending more than 1/8" perpendicular to the plane of the initial surface. • There are no open "V" entrapment angles on any part of the equipment. See Figs. A1.3-4 in ASTM F 1487.	10 10 10	○ ○ ○	
138. Head Entrapments (CPSC 9.6, ASTM 6.1): • No components fail the entrapment test. • There are no partially bounded openings. See Figs. A1.6a-A1.10 in ASTM F 1487.	10 10	○ ○	
139. Hardware: • Nuts and bolts are tight and not able to be loosened without tools. Upon close inspection, they show no loose play or excessive wear (CPSC 8.2).	10	○	

© NRPA/NPSI/PDRMA

Specific Conditions	Possible Index Points	Index Points Given	Comments

Swings, cont.

Specific Conditions	Possible Index Points	Index Points Given	Comments
139. Hardware, cont.:			
• Equipment is free of rust and chipping paint (CPSC 8.1).	5	○	
• Equipment is free of sharp edges, splinters or rough surfaces and shows no excessive wear (CPSC 9.1).	10	○	
• Ropes, chains and cables have not frayed or worn out (CPSC 7.2).	10	○	
• Equipment has not shifted or become bent (CPSC 8.1).	10	○	
• There is no corrosion or visible rotting at points where equipment comes into contact with ground surface (CPSC 7.2, 8.1).	10	○	
• No components are missing. All parts of the equipment are present and in good working order with no loose play or excessive wear in moving parts (CPSC 7.2, 8.1).	20	○	
• Handgrips are between 0.95" and 1.55" in diameter (CPSC 10.2.1).	10	○	
• Footings for equipment are stable and buried below ground level or covered by surfacing materials (CPSC 9.7).	20	○	
• Equipment is free of any litter, debris and surfacing material (ASTM 7.1.2).	20	○	
• Equipment use zone is free of litter and debris (CPSC 7.2).	10	○	
Section Subtotal	**422**	○	

Rotating and Rocking Equipment

Specific Conditions	Possible Index Points	Index Points Given	Comments
140. The seesaws seating surface does not reach more than 5' above the underlying surface ASTM 8.10.6).	10	○	
141. The seesaw fulcrum is fixed, enclosed or designed to prevent pinching (CPSC 12.3, ASTM 8.10.3).	10	○	
142. Seesaw handgrips intended to be gripped by one hand have a minimum length of 3" and 2-hands a minimum of 6" and pass the protrusion test (CPSC 12.3, ASTM 8.10.4.1).	10	○	

Specific Conditions	Possible Index Points	Index Points Given	Comments

Rotating and Rocking Equipment, cont.

Specific Conditions	Possible Index Points	Index Points Given	Comments
143. A rubber segment is buried in the surfacing under the seesaw seats unless seesaw uses a spring centering device (CPSC 12.3, ASTM 8.10.2).	10	N/A	
144. Log rolls (not recommended for 2-5yr. old users) have maximum ht. of 18" above the protective surface for 5-12 yr. old users (ASTM 8.12.2, 8.12.3).	20	N/A	
145. Spring rocking equipment seat height is between 14" and 28" (ASTM 8.11.5).	5	○	
146. There are no equipment parts that could cause a pinching or crushing injury on spring rocking equipment. Exemption is the attachment area of heavy duty coil springs to the body and base of spring rocking equipment (CPSC 12.5, ASTM 6.4.1.3 [2], 8.11.4).	10	○	
147. Handholds stay in place when grasped and pass the protrusion test (CPSC 12.5, ASTM 8.11.2).	10	○	
148. Footrests stay in place and pass the protrusion test (CPSC 12.5, ASTM 8.11.3).	5	○	
149. Merry-go-rounds are approximately circular, and the distance between the minimum and maximum radii of a noncircular platform does not exceed 2". See Fig. A1.25 in ASTM F1487 (CPSC 12.2, ASTM 8.8.1.1, 8.8.1.2).	10	N/A	
150. Components of the merry-go-round do not extend beyond the platform perimeter (CPSC 12.2, ASTM 8.8.1.2).	10	N/A	
151. There are no openings in the surface of the platform that permit the penetration of 5/16" rod through the surface of the merry-go-round (CPSC 12.2, ASTM 8.8.1.4).	10	N/A	
152. There are no accessible shearing or crushing mechanisms in the undercarriage of the equipment, and the platform does not provide an oscillatory (up and down) motion (CPSC 12.2, ASTM 8.8.1.5).	10	N/A	

© NRPA/NPSI/PDRMA

Specific Conditions	Possible Index Points	Index Points Given	Comments

Rotating Equipment, cont.

Specific Conditions	Possible Index Points	Index Points Given	Comments
153. The peripheral speed of the platform does not exceed 13 feet per second (CPSC 12.2, ASTM 8.8.1.6).	10	N/A	
154. There is a minimum of 9" between the protective surface and the underside of a merry-go-round platform with a max. ht. of 14" for the platform surface (CPSC 12.2, ASTM 8.8.1.2, 8.8.1.4).	10	N/A	
155. Pinch, Crush and Shear Points (CPSC 9.5, ASTM 6.4): • Equipment is free of sharp edges. • There are no open holes in the equipment forming traps (e.g. at the ends of the tubes). • There are no pinch, crush or shear points.	10 10 10	○ ○ ○	
156. Protrusions (CPSC 9.2, ASTM 6.2): • No components fail protrusion test. • Nuts, bolts and screws are recessed, covered or sanded smooth and level.	10 10	10 ○	Comment #19 All 3 rockers have hand hold protrusions
157. Entanglements/Entrapment Angles (CPSC 9.4, 9.6, ASTM 6.3): • No more than two threads of the fastener protrude through any nut. • No obstacles or protrusions project upwards from a horizontal plane extending more than 1/8" perpendicular to the plane of the initial surface. • There are no open "V" entrapment angles on any part of the equipment. See Figs. A1.3-4 in ASTM F 1487.	10 10 10	○ ○ ○	
158. Head Entrapments (CPSC 9.6, ASTM 6.1): • No components fail the entrapment test. • There are no partially bounded openings. See Figs. A1.6a-A1.10 in ASTM F 1487.	10 10	○ ○	
159. Hardware: • Nuts and bolts are tight and not able to be loosened without tools. Upon close inspection, they show no loose play or excessive wear (CPSC 8.2). • Equipment is free of rust and chipping paint (CPSC 8.1).	10 5	○ 5	Comment #20 Paint chipping on all three rocking animals.

Specific Conditions	Possible Index Points	Index Points Given	Comments

Rotating Equipment, cont.

Specific Conditions	Possible Index Points	Index Points Given	Comments
159. Hardware, cont.			
• Equipment is free of sharp edges, splinters or rough surfaces and shows no excessive wear (CPSC 9.1).	10	○	
• Ropes, chains and cables have not frayed or worn out (CPSC 7.2).	10	○	
• Equipment has not shifted or become bent (CPSC 8.1).	10	○	
• There is no corrosion or visible rotting at points where equipment comes into contact with ground surface (CPSC 7.2, 8.1).	10	○	
• No components are missing. All parts of the equipment are present and in good working order with no loose play or excessive wear in moving parts (CPSC 7.2, 8.1).	20	○	
• Handgrips are between 0.95" and 1.55" in diameter (CPSC 10.2.1).	10	10	Comment #21 All three diggers hand grips are <.95"
• Footings for equipment are stable and buried below ground level or covered by surfacing materials (CPSC 9.7).	20	○	
• Equipment is free of any litter, debris and surfacing material (ASTM 7.1.2).	20	○	
• Equipment use zone is free of litter and debris (CPSC 7.2).	10	○	
Section Subtotal	**385**	25	

Sand Play Area

Note: This section is only applicable to sand box areas designated for play. Ground level sand boxes and activity walls require a child to be at ground level. Such ground level activities are excluded from the recommendations for protective surfacing under and around playground equipment. Refer to CPSC revised handbook May, 1997.

Specific Conditions	Possible Index Points	Index Points Given	Comments
160. Sand play is located in a shaded area.	1	1	
161. The sand play area is inspected and raked at least every week for debris and to provide exposure to air and sun.	5	○	
162. If the sand play area is in a box, it is covered at night to prevent animal excrement contamination.	5	5	
163. The sand play area does not have standing water 24 hours after a rainfall.	5	○	

© NRPA/NPSI/PDRMA

Specific Conditions	Possible Index Points	Index Points Given	Comments

Sand Play Area cont.

Specific Conditions	Possible Index Points	Index Points Given	Comments
164. Elevated sand boxes have appropriate use zone with proper impact absorbing material (CPSC 4.4).	20	N/A	
165. Pinch, Crush and Shear Points (CPSC 9.5, ASTM 6.4): • Equipment is free of sharp edges. • There are no open holes in the equipment forming traps (e.g. at ends of the tubes). • There are no pinch, crush or shear points.	10 10 10	○ ○ 10	Comment #22 All 3 diggers appear to have pinch points between bucket and control arms
166. Protrusions (CPSC 9.2, ASTM 6.2): • No components fail protrusion test. • Nuts, bolts and screws are recessed, covered or sanded smooth and level.	10 10	○ ○	
167. Entanglements/Entrapment Angles (CPSC 9.4, 9.6, ASTM 6.3): • No more than two threads of the fastener protrude through any nut. • No obstacles or protrusions project upwards from a horizontal plane extending more than 1/8" perpendicular to the plane of the initial surface. • There are no open "V" entrapment angles on any part of the equipment. See Figs. A1.3-4 in ASTM F 1487.	10 10 10	○ ○ ○	
168. Head Entrapments (CPSC 9.6, ASTM 6.1): • No components fail the entrapment test. • There are no partially bounded openings. See Figs. A1.6a-A1.10 in ASTM F 1487.	10 10	○ ○	
169. Hardware: • Nuts and bolts are tight and not able to be loosened without tools. Upon close inspection, they show no loose play or excessive wear (CPSC 8.2). • Equipment is free of rust and chipping paint (CPSC 8.1). • Equipment is free of sharp edges, splinters or rough surfaces and shows no excessive wear (CPSC 9.1). • Ropes, chains and cables have not frayed or worn out (CPSC 7.2). • Equipment has not shifted or become bent (CPSC 8.1). • There is no corrosion or visible rotting at points where equipment comes into contact with ground surface (CPSC 7.2, 8.1).	10 5 10 10 10 10	○ 5 ○ ○ ○ ○	Comment #23 Hand holds and around moving parts have chipping paint and rust on all three diggers

Specific Conditions	Possible Index Points	Index Points Given	Comments

Sand Play Area, cont.

Specific Conditions	Possible Index Points	Index Points Given	Comments
169. Hardware, cont.			
• No components are missing. All parts of the equipment are present and in good working order with no loose play or excessive wear in moving parts (CPSC 7.2, 8.1).	20	○	
• Handgrips are between 0.95" and 1.55" in diameter (CPSC 10.2.1).	10	○	
• Footings for equipment are stable and buried below ground level or covered by surfacing materials (CPSC 9.7).	20	○	
• Equipment is free of any litter, debris and surfacing material (ASTM 7.1.2).	20	○	
• Equipment use zone is free of litter and debris (CPSC 7.2).	10	○	
Section Subtotal	**271**	21	

© NRPA/NPSI/PDRMA

Specific Conditions	Possible Index Points	Index Points Given	Comments

Specific Equipment Index Points Form (SEIP Form)
Equipment/Component Name: _N/A_

Specific Conditions	Possible Index Points	Index Points Given	Comments
Pinch, Crush and Shear Points (CPSC 9.5, ASTM 6.4): • Equipment is free of sharp edges. • There are no open holes in the equipment forming traps (e.g. at the ends of the tubes). • There are no pinch, crush or shear points.	10 10 10	N/A	
Protrusions (CPSC 9.2, ASTM 6.2): • No components fail protrusion test. • Nuts, bolts and screws are recessed, covered or sanded smooth and level.	10 10	N/A	
Entanglements/Entrapment Angles (CPSC 9.4, 9.6, ASTM 6.3: • No more than two threads of the fastener protrude through any nut. • No obstacles or protrusions project upwards from a horizontal plane extending more than 1/8" perpendicular to the plane of the initial surface. • There are no open "V" entrapment angles on any part of the equipment. See Figs. A1.3-4 in ASTM F 1487.	10 10 10	N/A	
Head Entrapments (CPSC 9.6, ASTM 6.1): • No components fail the entrapment test. • There are no partially bounded openings. See Figs. A1.6a-A1.10 in ASTM F 1487.	10 10	N/A	
Hardware: • Nuts and bolts are tight and not able to be loosened without tools. Upon close inspection, they show no loose play or excessive wear (CPSC 8.2). • Equipment is free of rust and chipping paint (CPSC 8.1). • Equipment is free of sharp edges, splinters or rough surfaces and shows no excessive wear (CPSC 9.1). • Ropes, chains and cables have not frayed or worn out (CPSC 7.2). • Equipment has not shifted or become bent (CPSC 8.1). • There is no corrosion or visible rotting at points where equipment comes into contact with ground surface (CPSC 7.2, 8.1).	10 5 10 10 10 10	N/A	

Specific Conditions	Possible Index Points	Index Points Given	Comments

SEIP Form, cont.

Specific Conditions	Possible Index Points	Index Points Given	Comments
Hardware, cont.			
• No components are missing. All parts of the equipment are present and in good working order with no loose play or excessive wear in moving parts (CPSC 7.2, 8.1).	20		
• Handgrips are between 0.95" and 1.55" in diameter (CPSC 10.2.1).	10	N/A	
• Footings for equipment are stable and buried below ground level or covered by surfacing materials (CPSC 9.7).	20		
• Equipment is free of any litter, debris and surfacing material (ASTM 7.1.2).	20		
• Equipment use zone is free of litter and debris (CPSC 7.2).	10		
Section Subtotal	**235**	N/A	

© NRPA/NPSI/PDRMA

Audit Summary:

Audit Section Headings	Questions	Possible Index Points	Actual Index Pts.	Index Pts. Given	Audit %Rating
Section A: General Conditions					
Playground Border Factors	3	70	70	11	
General Environment	4-14	103	103	6	
Age/Size Appropriateness Design	15-17	140	140	0	
Playground Protective Surface	18-22	150	150	25	
Use Zone	23-28	110	110	20	
Accessibility Design	29-43	171	171	41	
Section A Subtotal:		**744**	744	103	
Section B: Specific Conditions					
Slides	44-62	395	395	45	
Climbing Equipment	63-77	365	365	20	
Upper Body Climbing Equipment	78-96	390	390	10	
Stairways and Ladders	97-108	320	320	0	
Decks and Platforms	109-120	325	325	20	
Swings	121-139	422	422	0	
Rotating and Rocking Equipment	140-159	385	385	25	
Sand Play Areas	160-169	271	271	21	
Section B Subtotal:		**2873**	2873	141	

Section C: SEIP Forms **used for equipment not identified in specific conditions section**

SEIP Form _____		235*	N/A	N/A	
SEIP Form _____		235*	N/A	N/A	
SEIP Form _____		235*	N/A	N/A	
Section C Subtotal:			N/A	N/A	
Site Total: totals for sections A,B,C			3617	244	7%

*235 is the possible points for the Specific Equipment Index Points Form (SEIP Form).
Actual total may vary from playground site to playground site depending upon what type of equipment is present.

IMPORTANT

This information is for internal use only and is not to be released or otherwise diseminated to anyone other than an agency official, or designated representative.

COMMENTS SUMMARY

Auditor: Wendy Anderson / Camoron Bettin   Supervisor: Ken Kutska   Date: 2/20/98

Comment #1   (Maint.) Trim trees at least 7' above equipment and/or playground surface. Disregard upward growing branches. Concern is branches that can poke a child in the eye or that they can interact with while on the equipment.

Comment #2   (Maint.) Cut off protruding bolts and file down any rough edges. 6 benches and 9 tables had a total of 38 protruding bolts.

Comment #3   (Planning) Visibility is not as good as it could be from park road because it is in a sunken area. The fence and landscaping cuts down on visibility. Be careful locating shrubery in and around playgrounds. Don't remove anything.

Comment #4   (Maint.) Contact mft. and get more surface warning signs and put them at main access/egress points. Check installation recommendations of mft.

Comment #5   (Planning & Project) Check for 6' use zone around all diggers measure from digger bucket extended in all directions. Relocate as necessary.

Comment #6   (Planning) Accessible route from sidewalk to ramp and 5-12 year old play structure is 8%, walkway from main concrete transition platform to west walkway is 4.8%, and ramp from play deck to play deck is 8%. Check with new access board recommendations for future compliance issues. Play ramps are 12' long.

Comment #7   (Planning) This question relates to Question #114. Lower guardrail should be at a height of 24" not 19", but a handrail is required at height of 26"-28" for 2-5 year olds. Contact mft. to determine what should be done to be in compliance with ASTM and access board recommendations.

Comment #8   (Maint./Planning) It appears that our surfacing needs to be replenished at least 2"-4" to correct problems. These two station are located one in 2-5 year old play area and one in 5-12 year old play area. Adjust one sand transfer platform and step that has shifted. Step height is now 9". Two transfer platforms in play areas are triangles. They don't have 24"w x 14" deep trasition areas. Call mft. for a retrofit.

Comment #9   (Planning) Accessible route from playground entry (equip. ramp) to perimeter walkway loading to shelter with washrooms is at 7% grade without handrails. Check this against ADA access board recommendations.

Comment #10   (Maint.) Double tot slide in 2-5 year old area has exit at 14". Check surfacing. Fill in or add.

Comment #11   ((Planning/Maint.) Tot slide has gap between two single slides marking double slide. Slides are bolted together. Contact mft. to see if more bolts could be added to eliminate gap. Double slide on 5-12 year olds structure may appear to have a partially bounded opening ent., but not entanglement. There is no test for gaps or entanglement openings. only protrusions.

COMMENTS SUMMARY

Comment #12 (Planning) Two slides face west. Both are beige plastic and do not appear to absorb heat. Be aware of sun orientation when sitting slides on future playgrounds.

Comment #13 (Maint.) Contact mft. for replacements of rusted bolt/screw hardware on tunnel slide and tot double slide.

Comment #14 (Maint.) Grind smooth rough edges on concrete tunnel

Comment #15 (Inspector) Watch for wear on cargo net rubber coating and chain links. Order replacement part when it becomes a pinch concern or when chain shows wear.

Comment #16 (Planning/Maint.) Horizontal rungs first rung is 12" from loading edge of deck. Should be 10" - 8". Check with mft. on compliance with ASTM & CPSC.

Comment #17 (Planning) See Comment #7 or Question #34

Comment #18 (Planning) Check with mft. on guardrail/handrail compliance to CPSC/ASTM of components to be grabbed for balance between .95" - 1.55"

Comment #19 (Planning) Replace three old rocking animals with spring riders that have flat seats with back support in next years budget if funds are available.

Comment #20 (Maint.) Don't paint rockers. We will replace in next years budget. Talk to planning. Paint only if absolutely necessary.

Comment #21 (Planning) Check with back hoe digger mft. as to compliance of hand old controls which measure <95".

Comment #22 (Planning) Check with digger mft. on pinch point compliance at juncture of digging bucket and control arms.

Comment #23 (Maint.) Paint diggers as needed to control chipping paint and rust.

PLAYGROUND AUDIT SCORE SUMMARY FORM FOR ALL AGENCY SITES

Scores by Section for Each Playground Site

Audit Section Heading	Possible Index Points	Northside Park					
SECTION A: GENERAL CONDITIONS							
Playground Border Factors	70	11					
General Environment	103	6					
Age/Size Appropriate Design	140	0					
Playground Protective Surfacing	150	25					
Use Zone	110	20					
Accessibility Design	171	41					
SECTION A SUBTOTAL	**744**	103					
SECTION B: SPECIFIC CONDITIONS							
Slides	395	45					
Climbing Equipment	365	20					
Upper Body Climbing Equipment	390	10					
Stairways and Ladders	320	0					
Decks and Platforms	325	20					
Swings	422	0					
Rotating and Rocking Equipment	385	25					
Sand Play Areas	271	21					
SECTION B SUBTOTAL	**2873**	141					
SECTION C: SEIP FORMS							
SEIP Form _____	235*	0					
SEIP Form _____	235*	0					
SEIP Form _____	235*	0					
SECTION C SUBTOTAL		0					
Site Total: totals for Sections A, B, & C	4087*	244					
Index Points Given							
Acutal Index Points							
Index % Rating							

*235 is the possible points for the Specific Equipment Index Points Form (SEIP Form).
Actual total may vary from playground site to playground site depending upon what type of equipment is present.

IMPORTANT: This information is for internal use only and is not to be released or otherwise disseminated to anyone other than an agency official, or designated representative.

© NRPA/NPSI/PDRMA

Inspection Frequency Form

Playground Name/ID Number __Northside #26__ Form Completed By _____ Date __12/94__

The following guide weighs the most common use, materials, and environmental factors that will influence your playground inspection scheduling. Each factor has been weighted as to its importance and influence on the schedule. Put one of the factor numbers in the right hand column that best describes the conditions at the playground site.

Factors	Possible Points	Points Given
A. Use Factors		
1. Vandalism (Misuse/Abuse)		
High	10	
Moderate	5	5
Low	2	
2. Use Level (Community Use, Litter, Etc.)		
High	10	10
Moderate	5	
Low	2	
3. Age Design		
Preschool age (2-5 years)	2	2
School age (6-12 years)	4	4
All ages (2-12 years)	10	
Use Factors Total	30	21
B. Materials		
1. Resilient Surfacing		
Loose Materials	12	12
Synthetic Material	2	
2. Material (Major Components)		
Wood, Painted Steel	4	
Stabilized Plastics, Aluminum, Gal.Steel	2	2
Stainless Steel	0	
3. Equipment		
Moving (swing, spin around, spring rider, etc.)	6	
Static (Non-moving climbers)	2	
Both	6	6

© NRPA/NPSI/PDRMA

Factors	Possible Points	Points Given
4. Age of Equipment		
1-2 years old	0	
3-4 years old	3	3
5-9 years old	6	
10-14 years old	9	
15 years old and over	12	
Materials Factors Total	34	23
C. Environmental Factors		
1. Acid Soils/Rain/PH		
None (6-9)	0	0
Moderate (10, 11, 4, 5)	4	
High (Acid 1-3, Basic 12-14)	8	
2. Salt Air (Coastal Exposure)		
None	0	0
Moderate	4	
High	8	
3. Sun Exposure		
None	0	
Moderate	4	4
High	8	
4. Drainage		
Functioning underground drainage system	0	0
Moist Surface	4	
Seasonal Flooding	8	
Routine Standing Water	12	
Environmental Factors Total	36	4
Total Points for Site	**100**	48

IMPORTANT This information has been prepared to assist the Playground owners attorney in defending potential litigation. **Do not** release to any person except an agency official or designated claim representative or an investigating police officer.

Inspection Frequency Summary Form for all Agency Sites

Key to Inspection Frequency Chart		
Points	**High Frequency Inspections**	**Low Frequency Inspections**
71 or more	2 or more times per week	2-3 times per month
56-70	Weekly	Monthly
41-55	Biweekly	Bimonthly
40 & Below	Monthly	Seasonal

Once the inspection frequency form has been completed for each playground site, the results can be transferred to the blank inspection frequency summary form (Appendix A) so that all of your sites can be evaluated collectively. The total points for each site can then be compared to the key to inspection frequency chart (above) which will assist you in determining your most appropriate high and low frequency inspection schedule.

Local conditions may include other factors and in some cases affect seasonal adjustments to the schedule. Experience is your best guide.

Frequency of Inspection Summary Form (Sample)

Playground Site Name	Factors Evaluated					
	Use Factors	**Material**	**Environ-mental**	**Points Given**	**High Freq. Inspection**	**Low Freq. Inspection**
1. Northside 1995	21	23	4	48	Biweekly	Bimonthly
2. Presidents 1990	18	18	4	40	Monthly	Seasonal
3. Washington 1985	21	28	4	53	Biweekly	Bimonthly
4. Tasha 1980	24	31	6	61	Weekly	Monthly
5. Grant 1990	18	20	4	42	Biweekly	Bimonthly
6.						
7.						
8.						
9.						
10.						

1992 by NRPA

HIGH FREQUENCY INSPECTION FORM

Site Name/ID Number: **Northside Cove #26**

Inspector Name: **Dave Scarmardo**   Date: **2-23-98**   Start/Finish Times: **9:15 am 10:15 am**
Paul Pitts

Repairer name: _____ Date: _____ Start/Finish Times: _____

Use the following codes: 1 = Okay 2 = Needs Maintenance 3 = Request for Repair O = Supervisor notified and work order written   X = Corrective Action Complete

GENERAL INSPECTION ITEMS	CODE	INSPECTION COMMENTS	REPAIR COMMENTS
Vandalism: damage, graffiti, glass, trash, needles, etc.	X	Broken glass in chips	removed broken glass.
Loose or missing hardware	1		
Chains (kinked, twisted, broken)	X	Chain twisted on bucket seat.	untwisted chain
Guardrails/handrails secure	1		
Seats (cut, cracked, missing)	1		
Wood (rotten, cracked, missing)	1		
Remove foreign objects (ropes, chains, wood, etc.)	X	Sticks on chip surface	removed sticks
Sweep walkways, platforms, steps	X	Debris	Blew off all paths + walks
Footers (concrete) exposed	1		
Standing water	1		
Objects in surfacing material	1		
Rake level surfacing material	X	Low areas	filled in low areas with surfacing materials
Playground signage	1		
Need surfacing material for:	1		

FOR OFFICE USE ONLY
Reviewed by Assistant Superintendent of Parks **2/24/98**
(date)
Terry Parmenter (signature)

Reviewed by Superintendent of Parks and Planning **3/8/98**
(date)
Kenneth J. Hetzko (signature)

USE BACK OF FORM FOR ADDITIONAL COMMENTS
REPORT ALL VANDALISM TO ASST. SUPERINTENDENT OF PARKS OR YOUR MAINTENANCE SUPERVISOR

This form has been prepared to assist the District Attorney in defending potential litigation. DO NOT release to any person except an agency official, designated claim representative, or an investigating officer.

© NRPA/NPSI/PDRMA

ITEMIZED LIST
OF PLAY EQUIPMENT

DATE _____

INSPECTOR _____

EQUIPMENT LOCATION ___ **Northside Park** ___

PLAY EQUIPMENT AREA	PLAY COMPONENT	DESCRIPTION OF PLAY AREA OR COMPONENT	COMMENTS
Area A	Play	Play/Picnic Area	Iron Mountain Forge
		Timber Border Wood Surface	
	1	8' Steel Ramp with Safety Rails	Safety Rails & Curbs
	1	12' Steel Ramp with Barriers	
	7	Square Vinyl Clad Steel Decks	
	3	Triangular Vinyl Clad Steel Decks	
	2	Half Hex Punched Steel Decks	
	8	14' Post with Cap	
	7	12' Post with Cap	
	2	10' Post with Cap	
	4	8' Post with Cap	
	2	5' Post with Cap	
	1	360˚ Spiral Slide	
	1	Inverted Arch Climber	
	1	Step Ladder F/48" Deck	
	1	Step Ladder F/64" Deck	
	1	Tic-Tac-Toe Panel	
	1	Animal Panel	
	1	Triangular Transfer Station	
	1	20" Deck to Deck Step	
	1	Transfer Step	
	2	Polyethylene Safety Panels	
	1	Inter Deck Step	
	1	8" Deck Enclosure	
	1	Spelling Panel	
	1	Math Panel	

ITEMIZED LIST
OF PLAY EQUIPMENT

DATE _____

INSPECTOR _____

EQUIPMENT LOCATION ____ **Northside Park**

PLAY EQUIPMENT AREA	PLAY COMPONENT	DESCRIPTION OF PLAY AREA OR COMPONENT	COMMENTS
Area A (Cont.)	1	Double-wide Slide	
	1	"S" Pipe Climber	
	1	Steering Wheel	
	1	Elbow Tunnel Slide	
	1	Curly Climber	
	Entrance		
	2	9-Bar Safety Rails	
	1	Entrance Plate	
	100 LF	Railing Green	
	2	Concrete Ramps	
	3	Concrete Landings	
	110 LF	Diamond Block Retaining Wall	
		Safety Surface	
	1	Duck Spring Animal	
	1	Pelican Spring Animal	
	1	Frog Spring Animal	
	1	Access Ramp (NW Corner)	
	2	Playground Rules Signs	
	Picnic		
	6	Picnic Table 8' Long	
	5	Dumor Benches	
	4	Trash Cans	
	2	Planter Boxes Around Trees	

© NRPA/NPSI/PDRMA

ITEMIZED LIST OF PLAY EQUIPMENT

DATE _____

INSPECTOR _____

EQUIPMENT LOCATION ___<u>Northside Park</u>___

PLAY EQUIPMENT AREA	PLAY COMPONENT	DESCRIPTION OF PLAY AREA OR COMPONENT	COMMENTS
Area B	Swing Area		
		Timber Curb Border	
		Sand Base/Mulch Base	
	1	2-Bay 4-Seat Swing	2 Tot, 2 Belt
	3	Picnic Tables 8' Regular	
	2	Trash Cans	
	1	Dumor Bench	
	1	Planter Area	
Area C	Shelter Area		
	1	Shelter, Check Shingles	Vandalism
		Concrete Floor	Cracks Trip Hazards
			Clean
	5	Regular 8' Picnic Tables	In Shelter
	5	Accessive Picnic Tables	In Shelter
	4	Regular 8' Picnic Tables	By Sand Play Area
	4	Benches	
		Concrete Walk Crack & Trip Hazards	
	3	Trash Cans	
Area D	Water Play Area		
	1	Water Play Feature	
		Timber Border Sand Base	
	1	Drinking Fountain MDF	
	2	Planting Bed Areas	

© NRPA/NPSI/PDRMA

ITEMIZED LIST
OF PLAY EQUIPMENT

DATE _____

INSPECTOR _____

EQUIPMENT LOCATION ___ **Northside Park**

PLAY EQUIPMENT AREA	PLAY COMPONENT	DESCRIPTION AREA OR COMPONENT	COMMENTS
Area D	Water Play Area		
	1	Water Play Feature	
		Timber Border Sand Base	
	1	Drinking Fountain MDF	
	2	Planting Bed Areas	
Area E	Play Area 1		
		Iron Mountain Forge Play Structure	
		90˚ Crawl Tunnel	
		Arch Climber	
		Clatter Bridge	
		Chain Net Climber	
		Double-wide Wave Slide	
		Curly Climber	
		Steering Wheel	
		Pipe Climber	
		Sliding Pole	
		11'- 0 Double-wide Slide	
		Timber Border Sand Base	
			.
Area F	Play Area 2	Iron Mountain Forge Structure	
	1	Track Ride	
	1	Challenge Ladder	
	1	Burma Bridge	
		Timber Border Sand Base	
		Concrete Walk	

© NRPA/NPSI/PDRMA

ITEMIZED LIST
OF PLAY EQUIPMENT

DATE _____

INSPECTOR _____

EQUIPMENT LOCATION ___Northside Park___

PLAY EQUIPMENT AREA	PLAY COMPONENT	DESCRIPTION OF PLAY AREA OR COMPONENT	COMMENTS
Area G	Sand Play Area		
		Timber Border Sand Base	
	3	Backhoe Diggers	
	1	Crawl Tunnel	
	1	Dumor Bench	
	1	Sand Pile	
	4	Transfer Benches Trex Lumber	

© NRPA/NPSI/PDRMA

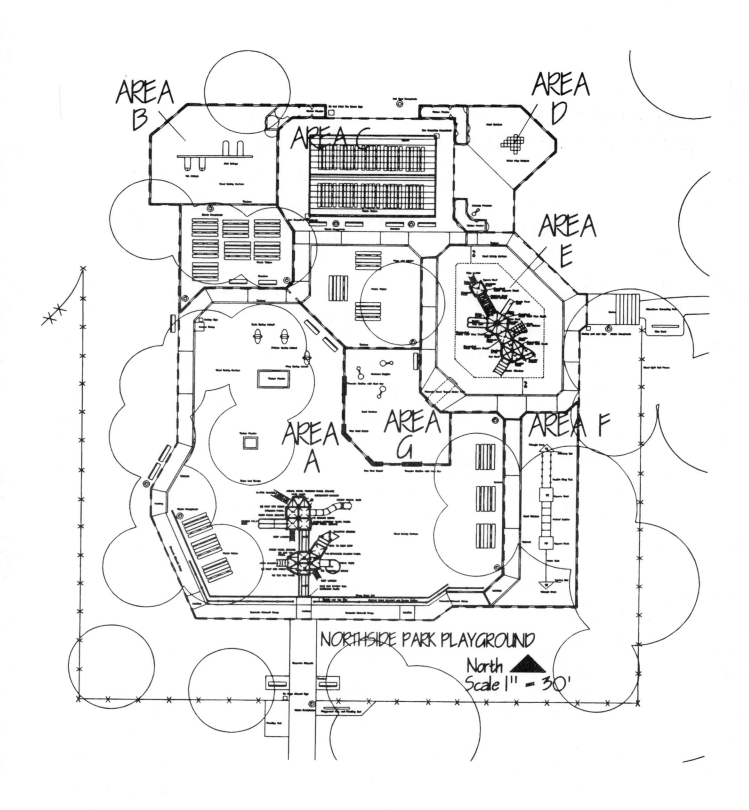

AREA B

AREA D

AREA C

AREA E

AREA A

AREA G

AREA F

NORTHSIDE PARK PLAYGROUND

North
Scale 1" = 30'

© NRPA/NPSI/PDRMA

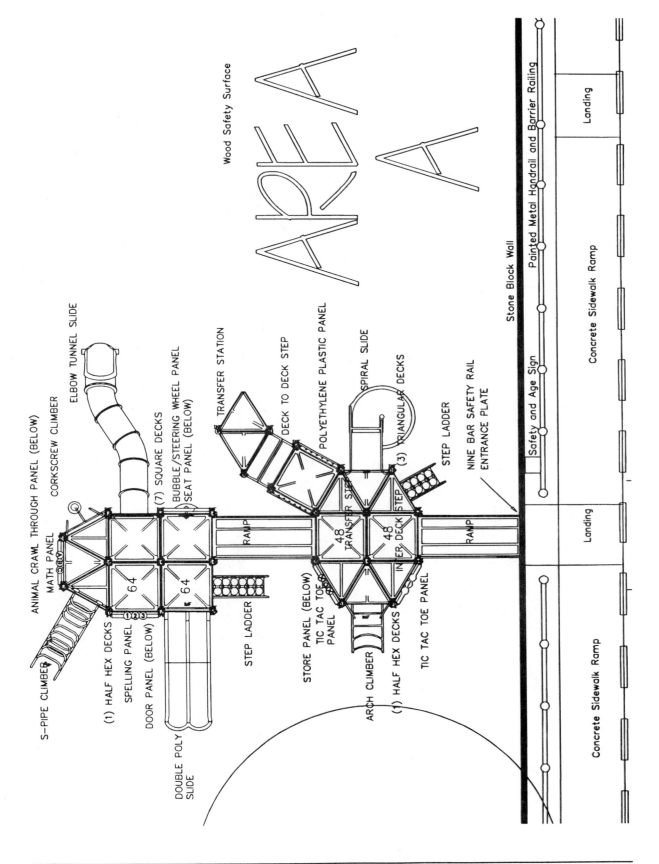

AREA

Wood Safety Surface

S-PIPE CLIMBER
ANIMAL CRAWL THROUGH PANEL (BELOW)
MATH PANEL
CORKSCREW CLIMBER
ELBOW TUNNEL SLIDE

(1) HALF HEX DECKS
SPELLING PANEL
DOOR PANEL (BELOW)
(7) SQUARE DECKS
BUBBLE/STEERING WHEEL PANEL
SEAT PANEL (BELOW)

DOUBLE POLY SLIDE

64
64

TRANSFER STATION
DECK TO DECK STEP
POLYETHYLENE PLASTIC PANEL
SPIRAL SLIDE
TRIANGULAR DECKS
(3)

RAMP
STEP LADDER

STORE PANEL (BELOW)
TIC TAC TOE PANEL

48
TRANSFER STEP

48
INNER DECK STEP

STEP LADDER

NINE BAR SAFETY RAIL
ENTRANCE PLATE

ARCH CLIMBER
(1) HALF HEX DECKS
TIC TAC TOE PANEL

RAMP

Stone Block Wall

Painted Metal Handrail and Barrier Railing

Safety and Age Sign
Concrete Sidewalk Ramp

Landing

Landing

Concrete Sidewalk Ramp
Concrete Sidewalk Ramp

© NRPA/NPSI/PDRMA

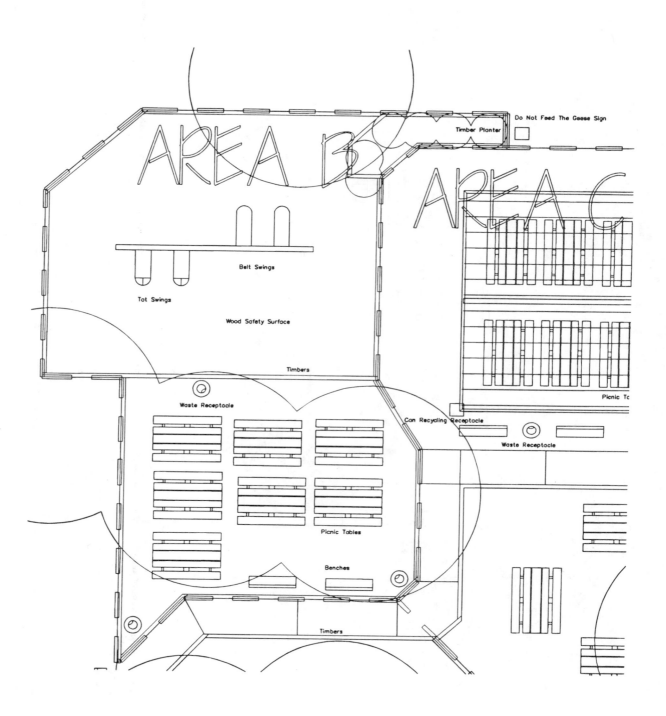

AREA B

AREA C

Do Not Feed The Geese Sign

Timber Planter

Belt Swings

Tot Swings

Wood Safety Surface

Timbers

Waste Receptacle

Can Recycling Receptacle

Picnic Tables

Waste Receptacle

Picnic Tables

Benches

Timbers

© NRPA/NPSI/PDRMA

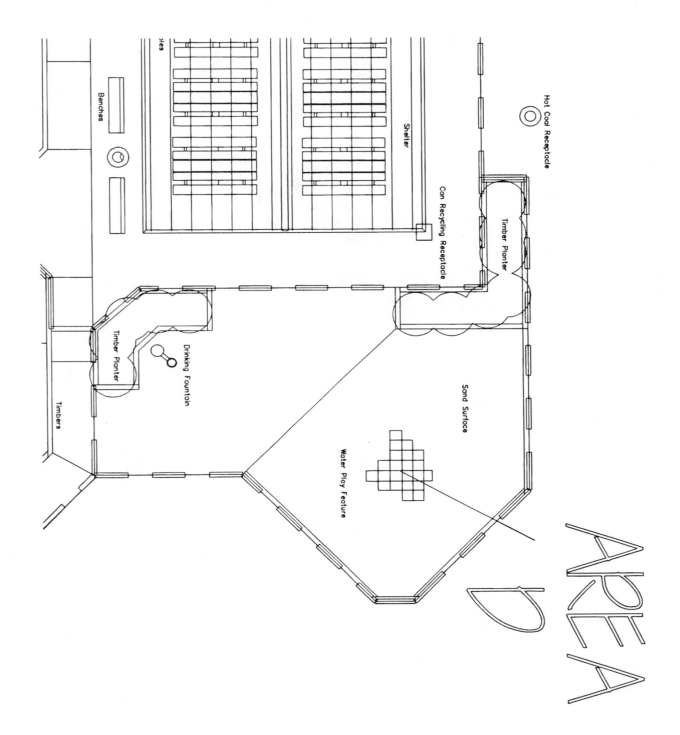

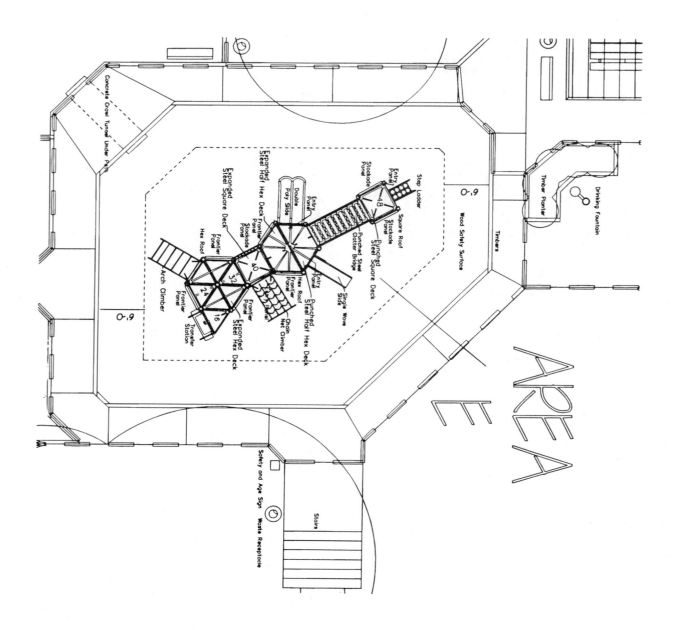

Concrete Crawl Tunnel Under Path

Expanded Steel Square Deck

Expanded Steel Half Hex Deck

Entry Panel

Stockade Panel

Square Roof Stockade Panel

Step Ladder

Double Play Slide

Entry Panel

Frontier Panel

Stockade Panel

Hex Roof

Frontier Panel

Punched Steel Clatter Bridge

Punched Steel Square Deck

0.9

Wood Safety Surface

Timbers

Timber Planter

Drinking Fountain

40

32

24

16

Arch Climber

Frontier Panel

Transfer Station

Frontier Panel

Expanded Steel Hex Deck

Frontier Panel

Chain Net Climber

Single Wave

Hex Roof

Entry Panel

Punched Steel Half Hex Deck

0.9

AREA

AREA

Safety and Age Sign

Waste Receptacle

Stairs

© NRPA/NPSI/PDRMA

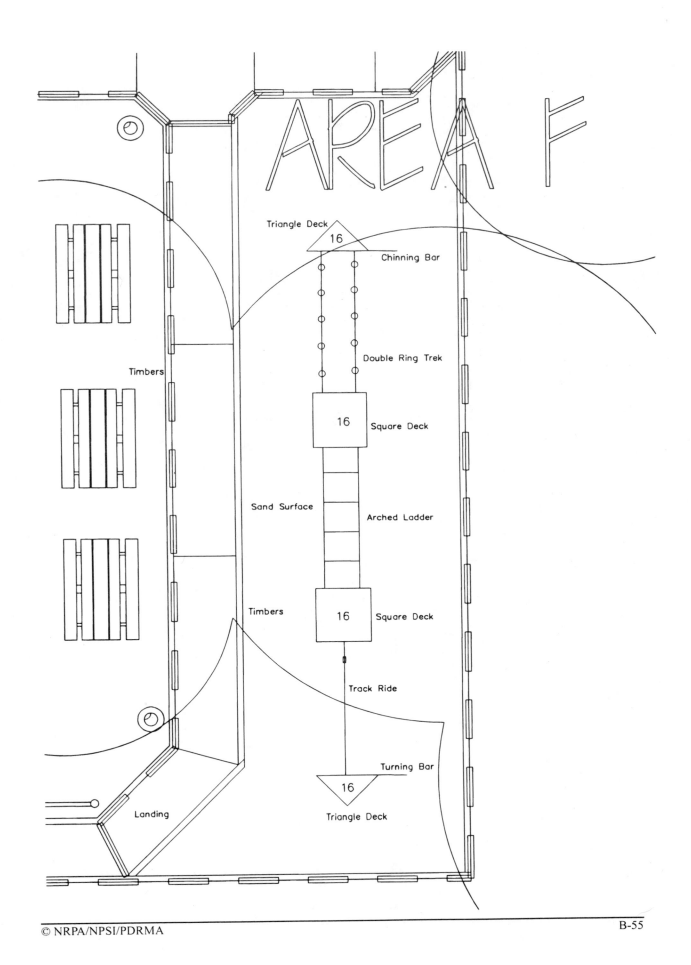

AREA F

Triangle Deck

16

Chinning Bar

Double Ring Trek

Timbers

16   Square Deck

Sand Surface

Arched Ladder

Timbers

16   Square Deck

Track Ride

Turning Bar

16

Triangle Deck

Landing

© NRPA/NPSI/PDRMA

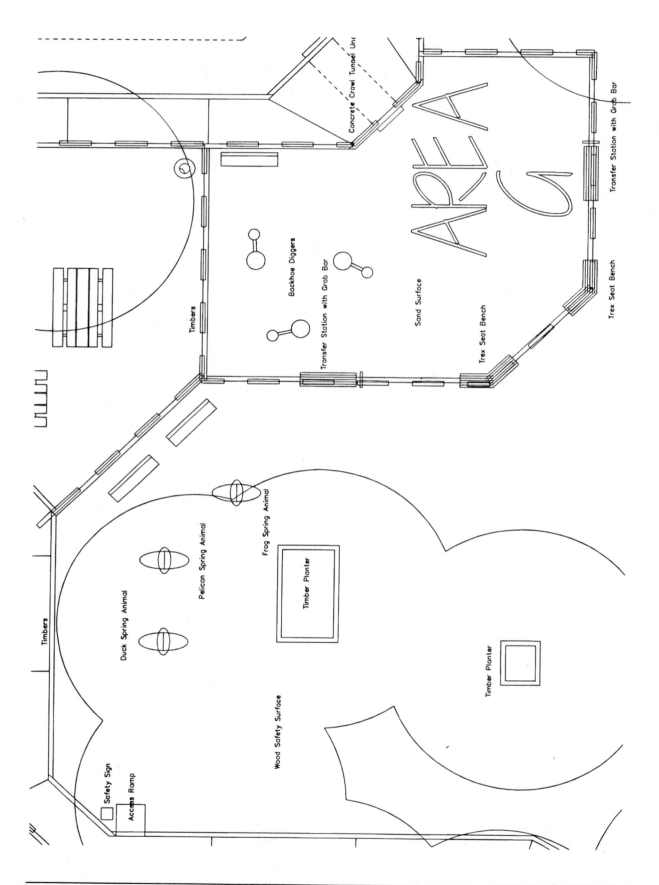

Concrete Crawl Tunnel Und

Transfer Station with Grab Bar

Trex Seat Bench

Backhoe Diggers

Transfer Station with Grab Bar

Sand Surface

Trex Seat Bench

Timbers

AREA 5

Frog Spring Animal

Pelican Spring Animal

Duck Spring Animal

Timber Planter

Timber Planter

Wood Safety Surface

Timbers

Safety Sign

Access Ramp

© NRPA/NPSI/PDRMA

LOW FREQUENCY SITE PLAN PLAYGROUND INSPECTION

Site Name/ID Number: **Northside Playground (026)**

Inspector Name: Dave Scarmardo _____ Date: 2-18-98 ____ Start/Finish Times: 7:45 am | 10:00 am
Paul Pitts

Repairer name: _____ Date: _____ Start/Finish Times: _____ | _____

Use the following codes: 1 = Okay   2 = Needs Maintenance   3 = Request for Repair
O = Supervisor notified and work order written   X = Corrective Action Complete

Area	#	Play Component	Code	Problem (if any)	Action Taken
A		**Play/Picnic Area**	X	Leaves, garbage + A broken tree branch	removed all debris from area
		Timber border/wood surface	X	Leaves, depressions in wood Surface	removed leaves, Raked Level wood chips.
	(1)	8' Steel ramp with safety rails	1		
	(1)	12' Steel ramp with barriers	1		
	(7)	Square vinyl clad steel decks	1		
	(3)	Triangular vinyl clad steel decks	1		
	(2)	Half hex punched steel decks	1		
	(8)	14' Post with cap	1		
	(7)	12' Post with cap	1		
	(2)	10' Post with cap	1		
	(4)	8' Post with cap	1		
	(2)	5' Post with cap	1		
	(1)	360 spiral slide	X	Goose manure inside slide entrance	removed manure + rinsed out slide entrance
	(1)	Inverted arch climber	1		

LOW FREQUENCY SITE PLAN PLAYGROUND INSPECTION - NORTHSIDE

Use the following codes: 1 = Okay   2 = Needs Maintenance   3 = Request for Repair
O = Supervisor notified and work order written   X = Corrective Action Complete

Area	#	Play Component	Code	Problem (if any)	Action Taken
A	(2)	9-bar safety rails	1		
	(1)	Entrance plate	1		
		110' diamond block retaining wall	1		
		Safety surface	X	Sticks, garbage, Leaves, Low areas	Removed all debris. Raked Level Low areas.
	(1)	Duck spring animal	X	Concrete footing exposed	Covered concrete with wood chips
	(1)	Pelican spring animal	1		
	(1)	Frog spring animal	X	Concrete Footing exposed	Covered Concrete with wood chips
	(1)	Access ramp (NW corner)	X	Goose manure on ramp.	removed manure
	(2)	"Playground Rules" signs	X	missing "No Dogs Allowed" Sign	Installed sign at entrance to playground.
	(6)	Picnic tables 8' long	1		
	(5)	Dumor Benches	1		
	(4)	Trash cans	X	Concrete container was Knocked over.	uprighted + releveled container.
	(2)	Planter boxes around trees	1		
B		**Swing Area**	1		
		Timber curb border	1		
		Sand base/Mulch base	X	Leaves, Sticks, garbage, Low areas	removed debris, raked Sand level
	(1)	2-bay 4-seat swing	1		

© NRPA/NPSI/PDRMA

LOW FREQUENCY SITE PLAN PLAYGROUND INSPECTION - NORTHSIDE

Use the following codes: 1 = Okay   2 = Needs Maintenance   3 = Request for Repair
O = Supervisor notified and work order written   X = Corrective Action Complete

Area	#	Play Component	Code	Problem (if any)	Action Taken
B	(3)	Picnic tables 8' regular	1		
	(2)	Trash receptacles	1		
	(1)	Dumor bench	1		
		Planter area	X	Timber rotten	replaced small top row timber.
C		**Shelter Area**	1		
	(1)	Shelter, check shingles	Ⓧ	Several leakes in roof.	Contracted with roofer. T.T. 4/24/90
		Concrete floor	X	Debris	blew off concrete floor.
	(9)	Regular 8' picnic tables	X	Anchors holding tables were missing	replaced 3 anchors
	(5)	Accessible picnic tables	1		
	(4)	Benches	1		
		Concrete walk; crack & trip hazards	X	Leaves	blew off walks + removed leaves
	(3)	Trash receptacles	1		
D		**Water play area**	X	Leaves, sticks, garbage	removed all debris
		Water play feature	Ⓧ	Closed for the season	
		Timber border sand base	1		
	(1)	Drinking fountain MDF	1	Closed for the season.	
	(2)	Planting bed areas	1		

LOW FREQUENCY SITE PLAN PLAYGROUND INSPECTION - NORTHSIDE

Use the following codes: 1 = Okay   2 = Needs Maintenance   3 = Request for Repair
O = Supervisor notified and work order written   X = Corrective Action Complete

Area	#	Play Component	Code	Problem (if any)	Action Taken
E		Play Area, Tot Lot	1		
		Iron Mountain Forge Play Str.	1		
	10	12' - 4" posts with caps (8 with extensions)	1		
	(7)	11' - 4" posts with caps	1		
	(1)	8' - 0" posts with caps	1		
	(1)	Expanded Steel half hex deck	1		
	(2)	Punched steel half hex deck	1		
	(1)	Punched steel square deck	1		
	(2)	Hex roofs	1		
	(1)	Square roof	1		
	(1)	Transfer station	1		
	(1)	Step Ladder	1		
	(5)	Frontier window panels	1		
	(3)	Frontier stockade panels	1		
	(1)	Frontier rustic entry panel	1		
	(1)	Single wave slide	1		
	(1)	8' Clatter bridge	1		

© NRPA/NPSI/PDRMA

LOW FREQUENCY SITE PLAN PLAYGROUND INSPECTION - NORTHSIDE

Use the following codes: 1 = Okay   2 = Needs Maintenance   3 = Request for Repair
O = Supervisor notified and work order written   X = Corrective Action Complete

Area	#	Play Component	Code	Problem (if any)	Action Taken
E	(1)	Double poly slide	I		
	(1)	Chain net climber	I	Coating on Chain showing wear. Safe at this time.	
	(1)	Arch climber	I		
		Timber border	I		
		Wood safety surface	X	Low areas	raked level
		Concrete walk	X	Debris on walk	Blew off walk
F		Play Area	I		
		Iron Mtn. Forge Play Structure	I		
	(1)	Track ride	I		
	(1)	Challenge ladder	I		
	(1)	Burma bridge	I		
		Timber border	I		
		Sand base	X	Leaves, rocks, tree branches	removed all debris
		Concrete walk	X	Leaves	blew off walk
G		Sand Play Area	I		
		Timber border	I		
		Sand base	I		

© NRPA/NPSI/PDRMA

LOW FREQUENCY SITE PLAN PLAYGROUND INSPECTION - NORTHSIDE

Use the following codes: 1 = Okay   2 = Needs Maintenance   3 = Request for Repair
O = Supervisor notified and work order written   X = Corrective Action Complete

Area	#	Play Component	Code	Problem (if any)	Action Taken
G	(3)	Sand Play Area	X	Leaves, Low areas	removed leaves raked level low areas
		Timber border sand base	1		
	(3)	Backhoe diggers	1		
	(1)	Crawl tunnel	1		
	(1)	Dumor bench	X	missing carriage bolts	replaced 2 carriage bolts + Nuts
	(1)	Sand pile	1		
	(4)	Transfer benches trex lumber	1		
	(2)	Grab bars	1		
		Playground signage	1		
		Playground Regulatory Sign (In park, North side of first circle)	1		

Directions:
1. List each piece of playground equipment in the "Play Components" column.
2. As each component is inspected indicate the appropriate codes in the Code column.
3. Describe the nature of any maintenance or follow-up repairs.
4. File each inspection report with your permanent records.

Work Order Numbers (list all that apply): _____

Supervisor: _Terry Turnquist_   Signature: _Kenneth S. Katsten_   Date: _2/20/98_

_2/24/98_

This form has been prepared to assist the District Attorney in defending potential litigation. *DO NOT* release to any person except an agency official, designated claim representative, or an investigating officer.

© NRPA/NPSI/PDRMA

WHEATON PARK DISTRICT PARKS AND PLANNING DEPARTMENT
PUBLIC PLAYGROUND COMMITTEE ANNUAL SAFETY/REVIEW MEETING
CENTRAL ADMINISTRATION BUILDING, JANUARY 21, 1997

I. CALL TO ORDER
Meeting called to order at 1:00 p.m.
Those attending: Ken Kutska, Dave Scarmardo, Paul Stanczak,
Beth Gravengood, Jerry Culp,Cameron Bettin,
Larry Bower, and Terry Turnquist

II. APPROVAL OF THE MINUTES
Motion to approve minutes of the January 9, 1996 meeting was moved by Cameron Bettin
and second by Terry Turnquist.
The minutes were approved by the whole committee.

III. OLD BUSINESS
Review of the 1996 projects and annual meeting minutes.

*Asphalt paths at Brighton, Scottdale and Briarknoll need repair.
- The paths at Brighton were completed.
- Scottdale's paths will be budgeted in 1997/98 fiscal year to be resurfaced.
  **Dave commented that the main pathway the porta-let company uses to get to
  the port-a-potty's location should be wider to accommodate trucks.**
- The paths at Briarknoll were completed.

*Purchase replacements for Northside's spring animal and tire swing.
- This has not been done. **If there is money in the 96/97 budget Jerry should order
  and get the equipment delivered before spring. If not, they should be
  purchased in 97/98.**

*Presidents Park playground replacement.
- The equipment is installed.
- **Jerry has a contractor to asphalt pave the walk when the weather clears.**
- _**Maintenance staff needs to round off/chamfer the corners of the concrete curbs.**_

*Sunnyside playground perennials to be ordered and planted.
- Hostas from Hurley Gardens and vinca from Seven Gables were transplanted at
  Sunnyside. Dead plant material was also removed.

*Replace Scottdale's worn wood decks.
- The decks are in decent shape so replacement can hold off until the playground is
  renovated in 1999. **In the mean time, for reference and if it is decided that
  replacing the decks is a better option than replacing everything,
  Cameron will talk to Jack Gleason of NuToys (rep for Landscape Structures)
  to see if recycled trex can be used on the decks, and if Landscape Structures
  will back it liability wise.**

OLD BUSINESS (cont.)

- *The Parks Department should schedule this as a maintenance repair when wood play surface is delivered.*
- *Maintenance is also to check the use zones of the totswing area.* The use zone is two times the height of the pivot to the bottom of the bucket.

* Need to replace timber steps to tot play area at Scottdale.
This was completed.

* Replace or repair panels at Community Center playground.
- *Maintenance staff replaced some that were bad, and flipped those that could. There are some gaps yet to fill.*

* Need to find replacement rope climber for Kelly playground.
- *The rope is in and will be installed by maintenance staff when the weather permits.*

* Replace sand playgrounds with wood mulch surface.
- *Maintenance is to do the tot lot area at Kelly playground first then another area of Kelly the following year and so forth. If maintenance can obtain the appropriate safety distance, timbers should be installed between the back hoes and tot structure in order to create a sand area that will remain after all the areas are wood mulched.*

* Check the drain at Kelly and replace if necessary.
This was completed.

* Purchase panels for under decks at Rathje and Northside.
This was completed.

* Write letter to Briarcliffe homeowners association about problems with playground at Hull Park. Surveys were sent to the residents near Hull Park and the responses were considered in the design. **Cameron is to get copies of all playground survey results to Terry so he can keep them in the master files.** Playgrounds surveyed were Herrick, Presidents, Prairie Path and Hull. A discussion on the water and heaving problem took place. Terry feels that the new equipment will heave as well. Dave mentioned that water seems to accumulate the most in the west side of the playground (southwest and south east corners being the most wet). There was further discussion on the installation of draintiles and french drainholes. The existing catch basin on the south side is part of the existing draintile system, and is not tied into the city storm sewer system. **Cameron will look into this while finishing the construction drawings.**

* Removal of the willow tree at Briarknoll that is destroying the walk.
- *Maintenance will remove the tree this winter, grind the stump and spray with Round Up.*

Reminder
**When tilling sand playgrounds do not till to deep and bring up soil.*

© NRPA/NPSI/PDRMA

* Transfer stations should be within 6-8" of both the bench and sand on the play
  surface side and 14" on the chair side.
  - **Cameron will get detailed construction drawings of transfer steps made of
    concrete and trex to the Maintenance Department.**
  - *Maintenance will construct concrete transfer steps at Atten and
    Sunnyside, and if need be, trex transfer steps at Briarpatch and Sunny side.*

* **Keep sand tunnel at Northside playground clear.**

* Pay attention to use zones on spring animals when designing play areas. Some
  spring animals are longer than others and require more than 6' from the center of
  the equipment. *The 6' safety distance should be measured from the ends and
  side of the equipment.*

* Check backhoe diggers use zones. When the bucket is extended while in use it is
  longer than when not in use, therefore the 6' use zone does not meet guidelines. This
  is a similar situation as the spring animals. **The use zone should probably be measured 6' from the extended backhoe.**
  - **Cameron is to check with Jack Gleason of NuToys on what Landscape
    Structures is requiring as the use zone.**

* Rathje playground grant reimbursement forms need to be sent into the state for the
  UPPY surface.
  - This was completed and the money has been sent back to us.

* *Check Rathje playsurface for cuts and burns during all high and low frequency
  playground safety inspections.*
  - Dave commented that it takes around two hours to complete large repairs, espe-
    cially when it is around equipment, and it takes 30 to 45 minutes for small
    repairs.

* Yellow playground caution street signs should be put on inspection forms.
  - This was completed.

* *Staff was reminded to fill out inspection forms completely including information
  such as time-in, time-out, who inspected, who repaired, what was done, etc.*

IV. **NEW BUSINESS**
Review progress of playgrounds

* Finish Presidents park playground.
  - *Maintenance is to round/chamfer edges of concrete curb.*
  - **Jerry's contractor is to asphalt pave the walk when weather permits.**
  - Gametime is hiring a contractor to replace the panels that were incorrect.

* Finish Prairie Path
    - 75% completed.
    - _**Work yet to be completed by the Parks Department is grading, installing the swing set and surfacing, and landscaping.**_

* Start Hull when weather permits.

Playgrounds to be replaced in 1997/98.
    * Brighton
        - Include a shelter similar to Kelly's.

    * Central
        - Look into incorporating an area by the volleyball courts for the 10-15 year old age group using 10 Plus equipment and gathering areas.
        - There was concern by the committee in having equipment for   this age group next to a tot play area. It would possibly create a higher safety risk to younger children that are not watched by their guardians. **It will be looked into further as the design of the site progresses.**
        - There was discussion regarding Central's park category.
          Is it a neighborhood or community park? No consensus was reached.
    * Surveys need to be sent out for both Brighton and Central.

V.   ADJOURNMENT
Meeting adjourned at 2:50 p.m.

SUMMARY OF MAINTENANCE ITEMS TO COMPLETE

*Presidents Park playground replacement.
    - _**Maintenance staff needs to round off/chamfer the corners of the concrete curbs.**_
*Need to replace sand play surface with wood mulch surface at Scottdale in tot swing area.
    -_**The Parks Department should schedule this as a maintenance repair when wood play surface is delivered.**_
    -_**Maintenance is also to check the use zones of the totswing area.**_ The use zone is two times the height of the pivot to the bottom of the bucket.

*Replace or repair panels at Community Center playground.
    - _**Maintenance staff replaced some that were bad, and flipped those that could. There are some gaps yet to fill.**_

*Need to find replacement rope climber for Kelly playground.
    - _**The rope is in and will be installed by maintenance staff when the weather permits.**_

*Replace sand playgrounds with wood mulch surface.
    - _**Maintenance is to do the tot lot area at Kelly playground first then another area of Kelly the following year and so forth. If maintenance can obtain the appropriate safety distance, timbers should be installed between the backhoes and tot structure in order to create a sand area that will remain after all the areas are wood mulched.**_

SUMMARY OF MAINTENANCE ITEMS TO COMPLETE CONT'D

* Removal of the willow tree at Briarknoll that is destroying the walk.
  - *Maintenance will remove the tree this winter, grind the stump and spray with Round Up.*

* *When tilling sand playgrounds do not till to deep and bring up soil.*

* Transfer stations should be within 6-8" of both the bench and sand on the play surface side and 14" on the chair side.
  - *Maintenance will construct concrete transfer steps at Atten and Sunnyside, and if need be, trex transfer steps at Briarpatch and Sunny side. Cameron will do the plans.*

* *Keep sand tunnel at Northside playground clear.*

* Pay attention to use zones on spring animals when designing play areas. Some spring animals are longer than others and require more than 6' from the center of the equipment. *The 6'safety distance should be measured from the ends and side of the equipment.*

* Check backhoe diggers use zones. When the bucket is extended while in use it is longer than when not in use, therefore the 6' use zone does not meet guidelines. This is a similar situation as the spring animals. The use zone should probably be measured 6' from the extended backhoe.

* *Check Rathje playsurface for cuts and burns during all high and low frequency play ground safety inspections.*

* *Staff was reminded to fill out inspection forms completely including information such as time-in, time-out, who inspected, who repaired, what was done, etc.*

SUMMARY OF PLANNING DEPARTMENT ITEMS TO COMPLETE

* Scottdale's paths will be budgeted in 1997/98 fiscal year to be resurfaced. **Dave commented that the main pathway the porta-let company uses to get to the porta-potty's location should be wider to accommodate trucks.**

*Purchase replacements for Northside's spring animal and tire swing.

  - **If there is money in the 96/97 budget Jerry should order and get the equipment delivered before spring. If not, they should be purchased in 97/98.**

*Presidents Park
  - **Jerry has a contractor to asphalt pave the walk when the weather clears.**

* Replace Scottdale's worn wood decks.
  - The decks are in decent shape so replacement can hold off until the playground is renovated in 1999. **In the meantime, for reference and if it is decided that replacing the decks is a better option than replacing everything, Cameron will talk to Jack Gleason of NuToys (rep for Landscape Structures) to see if recycled trex can be used on the decks, and if Landscape Structures will back it liability wise.**

* Surveys were sent to the residents near Hull Park and the responses were considered in the design.
  - **Cameron is to get copies of all playground survey results to Terry so he can keep them in the master files.** Playgrounds surveyed were Herrick, Presidents, Prairie Path and Hull.
  - The existing catch basin on the south side is part of the existing draintile system, and is not tied into the city storm sewer system. **Cameron will look into this while finishing the construction drawings.**

* Transfer stations should be within 6-8" of both the bench and sand on the play surface side and 14" on the chair side.
  - **Cameron will get detailed construction drawings of transfer steps made of concrete and trex to the Maintenance Department.**

* Pay attention to use zones on spring animals when designing play areas. Some spring animals are longer than others and require more than 6' from the center of the equipment. **The 6' safety distance should be measured from the ends and side of the equipment.**

* Check backhoe diggers use zones. When the bucket is extended while in use it is longer than when not in use, therefore the 6' use zone does not meet guidelines. This is a similar situation as the spring animals. *The use zone should probably be measured 6' from the extended backhoe.*
  - **Cameron is to check with Jack Gleason of NuToys on what Landscape Structures is requiring as the use zone.**

* Central
  - Look into incorporating an area by the volleyball courts for the 10-15 year old age group using 10 Plus equipment and gathering areas.
  - There was concern by the committee in having equipment for this age group next to a tot play area. It would possibly create a higher safety risk to younger children that are not watched by their guardians. **It will be looked into further as the design of the site progresses.**

* **Surveys need to be sent out for both Brighton and Central.**

© NRPA/NPSI/PDRMA

Bibliography

Books and Literature

Christiansen, Monty L. and Vogelsong, Hans (1996) *Play it Safe: Anthology of Playground Safe*; Alexandria, VA: National Recreation and Park Association.

Christiansen, Monty L. (1993 Second Edition) *Points About Playgrounds*, Third Edition.

Kutska, Ken and Hoffman, Kevin, (1993) *Playground Safety is No Accident*; Alexandria, VA; National Recreation and Park Association

Kutska, Ken. *Comprehensive Public Playground Safety Program*. (1991). Wheaton Park District, Wheaton, IL

MacIntyre, S., Goltsman, S.M. (1997) *Safety First Checklist: Audit and Inspection Program For Children's Play Areas*. MIG Communication, Berkeley, CA 94710.

1997 Handbook for Public Playground Safety, Publication Number 325. Consumer Products Safety Commission, Washington, DC 20207

Playground Maintenance, A Guide to Assist Staff in Establishing the Proper Frequency for Playground Safety Inspections. Landscape Structures, Inc. Route 3, 601 7th Street South, Delano, MN 55328 (modified by K. Kutska 1998).

Statewide Comprehensive Injury Prevention Program (SCIPP). Massachusetts Department of Public Health, 150 Trecoast Street, Boston, MA 92111.

Sources

ASTM, 100 Barr Harbor Dr.; West Conshohocken, PA 19428 (610-832-9500)

U.S.C.P.S.C., Washington, DC 20207   http://www.cpsc.gov

NRPA, National Playground Safety Institute, 22377 Belmont Ridge Road, Ashburn, VA 20148 (702-858-2148)

Videos

Safe Active Play: A Guide to Avoiding Play Area Hazards. © 1997
By Video Active Productions
Available From:
NRPA Professional Services
22377 Belmont Ridge Road
Ashburn, VA 20148
708-858-0784

Time Out for Safety © 1995
A Public Service of Game Time, Inc.
P.O. Box 121
Fort Payne, Alabama 35967
800-235-2440